T0001173

A Year of Puzzles, Fun Facts, Jokes, Crafts, Games, and More!

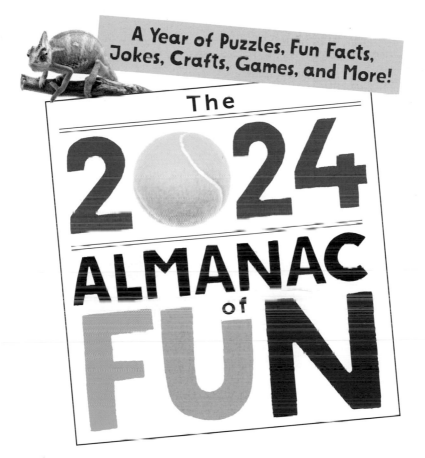

The **2024** ALMANAC of FUN

HIGHLIGHTS PRESS
Honesdale, Pennsylvania

SUNDAY	MONDAY	TUESDAY	WEDNESDAY

BIRTHSTONE
GARNET

NEW YEAR'S DAY **1**

World Introvert Day
Studies show that introverts make up 30 to 50 percent of the U.S. population. **2**

Festival of Sleep D
Get some shut-eye a staying up until midni to ring 20 **3**

Jupiter's Moons
In 1610, the astronomer Galileo discovered the first three of Jupiter's moons, now called Io, Europa, and Ganymede. **7**

National Bubble Bath Day
Grab your rubber ducky and scrub-a-dub-dub! **8**

NATIONAL APRICOT DAY
85 percent of our nation's apricots are grown in California. **9**

COMMON SENS
On this day in 1776, Thomas Paine publish his pamphlet *Commo Sense*, which argued fo American independen from England. **10**

National Dress Up Your Pet Day
Take pictures and share them with your friends! **14**

MARTIN LUTHER KING JR. DAY **15**

NATIONAL NOTHING DAY
Just enjoy doing absolutely NOTHING today! **16**

BENJAMIN FRANKLIN'S BIRTHDAY
It's also Kid Inventors' Day. What will you create? **17**

NATIONAL HUGGING DAY **21**

NATIONAL POLKA DOT DAY **22**

Catch!
In 1957, the toy company Wham-O produced the first Frisbees. **23**

GLOBAL BELLY LAUGH DAY
Why did the student e his homework?
Because his teacher told him it was a piece of cake! **24**

National Kazoo Day
No kazoo? No problem! Make your own with a comb and waxed paper. **28**

CURMUDGEONS DAY
Even the crankiest people need their own day to celebrate! **29**

NATIONAL CROISSANT DAY **30**

NATIONAL GORILLA SUIT DAY **3**

THURSDAY	FRIDAY	SATURDAY

WORLD BRAILLE DAY
4

George Washington Carver Recognition Day
This African American scientist developed hundreds of products using the peanut!
5

Feast of the Epiphany
Around the world, this day is also known as Three Kings' Day, Theophany, Denha, and Little Christmas.
6

National Step in a Puddle and Splash Your Friends Day
Don't forget your rain boots!
11

Avengers, assemble! Timely Comics (later called Marvel) was founded on this day in 1939.
12

MAKE YOUR DREAMS COME TRUE DAY
13

NATIONAL WINNIE THE POOH DAY
Celebrate this lovable bear and all his friends in the Hundred Acre Wood.
18

On your mark, get set, go! In 1903, the now popular bicycle race Tour de France was announced.
19

TAKE A WALK OUTDOORS DAY
20

NATIONAL FISH TACO DAY
25

NATIONAL OPPOSITE DAY
Definitely forget this day and *don't* celebrate.
26

International Holocaust Remembrance Day
27

JANUARY

ZODIAC SIGNS
CAPRICORN: DECEMBER 22– JANUARY 19

AQUARIUS: JANUARY 20– FEBRUARY 18

FLOWERS
CARNATION AND SNOWDROP

GET ORGANIZED MONTH

5 QUICK WAYS TO GET ORGANIZED

1. Keep a daily planner. Write down all the tasks you need to finish each day. Don't forget to check off each item as you complete it!

2. Clean out your backpack every Friday after school.

3. Keep all of your important papers in one place.

4. Each school night, get your backpack ready and lay out your clothes for the next day.

5. Use shoeboxes to store small knickknacks.

The first Get Organized Month was held **January 2005.**

A book never written: **How to Be Neat** by Mac K. Mess

PENCIL MEMO BOARD

1. Cut a large rectangle from **corrugated cardboard**. Cut a point at one end. Trace around the shape twice onto corrugated cardboard and cut out the pieces. Stack all three and glue them together.

2. For the pencil's tip, wood, body, metal band, and eraser, cut out **felt** pieces wide enough to wrap over the sides. Glue them on. Add details with a **marker**.

3. **Tape** some **yarn** to the back for a hanger.

For a fun way to store important messages, make this craft!

Meet at library 4:00 pm

Use thumbtacks to post important memos on your board!

NATIONAL OATMEAL MONTH

To make this yummy oatmeal, you don't even need to know how to cook! Just put this together the night before, and in the morning your breakfast will be all ready when you wake up.

NO-COOK OVERNIGHT OATMEAL

Before You Begin: Wash your hands.

1. Pour ¼ cup **old-fashioned rolled oats** into a **jar** or container with a tight lid.

2. Add ¼ cup **plain yogurt**, ¼ cup **milk**, 1 teaspoon **honey**, ½ teaspoon **ground cinnamon**, and a handful of **dried fruits** (raisins, cranberries, or chopped apricots).

3. Twist on the lid tightly. Shake until combined.

4. Refrigerate the oatmeal for at least 8 hours or overnight.

NATIONAL HOBBY MONTH

Use this month to enjoy old hobbies or begin new ones.

At the end of the month, get together with friends and share your hobbies with each other in a talent show!

Backstage at this talent show has gotten a little out of control. While the performers figure out who is up next, see how many silly things you can find in the scene.

Depending on a dog's breed, a pooch needs thirty minutes to two hours of exercise each day. A walk is a great way to get a dog moving — and you, too!

WALK YOUR DOG MONTH

These three friends took their dogs on a walk to the park. But their leashes got all mixed up! Follow the tangled leashes to figure out which dog belongs to which kid.

WHAT'S YOUR DOG IQ?

Are you a friend of Fido? A bestie of Barkly? Circle your answers and see how many you can fetch in this canine quiz.

1. **What is a schnoodle?**
   a. A mix between a schnauzer and a poodle
   b. A mix between a poodle and a sheepdog
   c. A long, buttery noodle

2. **At birth, dalmatians are:**
   a. Completely white
   b. Completely black
   c. Red-and-green striped

3. **The greyhound is the fastest type of dog on the planet. How fast can they run?**
   a. 30 miles per hour
   b. 45 miles per hour
   c. Faster than the speed of light

4. **Dogs can see best in what type of light?**
   a. Bright light
   b. Low light
   c. Strobe lights

5. **The Newfoundland has this unique characteristic:**
   a. Webbed feet
   b. No tail
   c. Ability to hula-hoop

January 3, 1959
65 YEARS AGO, ALASKA WAS ADMITTED TO THE UNION AS THE 49TH STATE.

Alaska's native peoples carve totem poles to tell stories. This scene shows poles at Ketchikan's Totem Bight State Historical Park. **Find all 7 matching pairs.**

ALASKA FACTS:

- The United States purchased Alaska from Russia on March 30, 1867, for $7.2 million dollars— about 2 cents per acre!

- Alaska has approximately 100,000 glaciers.

- Alaska has 33,904 miles of shoreline.

- On March 27, 1964, Alaska experienced the strongest earthquake ever recorded in North America. It was 9.2 on the Richter scale.

- Alaskan native Benny Benson won a contest to design Alaska's flag. He was only 13 years old when he won!

- Alaskan brown bears can eat 80 to 90 pounds of food per day!

DOGGONE IT!

Alaska's annual Iditarod Trail Sled Dog Race is about to start. But first Nick needs to figure out which one is his lead dog. Can you help him?

265 YEARS AGO, THE BRITISH MUSEUM OPENED IN LONDON.

Egyptian art, sculpture, and artifacts are some of the most popular items on display at the British Museum. **Can you find all the hidden objects in this Egyptian exhibit?**

needle

golf club

bell

pencil

pennant

banana

duck

crayon

acorn

toothbrush

eggshells

crescent moon

ruler

knitted hat

pitcher

The British Museum is **older than the USA!**

During World War II, priceless pieces in the collection were **evacuated** to a safe location.

People once had to take **extensive exams** in order to get a job here.

The museum has nearly **4.5 million objects** in its collection.

ROSE BOWL & ROSE PARADE

The Tournament of Roses, also known as the Rose Bowl, has been played in Pasadena, California, nearly every New Year's Day for over one hundred years. This game is when the top Big Ten and Pac-12 college football teams vie for the national championship. The Rose Parade occurs just before the game. What makes this parade special? Every single float is decorated in a variety of real flowers!

Make some flowers to decorate your house for the Rose Bowl.

1. **Glue** a piece of **lightweight fabric** to **poster board**, smoothing out any wrinkles.

2. Once it is dried, cut out petal shapes from the fabric-covered board.

3. Insert a **fuzzy stick** through one hole of a flat two-hole **button**. Then, continue by inserting it back down through the other hole.

4. Twist the ends together to make a stem.

5. Glue petals around the underside edge of the button. Let dry.

6. Decorate your house on New Year's Day in honor of the Rose Bowl Parade.

The first Rose Parade occurred in 1890. It was followed by a day of fun, including chariot races and foot races.

This is the oldest bowl game and known as the "**granddaddy of them all.**"

Find the following 18 objects hidden in this funny football scene: banana, horn, sailboat, comb, toothbrush, paper clip, fishhook, teacup, horseshoe, book, saw, pencil, light bulb, shovel, golf club, mitten, sock, and hockey stick.

BONUS
Can you find **5 water bottles** in this scene?

January 2024
WINTER X GAMES

Held every year in Aspen, Colorado, the Winter X Games are a competition in extreme winter sports, like snowboarding, skiing, and snowmobiling.

Can you find the 15 differences between these two snowboarding photos?

The first **Winter X Games** were held at Big Bear Lake, California, in **1997**. Now the games are held in Aspen, Colorado, each year.

There are also **Summer X Games,** which are held in Los Angeles, California. The sports you'll see there include skateboarding, BMX biking, and surfing.

The "X" in X Games has a few meanings:

 1 **Extreme** (as in *extreme sports*)

2 The **unknown**, as **X** is the mathematical symbol for the unknown

3 **Generation X** (those born between early 1960s and early 1980s), since this generation was the first to participate in the **X Games**

NATIONAL SCIENCE FICTION DAY

Read the letters in green to find out what term Isaac Asimov coined in his 1941 short story "Liar!"

Many science-fiction fans celebrate this unofficial holiday on the birthdate of famous science-fiction author Isaac Asimov. Use one of these story starters or your own idea to write a science-fiction story.

As Dad twisted knobs on the panel, the rocket started to shake and . . .

_____

_____

_____

_____

Knock, knock, knock. The door burst open, and . . .

_____

_____

_____

_____

We looked at the strange metallic substance, which suddenly started to . . .

_____

_____

_____

_____

January 18

NATIONAL THESAURUS DAY

Celebrate by spotting eight synonyms hidden in this scene. **Can you find the words SMART, BRAINY, INTELLIGENT, BRILLIANT, WISE, GENIUS, BRIGHT, and CLEVER?**

What do you call a dinosaur with an extensive vocabulary?

A thesaurus

January 24 is **National Compliment Day.** What synonyms could you use to compliment someone who is kind?

A thesaurus is a reference book that lists synonyms for words.

The author of *Roget's Thesaurus,* Peter Mark Roget, was born on January 18, 1779.

January 19

NATIONAL POPCORN DAY

This popcorn is hiding 20 dog bones.
Can you find them all?

Popcorn kernels can pop up to **3 feet** in the air!

Americans eat **17 billion** quarts of popcorn in a year, more than people in any other country.

Popcorn was a popular breakfast food during the **early 19th** and **late 20th** centuries.

What do you like to put on your popcorn? Pair it with one of January's other food holidays:

BITTERSWEET CHOCOLATE
DAY
JANUARY 10

BUTTERCRUNCH
DAY
JANUARY 20

HOT SAUCE
DAY
JANUARY 22

NATIONAL
SOUP
MONTH

Celebrate all month long with these soup jokes!

What is a duck's favorite meal?

Soup and quackers

If you leave alphabet soup on the stove and go out, it could spell disaster.

NATIONAL BLONDE BROWNIE (BLONDIES) DAY

There are chocolate chips hiding in the blondies below. **Can you find them?** The numbers in each grid tell you how many chips are touching the numbered square—above, below, left, right, and diagonally. **Place an X on squares that can't have a chip.**

Solve this practice puzzle.

Here's the answer.

Solve this puzzle with 10 chocolate chips.

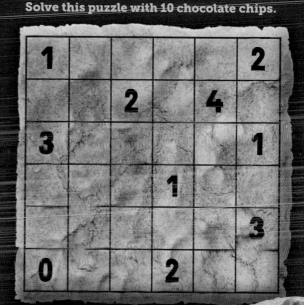

Hints:
- Put an X on all the squares touching a zero.
- Look in the corners where a numbered square may make it more obvious where a chocolate chip is hiding.
- A chip cannot go in a square that has a number.

Why are you eating alphabet soup?

Because if I were eating number soup, I'd be a cow-culator.

Knock, knock.
Who's there?
Jupiter.
Jupiter who?
Jupiter fly in my soup?

WHAT IS YOUR NEW YEAR'S RESOLUTION?

January 1

NEW YEAR'S DAY

MAKE A NOISEMAKER
TO RING IN THE NEW YEAR.

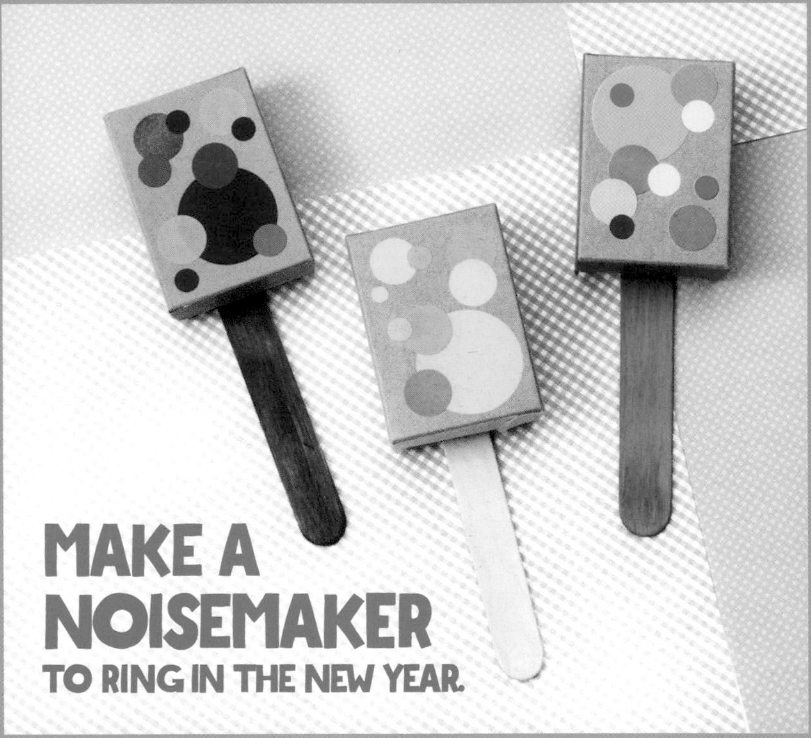

1. Place large **buttons** into a small **jewelry box**.
2. **Tape** the box tightly closed.
3. Tape a **craft stick** to the back of the box.
4. Decorate your box with **stickers** or **markers**.

Then shake it!

1
2
3
4

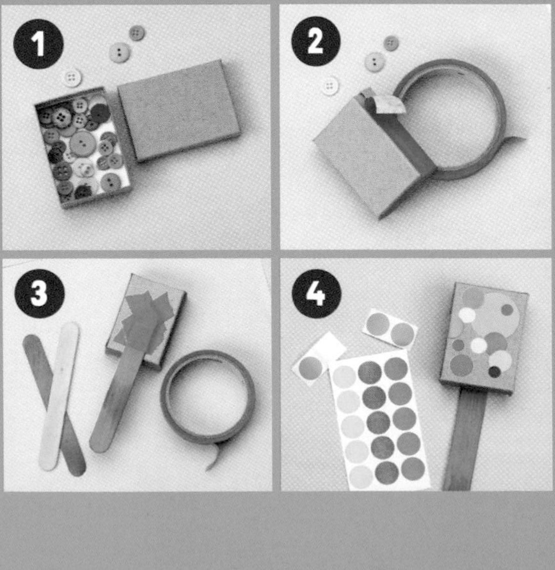

PASS THE LUCK, PLEASE!

Many countries around the world have foods that they consider to bring good luck when eaten at the start of the new year. **Can you match each food with the country it belongs to?**

1

Black-eyed peas and collard greens:
The peas represent coins, while the greens stand for "folding money."

Saint Basil's Day cake:
The cook sprinkles coins and other trinkets into the cake before baking. Whoever finds the treasure in their slice of cake gets good luck!

2

Pork sausages and lentils:
The fat, rich sausage is a symbol of plenty, while the green, coin-shaped lentils represent money.

3

4

Grapes:
As the clock strikes midnight, 12 grapes are eaten for each chime of the clock, in hopes of 12 months of prosperity.

Soba noodles:
To ensure a long life, noodles must be sucked up and swallowed without breaking or chewing them.

5

  Italy

 Japan

United States

 **Spain**

 Greece

Martin Luther

The holiday is observed on the third Monday of January each year.

Sonnet for a King

This January day was set aside

to celebrate the birthday of a man,

a gentle man, who bravely lived and died

too soon, but left a challenge and a plan.

He was a man of strength and grace and will

who stood for honor, character, and grit,

a man who sought and fought for freedom till

he gave his life, in faith, defending it.

He had a dream of hope, a dream that we,

though different in creed, belief, and race,

could live, as friends, in peace and harmony

and make the world a better place.

"Hold fast to dreams": together we must strive

to understand, and keep the dream alive.

The line *Hold fast to dreams* is from the poem "Dreams" by Langston Hughes.

Read the poem, then write your own poem to honor Dr. King.

MLK DAY OF SERVICE

Corporation for NATIONAL & COMMUNITY SERVICE

The MLK Day of Service was created to inspire Americans to turn Martin Luther King Jr. Day into a day of citizen action volunteer service in King's honor.

Talk with your parents about ways you can volunteer. Here are some ideas:

- Walk a neighbor's dog or wash their car.
- Help do yardwork for people who can't.
- Make welcome kits for new kids at school.
- Read books to others during your library's story hour.

King Jr. Day

The Martin Luther King Jr. Memorial opened in Washington, D.C., in 2011. It features a granite statue of the civil rights leader called the *Stone of Hope*.

- Why do we build memorials?
- Name some people and events with memorials built in their honor.
- How else do we remember important people and events?
- Are there any memorials or monuments near where you live? If so, what do they honor?

Martin Luther King Jr. was born on **January 15, 1929.**

January 20, 1986, was the first time Martin Luther King Jr. Day was observed.

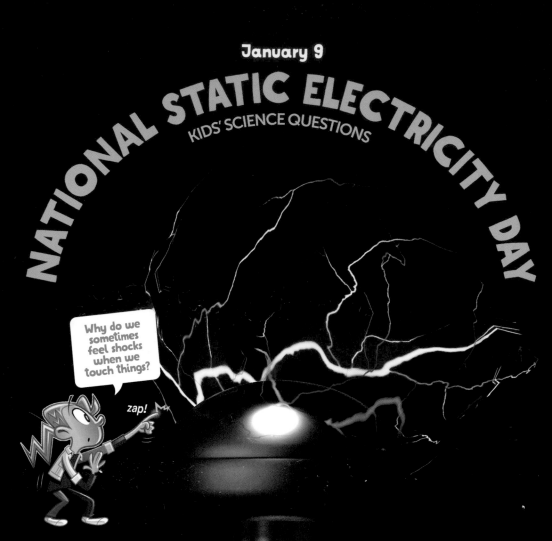

NATIONAL STATIC ELECTRICITY DAY

January 9

KIDS' SCIENCE QUESTIONS

Why do we sometimes feel shocks when we touch things?

zap!

That ZAP happens when static electricity gets moving! As you scuff across a rug, your socks may pick up a charge. That's from electrons, negatively charged bits that are part of all atoms. Usually they stay with their atoms, nicely balanced by positive charges. But if they rub onto an object, it gets extra negativity!

Robert Van de Graaff, an American physicist, invented the Van de Graaff generator in 1931. A Van de Graaff generator is an electrostatic generator that can create static electricity for experiments.

Negative charges push away from each other. So the extra electrons move away from that charged sock. Destination: Earth's big surface, where they can spread out (or *ground*). To get there, they need *conductors*—things that a charge can easily move across. Unlike your socks and rug, YOU are a conductor. A charge can flow across you, but it's *static*; it can't keep going until you are almost touching another conductor. Then, ZAP! Electrons leap through the air as a spark. Shocking, huh?

PENGUIN AWARENESS DAY

Knock, knock.
Who's there?
Arthur.
Arthur who?
**Arthur-mometer
is broken.**

PENGUIN PATTERN

The numbers on these penguins follow a pattern. **Figure out the pattern and then fill in the blanks.**

PENGUIN PUZZLER

It's lunchtime, but Ben can't get to his lunchbox. He has forgotten his locker combination! Luckily, he remembers some clues that might help. **Using the clues, can you figure out the three numbers in Ben's locker combination?**

CLUES:

1. The first number equals the number of months in a year.
2. The second number falls halfway between the first number and the last number.
3. The last number is double the first number.

January 16
APPRECIATE A DRAGON
DAY

Knock, knock.
Who's there?
Dragon
Dragon who?
Dragon easy chair over here and let's talk.

Henry's pet dragon has really made a mess of his room.
You'll truly be the hero of this *roar*-ific scene if you can find all the hidden objects in the chaos.

necktie

heart

can

flag

slice of pie

olive

needle

bagel

lightning bolt

slice of bread

stick of gum

ruler

teacup

crescent moon

sailboat

lollipop

coat hanger

wishbone

cracker

fan

pea pod

envelope

barbell

domino

slice of pizza

jar

saltshaker

party hat

NATIONAL PUZZLE DAY

Can you find these hidden jigsaw pieces in this photo of building blocks?

Jigsaw puzzles were invented in the **1760s** by mapmaker John Spilsbury. He glued maps onto wood and cut them into pieces.

January 28 is National Lego Day!

Puzzles became a popular hobby during the Great Depression as an affordable, reusable activity. In **1933**, over **10 million** puzzles were sold per week!

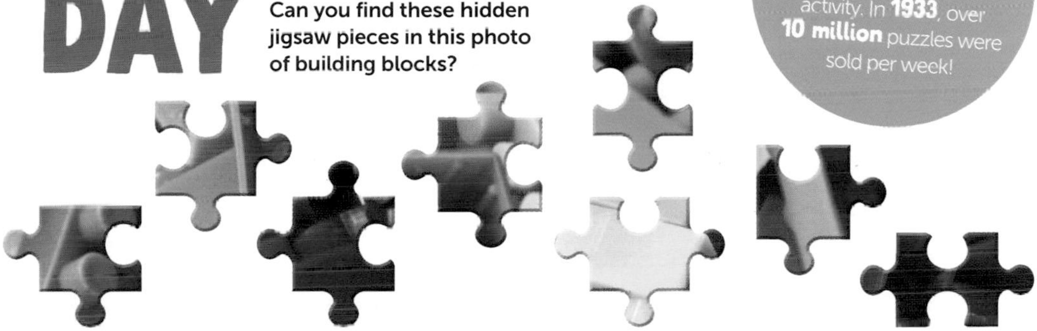

AROUND

Take a spin around the globe to see how

January 13

📍 SAINT KNUT'S DAY

In Sweden, Saint Knut's Day is the day to get rid of Christmas trees. Swedes eat any edible ornaments, smash gingerbread houses, and put away decorations. In Swedish, this is called *julgransplundring*, which translates to "Christmas tree plundering."

Can you match these other Swedish words with their English translation? *God jul!* **(Merry Christmas!)**

SWEDISH	ENGLISH
julstjärna	Christmas stocking
julklappsstrumpa	Christmas star
julgranskula	Christmas tree lights
julgransbelysning	Christmas ornament

January 15–16, 2024

📍 PONGALO PONGAL!

In Sri Lanka, Tamil Thai Pongal Day is a two-day harvest festival dedicated to the Sun God. On the first day of the festival, Sri Lankans make rice in large clay pots, outside under the sun. They boil the rice in milk and spices. As the milk boils over, people shout, "Pongalo pongal!" An overflowing pot brings good luck.

The second day of the festival honors the oxen who provide milk, transportation, and help with harvesting rice and other crops. The oxen are bathed and given special food to eat. Then they have their horns painted beautiful colors and are given garlands to wear.

This ox is ready for Tamil Thai Pongal Day!

THE WORLD

people around the world celebrate in January.

January 18

♀ HAPPY BIRTHDAY, LIMA!

On January 18, 1535, the conquistador Francisco Pizarro founded Lima, Peru, as "Ciudad de los Reyes" (City of the Kings). Major celebrations and civic events take place across Lima to mark the capital's foundation, including parades, food, dancing, and fireworks!

January 27

♀ SAINT DEVOTA'S DAY

In Catholicism, Saint Devota is the patron saint of Monaco. The Catholic Church has many patron saints who they believe work to protect different things. **The following are some patron saints. Can you match them with what they protect?**

SAINTS

1. Francis of Assisi
2. John the Baptist
3. Joseph
4. Florian
5. Patrick
6. Anthony
7. Joan of Arc
8. Sebastian

WHAT THEY PROTECT

A. firefighters
B. France
C. animals
D. lost items
E. soldiers
F. carpenters and laborers
G. Ireland
H. baptism

SUNDAY	MONDAY	TUESDAY	WEDNESDAY

FLOWERS
PRIMROSE AND VIOLET

ZODIAC SIGNS
AQUARIUS: JANUARY 20– FEBRUARY 18

PISCES: FEBRUARY 19– MARCH 20

Thank a Mail Carrier Day
Whether sun, rain, or snow, they'll still deliver your mail!
4

WESTERN MONARCH DAY
Here ye, here ye! All hail the western monarch butterfly on this day.
5

FORE! On this day in 1971, Alan Shepard became the first (and so far only) person to hit a golf ball on the moon.
6

BALLET DAY
7

Don't Cry Over Spilled Milk Day
Instead, think positive and mop up that milk with some cookies!
11

Blades of glory! In 1879, skaters glided on North America's first artificial ice rink, set up in New York City's Madison Square Garden.
12

GET A DIFFERENT NAME DAY
If you could choose a different name for yourself, what would it be?
13

Valentine's Day

ASH WEDNESDAY
First day of Lent
14

PLUTO DAY
In 1930, Clyde Tombaugh discovered the tiny, distant dwarf planet using a cool tool called a blink microscope.
18

International Tug-of-War Day
Grab a rope and some friends, then dig in your heels!
19

NATIONAL CHERRY PIE DAY
20

WASHINGTON BIRTHDAY
George often shares his birthday celebration with Abe and others.
21

Celebrate Revels! On this day in 1820, Hiram Revels from Mississippi was the first African American to be sworn into Congress.
25

Tell a Fairy Tale Day
Make up your own! (Add an ogre or two.)
26

INTERNATIONAL POLAR BEAR DAY
27

NATIONAL TOOTH FAIRY DAY
28

FEBRUARY

...binson Crusoe Day

...gine what you'd do if ...found yourself alone ...a deserted island— with no Wi-Fi.

1

GROUNDHOG DAY

Will Punxsutawney Phil or Staten Island Chuck see their shadows?

2

Is it cold, or is it me? In 1947, Snag, Yukon, snagged the record for the coldest temperature ever recorded in North America: 81°F below 0!

3

...ational Girl Scout Cookie Day

...moas or Thin Mints? ...at will it be?

8

Get served! Mintonette, better known today as volleyball, was created by William G. Morgan on this day in 1895.

9

LUNAR NEW YEAR

Happy Year of the Dragon!

10

...san B. Anthony Day

...an B. Anthony fought ...women's rights, ...uding the right to ...e, her whole life. ...cause of activists like ..., women ...n the ...t to vote ...920.

15

Tim Tam Day (Australia)

A chocolate-cookie sandwich dipped in chocolate—what's not to love?

16

RANDOM ACTS OF KINDNESS DAY

Nice!

17

NATIONAL WALKING THE DOG DAY

22

Chew on this! In 1896, Leo Hirschfield gave us the Tootsie Roll, named after his five-year-old daughter Clara, whose nickname was "Tootsie."

23

National Tortilla Chip Day

What's this chip's favorite type of dance? Salsa, of course!

24

LEAP DAY!

...only happens every ...our years, so have a ...hopping good time.

29

BIRTHSTONE
AMETHYST ----›

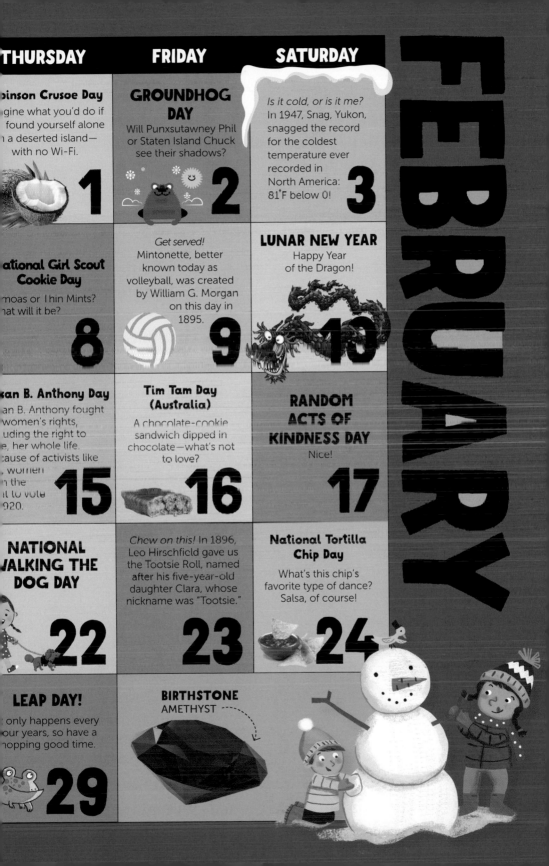

BLACK HISTORY MONTH

Travel through this timeline of influential African Americans.

Frederick Douglass

Harriet Tubman

Madam C.J. Walker

W.E.B. Du Bois

George Washington Carver

Jackie Robinson

Rosa Parks

Judge Thurgood Marshall

Oprah Winfrey

Mae Jemison

Toni Morrison

Colin Powell

Barack Obama

Misty Copeland

1847 Abolitionist, author, and orator **Frederick Douglass** publishes the antislavery newspaper the *North Star*.

1849 **Harriet Tubman** escapes from slavery and leads others to freedom through the Underground Railroad.

1905 **Madam C.J. Walker** launches a business creating hair-care products, eventually becoming the first Black woman millionaire.

1909 **W.E.B. Du Bois** co-founds the NAACP (National Association for the Advancement of Colored People).

1921 Inventor **George Washington Carver** addresses Congress about the hundreds of uses he discovered for peanuts, including flour, milk, dyes, and cheeses.

1947 **Jackie Robinson** joins the Brooklyn Dodgers, a Major League Baseball team.

1955 **Rosa Parks** takes a stand against segregation and is arrested for refusing to give up her bus seat.

1967 **Judge Thurgood Marshall** is appointed to the Supreme Court.

1986 **Oprah Winfrey** first goes on the air with her national TV show.

1992 Astronaut **Mae Jemison** blasts off on the space shuttle Endeavor.

1993 Author **Toni Morrison** wins the Nobel Prize in Literature.

2001 Four-star general **Colin Powell** is appointed U.S. secretary of state.

2008 **Barack Obama**—a senator from Illinois, born in Hawaii—is elected the 44th president of the United States.

2015 **Misty Copeland** is named a principal dancer with the American Ballet Theatre.

BAKE FOR FAMILY FUN MONTH

Grab an apron and get baking!
How many of your family's favorites can you make this month?

Ask an adult to help with anything sharp or hot.

Tapioca flour gives this gluten-free treat its chewy texture.

BRAZILIAN CHEESE BREAD

You Need:

- 24-cup mini-muffin tin
- Non-stick spray
- 2/3 cup milk
- 1/3 cup vegetable oil
- 1 egg
- 1/2 teaspoon salt
- 1 1/2 cups tapioca flour
- 1/2 cup shredded Parmesan cheese

Directions:

1. Preheat the oven to 350°F. Spray a **24-cup mini-muffin tin** with **non-stick spray**.

2. Whisk together the **milk**, **vegetable oil**, **egg**, and **salt**.

3. Whisk in the **tapioca flour** a little at a time until blended. Mix in the shredded **Parmesan cheese**.

4. Fill muffin cups with batter until they are two-thirds full.

5. Bake for 20–25 minutes until golden brown and puffy. If using a 12-cup muffin tin, bake for 30–35 minutes.

NATIONAL CHERRY MONTH

In 1912, Japan gifted the United States 3,000 cherry trees to be planted in the nation's capital. This was meant to show the friendship between the two nations. Every year, people love coming to Washington, D.C., for its famous Cherry Blossom Festival.

What's a turkey's favorite dessert?

Cherry gobbler

CHERRY FIZZ

Sit back and relax with one of these bubbly cherry drinks.

You Need

- Ginger ale
- Cherry juice
- ¼ cup half-and-half
- Whipped cream

1. Fill a glass two-thirds of the way full with equal parts **ginger ale** and **cherry juice**. Let it stand for 5 minutes.

2. Pour the **half-and-half** into the glass. Top with **whipped cream**.

Cherries were brought to the Americas by European colonists in the **1600s.**

CHERRY MATCHUP

Draw a line to connect each pair of cherries to its exact match.

CHILDREN'S DENTAL HEALTH MONTH

Sink your teeth into this! **Can you find the 20 non-beaver teeth hidden in this scene?**

RIDDLE SUDOKU

Fill in the squares so that the six letters appear once in each row, column, and 2 x 3 box. Then read the yellow squares to find out the answer to the riddle.

Letters: C N O R S W

			W		
		N	O		
S	W				
				S	O
	S		R		
	N			C	

RIDDLE: Why do kings and queens go to the dentist?

ANSWER: To get ___ ___ ___ ___ ___ ___

What time do you go to the dentist?

Tooth-hurty

The first toothbrushes were tree twigs. Chewing on the tips of the twigs spread out the fibers, which were then used to clean the teeth.

February 9, 1964

60 YEARS AGO, THE BEATLES APPEARED ON THE ED SULLIVAN SHOW, MARKING THE OFFICIAL START OF BEATLEMANIA IN THE UNITED STATES.

About **73 MILLION** Americans tuned in to watch the Beatles in their U.S. debut.

There were four Beatles:
- John Lennon
- Paul McCartney
- George Harrison
- Ringo Starr

The Beatles wrote nearly 200 songs and sold hundreds of millions of records. **See if you can figure out the names to some of their hits in the puzzle below. We've finished one for you.**

1. **Here Comes the** ___
2. **Sergeant** _____**'s Lonely Hearts Club Band**
3. **Let it** ___
4. **I Want to Hold Your** ____
5. _____ **Lane**
6. **BLACKBIRD**

7. **While My** _____ **Gently Weeps**
8. **Yellow** _____
9. _____ **Fields Forever**
10. **Lucy in the Sky with** _____
11. **I am the** _____
12. **Drive My** ___

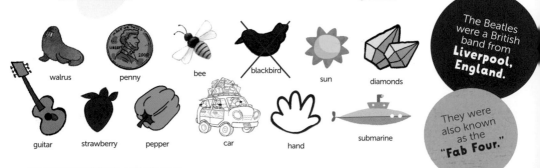

walrus · penny · bee · blackbird · sun · diamonds · guitar · strawberry · pepper · car · hand · submarine

The Beatles were a British band from **Liverpool, England.**

They were also known as the **"Fab Four."**

February 15, 1564
460 YEARS AGO, GALILEO WAS BORN.

Galileo was an Italian astronomer and mathematician who was most well-known for the telescope he invented that let him see the moons of Jupiter, the rings of Saturn, and the phases of Venus.

Before you gaze out over the universe with this telescope, scan this scene and find all the hidden images.

roller skate

belt

flashlight

pizza

mop

envelope

ring

hockey stick

Knock, knock.
Who's there?
Venus.
Venus who?
Venus discuss the best way to launch this spaceship.

IMAGINE
AND
DRAW

Draw what you think you'd see if you looked through this telescope.

February 7, 2024

NATIONAL GIRLS & WOMEN IN SPORTS DAY

Since 1987, National Girls & Women in Sports Day has spotlighted the history of women's athletics. Held the first Wednesday of February, it also recognizes the progress made since the passing of Title IX of the Education Amendments of 1972, which ensures that students receive educational—and athletic— opportunities free from discrimination based on gender.

Alex, Brooke, and Claire are about to dive into the pool. Circle the correct answers to the questions below about famous female firsts. Then for each answer, shade in a square in the matching swim lane (A, B, or C). The first swimmer to reach the end of her lane wins!

	A	**B**	**C**
1. At age 13, Donna de Varona was the youngest to compete on the 1960 U.S. Olympic _____ team.	discus	swimming	boxing
2. Fore! In 2014, 11-year-old Lucy Li was the youngest girl to qualify to compete in the Women's U.S. Open _____ tournament.	snowboard	polo	golf
3. Goal! In 1987 at age 15, Mia Hamm became the youngest member ever of the U.S. women's national ___ team.	soccer	ice hockey	judo
4. Tatyana McFadden was 15 when she won two gold medals at the Paralympics on the U.S. _____ team.	wheelchair racing	wheelchair rugby	wheelchair boccia
5. In 1904, teenager Amanda Clement became baseball's first paid female _____.	cheerleader	quarterback	umpire
6. In 1948, Alice Coachman became the first African American woman to win an Olympic track-and-field gold medal for the _____.	beanbag toss	high jump	bobsled
7. Nadia Comăneci of Romania was the first female to be awarded a perfect score of ___ in an Olympic gymnastics event.	100	10	25
8. Wilma Rudolph, once considered the fastest woman in the world, was the first American woman to win three gold medals in a single Olympics for _____.	running	skiing	curling
9. Janet Guthrie was the first woman racecar driver to earn a starting spot in both the Daytona 500 and the _____ 500.	Cincinnati	Peoria	Indianapolis
10. Tara Lipinski glided into history as the youngest person ever to hold the titles of world and Olympic champion in _____.	ice-skating	basketball	canoeing

February 11, 2024
SUPER BOWL LVIII

It's been a windy day in the stadium. With the game tied and just a few seconds left on the clock, Chase Gridiron must get to the end zone to score the winning touchdown. Help him find his way around the other players and also the objects that have blown onto the field.

That's 58 Super Bowls since the first in 1967. Each year, the two winningest teams of the American Football Conference and the National Football Conference face off in a championship game. This year, Super Bowl LVIII kicks off at Allegiant Stadium in Las Vegas, Nevada.

SUPER BOWL
SUPER
STATS

Tackle this quiz!

1. Which city has hosted the most Super Bowls?

    a. Los Angeles

    b. New Orleans

    c. Miami

2. Which team has competed at the most Super Bowls?

    a. New England Patriots

    b. Pittsburgh Steelers

    c. Dallas Cowboys

3. Which was the most watched Super Bowl of all time?

    a. XLV (2011)

    b. XLIX (2015)

    c. LIII (2019)

4. Who has appeared at the most halftime shows?

    a. World Famed Tiger Marching Band

    b. Justin Timberlake

    c. Beyoncé

BONUS! Unscramble the letters on the 10 foam fingers to answer the riddle: What do football champions put their cereal in?

_____ _____

START

SNACK BOWL

Super Bowl Sunday is second only to Thanksgiving as America's biggest food holiday. Maybe that's why February is also National Snack Food Month! Here's what people have eaten, by the numbers, on recent Super Bowl Sundays:

More than **1.35 billion** wings

More than **12.5 million** takeout pizzas

29 million pounds of chips (with dip)

160 million avocados (Holy guacamole!)

3.8 million pounds of popcorn

OPERA DAY

Marian Anderson was a famous African American opera singer. She performed with renowned orchestras all over the world. Two of her most famous performances were at the Lincoln Memorial in 1939 and with the Metropolitan Opera in 1955. **Can you find the hidden objects?**

The first opera was Jacopo Peri's *Dafne*, first performed in Italy in 1597.

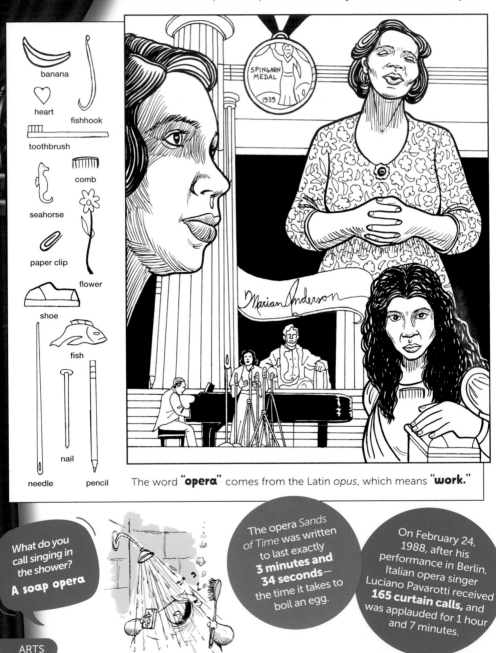

banana

heart

fishhook

toothbrush

comb

seahorse

paper clip

flower

shoe

fish

nail

needle

pencil

The word **"opera"** comes from the Latin *opus*, which means **"work."**

What do you call singing in the shower?

A soap opera

The opera *Sands of Time* was written to last exactly **3 minutes and 34 seconds**— the time it takes to boil an egg.

On February 24, 1988, after his performance in Berlin, Italian opera singer Luciano Pavarotti received **165 curtain calls,** and was applauded for 1 hour and 7 minutes.

February 11
GET OUT YOUR
GUITAR DAY

Every groovy guitar here has one that looks just like it.
Find all 10 matching pairs.

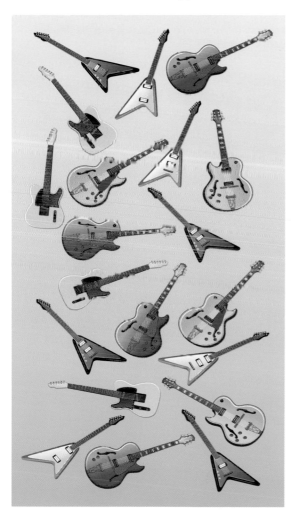

What did the guitar say to the musician?

Stop picking on me!

?

NAME
THAT
GUITAR

**Some instruments are
nearly as famous as the
musician who played them.
Which guitarist plucked
which guitar?**

Willie Nelson	Blackie
B.B. King	Red Special
Eric Clapton	Frankenstrat
Eddie Van Halen	Lucille
Brian May	Trigger

ANATOMY OF A
GUITAR

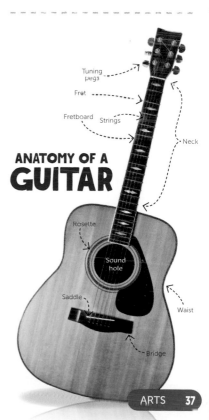

Tuning pegs
Fret
Fretboard Strings
Neck
Rosette
Sound hole
Saddle
Waist
Bridge

NATIONAL FROZEN YOGURT DAY

Most people may not crave this frozen treat in the middle of winter, but it's still a day to celebrate!

What do the frozen-yogurt cups in each row (horizontally, vertically, and diagonally) have in common?

Yogurt has been around for thousands of years, but it didn't become commercially frozen until the **1970s**. Frozen yogurt picked up in popularity twelve years ago, in **2012**. What are your favorite toppings?

CHILI DAY

Chili peppers have more vitamin C than oranges.

For Chili Day, try this twist on a traditional "sloppy joe" by making a "chili joe." **Here's how:**

Ask an adult for help with anything **HOT** or **SHARP.**

A chili pepper's heat is ranked on a special scale called the Scoville scale. Bell peppers are up to 100 Scoville heat units, while habanero peppers can be up to **350,000 SCOVILLE** heat units.

Chili Joe

1. Cut a **corn muffin** in half.
2. Scoop a spoonful of **turkey chili** on the bottom half of the muffin. Sprinkle on **corn chips**, **chopped bell peppers**, and shredded **cheddar cheese**.
3. Replace the top half of the muffin.

Dig in!

February 10, 2024
LUNAR NEW YEAR

Happy 4722—the Year of the Dragon! This holiday, known as the Spring Festival in China, celebrates the beginning of a new year on the Chinese calendar and lasts for 15 days. People celebrate by visiting their families, decorating their houses, and setting off fireworks and firecrackers. Kids often receive a gift of money in a red envelope.

Join the dragon-dance parade and find the 12 hidden objects in this Hidden Pictures puzzle.

bat   leaf   skateboard   clipboard   pumpkin

toothbrush   paper clip   pencil   bowl   needle

tweezers

carrot

What Is Your Zodiac Animal?

Below is a list of the 12 Chinese zodiac animals. Every year is assigned an animal. Look for the year you were born and see which is your zodiac animal. The cycle repeats itself every 12 years.

RAT
1996, 2008, 2020

OX
1997, 2009, 2021

TIGER
1998, 2010, 2022

RABBIT
1999, 2011, 2023

DRAGON
2000, 2012, 2024

SNAKE
2001, 2013, 2025

HORSE
2002, 2014, 2026

GOAT/RAM
2003, 2015, 2027

MONKEY
2004, 2016, 2028

ROOSTER
2005, 2017, 2029

DOG
2006, 2018, 2030

PIG
2007, 2019, 2031

February 14
VALENTINE'S DAY

Amy's class is enjoying their big Valentine's Day party. To add to the fun, someone played matchmaker with the cookies! Each cookie on Amy's tray has one exact match somewhere in the room. **Can you find all six matches?**

VALENTINE'S DAY "FORTUNE" HEARTS

1. Cut out a pair of hearts from **cardstock**. Glue the edges together.

2. Write a Valentine's Day "fortune" on a narrow strip of **paper**.

3. Cut the heart down the center, leaving a small connection at the point.

4. Glue the left side of the fortune into the left half of the heart. Fold the fortune and insert it into the right half of the heart.

5. Write a name on a small strip of paper. Glue it to the heart to hold the left and right sides together.

Natalie

Sam

Ryan

May you always be surrounded by good friends. Valentine!

What do you call two birds in love?

Tweet-hearts

WASHINGTON'S BIRTHDAY

Since 1885, this federal holiday has honored the February 22 birthday of the first U.S. president. The holiday was later moved to the third Monday of the month to give government workers—and schoolkids—a three-day weekend. Today it is often called Presidents' Day and celebrates Abraham Lincoln (born February 12) and all U.S. presidents, past and present. However, officially, it still is just George Washington's day.

Spell out the last name of each U.S. president below to find something that was named for him or built in his honor. Start each name on a letter in the yellow column, then move in any direction, including diagonally. We've found HOOVER for you.

Two other presidents were also born in February: William Henry Harrison (February 9, 1773) and Ronald Reagan (February 6, 1911).

ROOSEVELT

HOOVER

WASHINGTON

LINCOLN

KENNEDY

JEFFERSON

H	E	V	R	T	Y	L	N
K	O	O	E	D	F	I	S
R	E	S	E	A	J	G	T
E	O	N	N	V	A	L	O
F	I	N	C	W	E	S	N
L	S	H	F	O	R	I	T
J	A	F	H	E	L	G	O
W	E	S	G	I	N	W	N

BONUS!
In what order did these six presidents serve?

LEAP DAY

How many days are there in a year? If you said 365 days, you'd *almost* be right. Technically, it takes Earth 365 and ¼ days to travel around the sun. To compensate for that extra ¼ of a day, we add on one full day to the calendar every four years. This added-on-day is February 29 and is called Leap Day.

Don't leap past this page without testing your skills on one of these leap-themed puzzles

LEAPING LEMURS

These trees are loaded with lemurs! Every row of trees across, down, and diagonally has 30 lemurs in all. We've provided the exact number of lemurs hanging out in some of the trees. **Can you figure out how many are hanging on each of the other ones?**

A LEAP OF LOGIC

It's time for the annual Lakeside County frog-jumping contest. Taylor and two of her friends have entered their frogs. Using the clues below, can you figure out whose frog is whose and what place each frog took in the contest?

Use the chart to keep track of your answers. Put an **X** in each box that can't be true and an **O** in boxes that match.

	Freddie	Spot	Hoppy	1st	2nd	3rd
Taylor						
Madison						
Cameron						

1. Taylor's frog finished after Hoppy.
2. Madison's frog finished before Cameron's frog and Spot.
3. Freddie finished second.

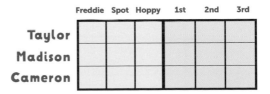

NATIONAL WEATHERPERSON'S DAY

Try your hand at being a meteorologist—a scientist who studies the weather and uses patterns to predict future weather conditions. Keep track of the weather where you live for a week.

Use this calendar. Draw or write about the weather every day.

Day 1

Day 2

Day 3

Day 4

Day 5

Day 6

Day 7

Talk About It!

- How many cloudy days did you record? How many sunny days?
- Were there any windy days?
- Can you find any patterns?
- Predict what your calendar might look like if you kept track of the weather in a different season.

WEATHER STUMPER

Every type of weather should only appear once in each row, column, and 2 x 3 box. Fill in the squares by drawing or writing the name of each weather type.

KIDS' SCIENCE QUESTION

Why does the temperature go up a few degrees after it rains?

Air temperature sometimes rises after it rains, but not always. Rain falls when winds mix a mass of cold air with a mass of warm air that's carrying *water vapor*, water in gas form. The cold air makes the water vapor condense into drops, which fall as rain.

If the winds push the warm air into the cold air, then the warm air replaces the cold air. In that case, the temperature goes up. If the winds push the cold air into the warm air, then the temperature goes down.

Why did the woman stand outside with her purse open?

Because she expected some change in the weather.

BE ELECTRIC DAY

Today's Thomas Edison's birthday. In honor of the inventor of the electric light bulb,
we celebrate Be Electric Day today!

HYDROELECTRIC
PLANTS

There are many ways that people get electricity to use in their homes and businesses. Hydroelectric plants are one of them. These plants make electricity from hydro power. *Hydro* means "water." At these plants, people build a large dam to hold back water. Then some of the water is forced through a pipe. As it moves through the pipe, it turns the blades on a turbine. This turbine then spins a generator to produce electricity. This is a clean energy source because it doesn't use any fossil fuels to make the electricity.

There's enough cement in the Hoover Dam to build a **FOUR-FOOT-WIDE SIDEWALK AROUND THE EARTH'S EQUATOR.**

The Hoover Dam is **726 FEET HIGH**—as tall as a **60-STORY BUILDING.**

About 21,000 men built the Hoover Dam in the 1930s.

THE
HOOVER DAM

The hydroelectric plant at the Hoover Dam in Nevada brings electricity to about 1.3 million homes in the American West. Scan this scene. **Can you find the objects hidden in and around the Hoover Dam?**

ruler

paper clip

sailboat

ice-cream cone

loaf of bread

banana

hand rake

cookie

February 3, 2024
SETSUBUN

Setsubun (節分, or "seasonal division") marks the day before the start of spring according to the Japanese lunar calendar. For many centuries, the people of Japan have been performing these Setsubun rituals to chase away evil spirits, or *oni*, at home and in temples to ensure good luck in the year ahead. Here's how to get into the non-evil spirit:

ON*I* IT! One family member wears the demon mask.

TOSS IT! In the *mamemak*i (bean-throwing) ceremony, roasted soybeans, gathered in an *asakemasu* (a wooden box), are thrown at the oni.

SHOUT IT! While flinging, chant *"Oni wa soto! Fuku wa uchi!"* ("Demons out! Happiness in!")

CHASE IT! Once the oni is outside, slam the door!

CHEW IT! Afterward, pick up and eat the number of beans equal to your age, plus one.

QUIET! Eat an entire uncut sushi roll, *in silence*, facing toward the year's "lucky direction." (The direction depends on the zodiac sign of the year. For 2024, it's east-northeast!)

February 6
NATIONAL CHOPSTICKS DAY

Today, try eating all your meals (okay, maybe not a bowl of soup or a sandwich) with chopsticks. Here's how.

The earliest chopsticks were likely in use around 5,000 years ago!

1 Tuck the first (lower) chopstick in the nook between your thumb and your index (pointer) finger. Hold it against your thumb and bent ring finger. This chopstick does not move while eating.

Hold the chopsticks near the tops, toward the wider ends, with the tips lined up.

2 Hold the second (upper) chopstick between your index finger and thumb, as you would if holding a pencil—only higher up. Brace this chopstick against your middle finger.

3 Open up the chopsticks by moving just the upper chopstick with your index and middle finger.

4 Moving the upper chopstick down with your index and middle fingers, close the chopsticks over your morsel of food.

February 7, 2024

SEND A CARD TO A FRIEND DAY

A handwritten letter is the perfect way to tell a friend a funny story or just say hello. This outline will give you some ideas of what to write and how to form your letter.

Put your address at the top right so your friend can write you back.

Ask what is new with your friend.

Add the date you wrote the letter.

Explain why you are writing.

End your letter with a wish for the future.

Close a letter to a friend with a short expression like *Your friend* or *Take care*.

If there's something you forgot to say, add it at the bottom with *P.S.*

75 Willow Street
Flisk, MT 55562
July 1, 2024

Dear Alex,

How are you? My summer is great but I'm super bored today. I could have texted you, but a letter seemed more special. Plus, it takes more time to write!

I miss talking about joking around with you. Remember the skateboards we made for Horatio Hamster? I hope we can see each other soon.

Your friend,
Ava

P.S. Write me back!

February 20

NATIONAL LOVE YOUR PET DAY

A dog's nose print is unique, much like a human's fingerprint.

Hamsters' teeth never stop growing.

Hooray for pets! These critters bring all kinds of joy, even when they're causing mischief. One of the pets in this picture knocked over a houseplant. **Use the clues to figure out which one made the mess.**

THE MISCHIEVOUS PET...

- has white paws.
- has brown ears.
- doesn't have a pink nose.

Take a spin around the globe to see how

February 6
WAITANGI DAY

On this day in 1840, the British government and 540 Māori chiefs signed the Treaty of Waitangi (named after the region where this took place) to create the nation of New Zealand. Māori cultural performances, speeches from Māori and Pakeha (European) dignitaries, and a naval salute are part of the activities.

1. Roll **polymer clay** into a 9-inch-long "snake," wide at one end and thin at the other.

2. On **foil** on a **baking sheet**, arrange the shape into a spiral. With an adult's help, bake the clay according to the instructions. Let the spiral cool.

3. Loop **string** or **cord** to make a lanyard.

Make a Māori koru pendant, inspired by the art of the Māori people of New Zealand.

Often, lanterns will have a riddle written on them. Whoever solves the riddle gets a gift!

February 24, 2024
LANTERN FESTIVAL

While the origin of the Lantern Festival is unknown, one theory says that it began two thousand years ago with Han Mingdi. Han Mingdi was a Chinese emperor who wanted to spread Buddhism throughout China. Buddhist monks would hang lanterns in their temples to honor Buddha on the fifteenth day of the first lunar month. Emperor Han Mingdi said people throughout the country should do the same. Today, the Lantern Festival has become a nationwide tradition where Chinese citizens light and admire lanterns, watch firework shows, eat *tangyuan* (a rice ball with fillings), and enjoy lion dance performances.

Decorate your own lantern for the Lantern Festival!

THE WORLD

To celebrate Fastelavn, Danes eat *fastelavnsboller*, sweet buns filled with cream.

February 11, 2024

FASTELAVN

One popular tradition to celebrate this pre-Lenten festival is for Danish children to dress up in fanciful costumes and try to "beat the cat out of the barrel." Don't worry—the wooden barrel only has images of black cats, which represent evil spirits. The person who knocks out the bottom of the barrel is crowned *Kattedronning* ("Cat Queen"), and the person who knocks down the last piece of the barrel is crowned *Kattekonge* ("Cat King")

February 24, 2024

NAVAM FULL MOON POYA DAY

This Buddhist holiday usually takes place on the first full moon in February. The tiny country of Sri Lanka, a raindrop-shaped island off the tip of India, celebrates in a big way: Its capital, Colombo, hosts a joyous parade, or *perahera*, featuring thousands of fire dancers, flag bearers, traditional dancers, musicians, and dozens of dazzlingly dressed elephants. Can you find where the three jigsaw pieces fit into this photo of a typical Navam Perahera sight?

SUNDAY	MONDAY	TUESDAY	WEDNESDAY

BIRTHSTONES
AQUAMARINE ----

BLOODSTONE ---

H ----> PISCES: FEBRUARY 19–MARCH 20

ZODIAC SIGNS Y ----> ARIES: MARCH 21–APRIL 19

National Anthem Day
Sing along as you raise the Stars and Stripes.
3

Marching Band Day
Today's the perfect day to grab an instrument and "march forth!"
4

NATIONAL CHEESE DOODLE DAY
This crunchy snack hits the spot!
5

NATIONAL WHITE CHOCOLATE CHEESECAKE DAY
6

RAMADAN

Daylight Saving Begins
*Not for you, Arizona and Hawaii
10

Moshoeshoe Day (Lesotho)
This holiday honors King Moshoeshoe I, the founder and national hero of Lesotho.
11

NATIONAL PLANT A FLOWER DAY
There are over 400,000 types of flowering plants!
12

National Good Samaritan Day
Do something nice for someone else today.
1

SAINT PATRICK'S DAY
17

Far out!
In 1965, Alexei Leonov became the first man to walk in space.
18

First Day of Spring
What is the best smell in spring?
19

International Day of Happiness
Don't worry! Just be happy!
20

24
Palm Sunday
Easter
31

Ciao, Venezia!
In 421—1,603 years ago!—the city of Venice was founded at the stroke of noon.
25

Make Up Your Own Holiday Day
You know what to do!
26

National Scribble Day
What art can you make with a few scribbles?
27

THURSDAY	FRIDAY	SATURDAY

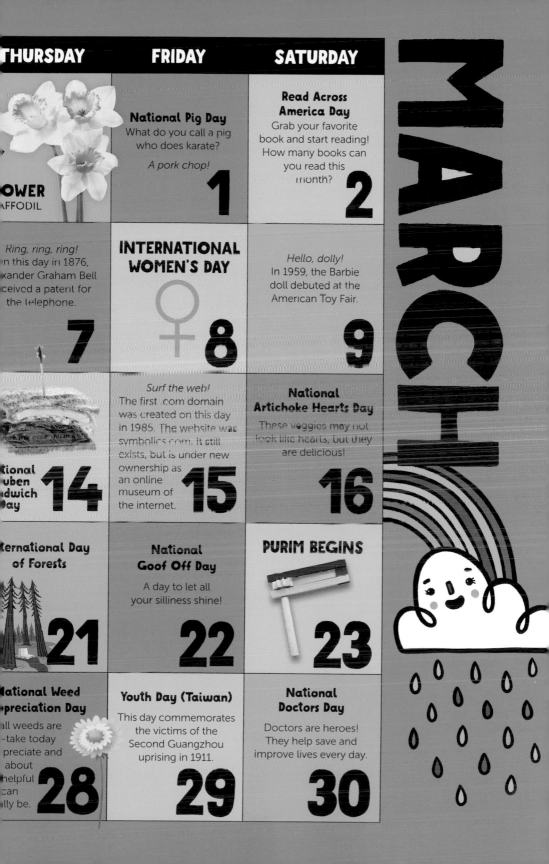

FLOWER
DAFFODIL

National Pig Day
What do you call a pig who does karate?

A pork chop!

1

Read Across America Day
Grab your favorite book and start reading! How many books can you read this month?

2

Ring, ring, ring!
On this day in 1876, Alexander Graham Bell received a patent for the telephone.

7

INTERNATIONAL WOMEN'S DAY

8

Hello, dolly!
In 1959, the Barbie doll debuted at the American Toy Fair.

9

National Reuben Sandwich Day

14

Surf the web!
The first .com domain was created on this day in 1985. The website was symbolics.com. It still exists, but is under new ownership as an online museum of the internet.

15

National Artichoke Hearts Day
These veggies may not look like hearts, but they are delicious!

16

International Day of Forests

21

National Goof Off Day
A day to let all your silliness shine!

22

PURIM BEGINS

23

National Weed Appreciation Day
Not all weeds are bad—take today to appreciate and learn about how helpful they can really be.

28

Youth Day (Taiwan)
This day commemorates the victims of the Second Guangzhou uprising in 1911.

29

National Doctors Day
Doctors are heroes! They help save and improve lives every day.

30

MARCH

Kamala Harris

Marie Curie

Mo'ne Davis

Amelia Earhart

WOMEN'S HISTORY MONTH

Celebrate by matching each pioneering woman with her historic achievement.

Aretha Franklin

1. Who was the first woman to win a Nobel Prize (1903)?

2. Who was the first woman to make a nonstop solo airplane flight across the Atlantic Ocean (1932)?

3. Who is considered to be America's first prima ballerina (1940s)?

4. Who was the first woman to fly into outer space (1963)?

5. Who was the first woman to reach the summit of Mount Everest (1975)?

6. Who was the first woman to serve on the Supreme Court (1981)?

7. Who was the first woman to be inducted into the Rock & Roll Hall of Fame (1987)?

8. Who was the first girl to pitch a shutout in the Little League World Series (2014)?

9. Who was the first woman elected vice president of the United States (2020)?

INTERNATIONAL WOMEN'S DAY IS MARCH 8. This global day celebrates women's achievements and calls for gender equality.

Sandra Day O'Connor

Maria Tallchief

Junko Tabei

Valentina Tereshkova

NATIONAL UMBRELLA MONTH

	1	2	3	4	5
A	W	H	O	E	N
B	C	T	H	O	E
C	S	E	U	N	T
D	R	I	T	P	S
E	O	L	U	T	D

Umbrella Fun

Black out the squares listed for each row. When you're done, the remaining letters will spell out the answer to the riddle.

- **Row A:** Black out **3**.
- **Row B:** Black out **1** and **4**.
- **Row C:** Black out **2** and **5**.
- **Row D:** Black out **1**, **3**, and **4**.
- **Row E:** Black out **2** and **5**.

When can 6 people share one umbrella without getting wet?

__ __ __ __ __

__ __ __

__ __ __ __

__ __ __

NATIONAL MUSIC IN OUR SCHOOLS MONTH

Celebrate by finding these six WORDS (not pictures) hidden in the scene below. Can you find BEAT, CHORUS, CONDUCT, MUSICIAN, NOTE, and PIANO?

The most popular instruments to play are:
1. Piano
2. Guitar
3. Violin
4. Drums
5. Saxophone

NATIONAL NOODLE MONTH

No one knows for sure where noodles were first invented, but they are believed to have existed in some form in ancient China and Greece. Today, there are noodles of all shapes and sizes, including gluten-free and wheat-free versions, and even noodles made from vegetables.

Use your noodle to take this quiz and figure out which facts are true and which are im-pastas!

T F In Italian, *orecchiette* means "little ears" and *linguine* means "little tongues."

T F Noodles that are cooked *al dente* means they were cooked in a pot without any dents in it.

T F Thomas Jefferson helped popularize macaroni and cheese by serving it to his dinner guests.

T F Although used interchangeably, pasta and noodles are technically two different foods.

T F The name *macaroni* comes from the song "Yankee Doodle."

T F In Japan, somen noodles are hung outside to dry in the sun.

T F It is scientifically impossible to eat spaghetti and meatballs without making a mess.

T F In 1848, the first commercial pasta plant in the U.S. was founded in Brooklyn.

NATIONAL NUTRITION MONTH

Nutritious food is good for you—it helps your body grow strong, it helps you feel good, and it tastes great, too!

To make these healthy cucumber snacks, have an adult help you slice the cucumbers. Then, top them with Greek yogurt or cottage cheese. Last, add some of your favorite toppings. Here are some ideas:

Turkey

Pretzel

Peas

Cranberries

Tasty!

Olives

Pickle

Pepperoni

Raspberries

What will you choose to make?

NATIONAL CRAFT MONTH

**March is a perfect month to plant some flowers.
It's also the perfect month to make some flower crafts!**

Once your flowerpot is completely dry, plant your favorite flower or succulent inside!

DRIP POTS

1. Paint **clear sealer** onto the inside and outside of a **terra-cotta pot**. Let it dry.

2. Paint the outside of the pot with white **acrylic paint**. Let it dry.

3. Mix another color of paint with a few drops of **water** so that it drips like milk.

4. Place the pot upside down on a covered surface. Drip the watery paint onto the pot. Let it dry.

5. Add a coat of clear sealer.

PAPER FLOWERS

If you'd rather fill your pot with flowers that don't need to be watered, try making them instead!

DAFFODIL

1. Flatten three **cupcake liners**. On each, draw a shape with three petals.

2. Stack and arrange them to form a circle. **Glue** them together.

3. Glue a **mini cupcake liner** and a **pompom** on top. **Tape** a **paper straw** to the back.

DAISY

1. Cut out a long strip of **cardstock**. **Glue** the ends together to form a loop. Make three more loops.

2. Stack and arrange the loops to form a circle. Glue them together.

3. Add a small **cardstock** circle. Tape a **paper straw** to the back.

POPPY

1. Cut out six circles from **tissue paper**. Glue them together to form a big circle.

2. Cut out two small **cardstock** circles. Punch a hole in each and in the tissue-paper circle.

3. Push a **fuzzy stick** through one cardstock circle, then the tissue-paper circle, and then the other cardstock circle. Bend the end.

4. Slide a **paper straw** onto the fuzzy stick. Bend the end.

March 21, 1999

25 YEARS AGO, BRIAN JONES AND BERTRAND PICCARD FINISHED THE FIRST NON-STOP FLIGHT AROUND THE WORLD IN A HOT-AIR BALLOON.

They started in Switzerland, traveled for 20 days, and then finally landed in Africa.
At their fastest speed, they were traveling about 170 miles per hour.

Jackie and her friends are traveling in this hot-air balloon, and the only way they can land is if you find your way from start to finish. Be careful! There's sure to be lots of tricks along the way.

The first known passengers aboard a hot-air balloon were a duck, a sheep, and a rooster.

March 31, 1889

135 YEARS AGO, THE EIFFEL TOWER OPENED.

Gustave Eiffel and his team constructed the Eiffel Tower in Paris, France, in exactly two years, two months, and five days. They built it out of over 7,000 tons of steel with 2.5 million rivets holding it all together. Today, approximately 7 million people visit the Eiffel Tower every year.

Gustave Eiffel built a private apartment at the top of the tower so he could entertain guests.

Visitors can ride an elevator all the way to the top. It travels at an angle at first, and then goes straight up!

Can you find each hidden object in and around the Eiffel Tower?

Learn to say the objects in French, too!

heart	**grapes**
un coeur	une grappe de raisin
uhn kurr	ewn grahp duh ray-ZAHN

fish
un poisson
uhn pwah-SONE

banana
une banane
ewn bah-NAHN

spoon
une cuillère
ewn KWEE-yair

ruler
une règle
ewn REHG-luh

sailboat
un voilier
uhn vwall-ee-AY

ice-cream cone
un cornet de glace
uhn kore-nay duh GLASS

star
une étoile
ewn ay-TWAL

comb
un peigne
uhn PEN-yuh

toothbrush
une brosse à dents
ewn bruhss-ah-DAHN

tomato
une tomate
ewn toh-MOTT

bell
une cloche
ewn clush

candle
une bougie
ewn booge-EE

Say it in French:
Awesome!
Génial!
jeay-NYAL

MARCH MADNESS

Throughout the month of March every year, both men and women college teams play in a single-elimination **National Collegiate Athletic Association (NCAA) Division I Basketball Tournament**, also known as March Madness. The final championship game determines the #1 men's and women's teams in the nation.

SPACE BASKETBALL

Earth isn't the only place that is "mad" for basketball in March. The Astros and the Rockets battle it out in space, too! Well, not really, but it sure is fun to imagine. Can you find all the hidden objects in this puzzle?

olive   sock   banana   tack   drinking straw   knitted hat   broccoli   mug   cane

artist's brush   flowerpot   heart   ruler   boomerang   butter knife   golf club

10	33	5	20	12	8	21	16	25	41	3
T	I	H	E	C	Y	N	R	E	A	W
13	9	37	24	19	52	36	14	38	6	40
L	E	W	K	A	Y	M	S	D	F	R
99	7	50	30	26	35	15	4	23	60	11
G	I	B	D	B	L	V	I	N	Y	G

TO THE HOOP!

Cross out all the boxes in which the number can be evenly divided by 3. Then write the leftover letters in the spaces to spell the answer.

Why are basketball players messy eaters?

_ _ _ _ _ _ _ _ _ _

_ _ _ _ _ _ _ _ _

MLB SPRING TRAINING

Every March, Major League Baseball teams from throughout the country descend on the sunny states of Arizona and Florida to start their spring training. They play practice games amongst the other teams who also came to the area. The teams who come to Arizona are called the Cactus League, and the teams who come to Florida are the Grapefruit League.

HOME RUN!

Take a break from Spring Training to find **8 hidden objects** in this out-of-this-world baseball game.

ice-pop

pencil

spoon

book

drum

tack

peanut

duster

IMAGINE AND DRAW

It you could design any space baseball uniform, what would it look like? Design yours here!

Why won't the Stegosaurus invite the baseball team for dinner?

They're always stepping on his plates.

READ ACROSS AMERICA DAY

There are 12 objects hidden in this library scene. Can you find them all?

OBJECT LIST

- COFFEEPOT
- ICE-CREAM BAR
- ELEPHANT
- LIGHT BULB
- OILCAN
- OWL
- PENNANT
- ROLLER SKATE
- SOCK
- BRIEFCASE
- TOP HAT
- UMBRELLA

March 28

WORLD PIANO DAY

World Piano Day is celebrated on the 88th day of the year, which is the same number of keys on the piano.

PIANO PATH

Lina is late for her piano lesson today. Help her make her way through the maze so she can get there on time.

START →
FINISH

Knock, knock.
Who's there?
Tuna.
Tuna who?
Tuna piano and it'll sound better.

March 27

WORLD THEATER DAY

Have you been to a theater? If so, what did you see?

If you were to write your own play, what would it be about?

World Theater Day is celebrated annually on March 27 with theater events around the world. Theater people can be pretty superstitious, so read up on these seven tips to avoid bad luck in the theater.

1. **"Good luck" is bad luck!** Say "break a leg" to wish someone in theater well.

2. **Leave the ghost light on.** A single lit bulb upstage center helps ward off theater ghosts—and helps the crew see in the dark!

3. **Don't say "Macbeth!"** To avoid saying the famous Shakespeare play's title, which supposedly brings bad luck, theater people call it "The Scottish Play."

4. **Mirror, mirror, on the wall—not on stage.** If a mirror breaks on stage, it brings bad luck, so most sets don't include real mirrors.

5. **Don't whistle while you work!** Stagehands once communicated with coded whistles, so whistling backstage could lead to accidents.

6. **What's under your pillow?** Superstitious performers sleep with a script under their pillow to help them memorize lines faster. Just don't try it for your next history exam!

7. **Lucky lefty.** In theater, the left foot is luckier than the right foot, so actors should always walk left foot first into a dressing room.

Top Act

Here's a list of the top 10 most frequently performed musicals in North American high schools, with a twist—we replaced one word in six of the titles with a synonym in blue. Can you figure out the real names of the six silly musicals?

What performances did your school do this year?

1. Beauty and the Monstrosity
2. The Addams Clan
3. The Miniature Mermaid
4. Into the Forest
5. Cinderella
6. Shrek
7. Seussical
8. Little Boutique of Horrors
9. The Magician of Oz
10. Annie

NATIONAL PI DAY

March 14 (3/14) is celebrated as Pi Day because 3, 1, and 4 are the first three digits of the mathematical symbol π. Seventeen types of pie are hidden up, down, across, backward, and diagonally. Dig in!

```
        C O C O N U T
      Y I C E C R E A M
  Y P M I N C E M E A T
U O E P R U N E W H I P R
T U A Y E L E M O N C E T
H C R N R E Q B N A P E A R B
Q H T U R T R K E Y L I M E P
Y E E T E A M Y     N A C E P
U R E B B L P L         E O
M R T U Q O U F         S
Y H T A C M O
R A T P O P O T
  H E P H K H B
  R L C I S L
  E A N E X
```

What's the best thing to put in a pie?

WORD LIST

APPLE	MINCEMEAT
BERRY	PEACH
CHERRY	PEANUT BUTTER
CHOCOLATE	PEAR
COCONUT	PECAN
ICE CREAM	PRUNE WHIP
KEY LIME	PUMPKIN
LEMON	RHUBARB
	SHOOFLY

A Never-Ending Number

The number pi is infinitely long, but that hasn't stopped people from trying to calculate it. A new record was set in March 2019 when Emma Haruka Iwao calculated pi to 31,415,926,535,897 digits! Why is that number significant? Here are the first 100 digits:

3.1415926535897932384626433832795028841971693993751058209749445923078164062862089986280348253421170 67

More Treats for Your Tongue

Say these tongue twisters three times, fast!

Three slices of pumpkin pie, please!
Pecan pie is perfect for a party.
Crisscrossed crispy piecrust.

March 25

INTERNATIONAL WAFFLE DAY

Here are four meals you can make to celebrate. Rate each recipe you try by filling in the stars.

☆☆☆☆
Cornbread-and-Chili Dinner

Pour **cornbread batter** onto a waffle iron. Cook until lightly browned, about 1½–2 minutes. Top with **chili**, **cheese**, **lettuce**, and **sour cream**.

☆☆☆☆
Waffled-Egg Breakfast

Beat 3 **eggs**. Add **salt** and **pepper**. Pour the eggs onto a waffle iron. Cook through, about 2–3 minutes.

☆☆☆☆
Mini-Pizza Lunch

Add **pizza sauce**, **cheese**, and **mini pepperoni** to the bottom half of a **refrigerated biscuit**. Put on the top half and squeeze the edges together. Cook in a waffle iron for 1–1½ minutes.

☆☆☆☆
S'more Dessert

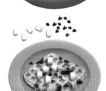

Mix **chocolate chips** and **mini marshmallows** into **waffle batter**. Cook until the waffles are done.

We hope you're hungry! There are lots of fun food holidays in March. Here are just a few:

March 1
NATIONAL PEANUT BUTTER LOVERS' DAY

There are about 540 peanuts in a 12-ounce jar of peanut butter.

March 7
NATIONAL CEREAL DAY

Most Americans eat around 160 bowls of cereal per year.

March 16
NATIONAL ARTICHOKE HEARTS DAY

Artichokes are flowers. They're part of the daisy family.

March 26
NATIONAL SPINACH DAY

If you see *Florentine* on a menu or in a recipe, there's probably spinach in the dish.

ST. PATRICK'S DAY

A prankster is on the loose! Someone took an item from one of the shops and hid it. Luckily, he or she left some clues behind. Can you figure out WHO the mischief-maker is, WHAT was taken, and WHERE it was hidden?

Clues

WHO
I am a prankster,
red-haired am I,
with golden shoes
and bright-green
eyes.

WHAT
I'm made of wood
and pegs and
string.
You can play me
while you sing.

WHERE
A place with
a chimney and
mushrooms galore.
Look above a
spotted door.

BONUS!
Find 5 gold coins,
4 four-leaf clovers,
3 horseshoes,
2 rainbows,
and 1 harp.

March 23-24, 2024

PURIM

This Jewish holiday honors Queen Esther, who persuaded her husband, King Ahasuerus, to save the Jewish people of Persia from the villain Haman. It's a festive day, during which people dress up in costumes, exchange gifts, and give to the poor.

From the Middle Ages onward, actors have performed funny plays called *spiels* that tell the Purim story, known as the Megillah. (*Spiel* means "play" or "skit" in Yiddish, the language Jews spoke in Central and Eastern Europe.) To this day, the name *Haman* is met with boos and the sounds of *groggers* (noisemakers) during these plays—and even during religious services.

MAKE HAMANTASCHEN

Hamantaschen, which means "Haman's pockets" in Yiddish, are traditional treats eaten at Purim. This three-sided pastry looks like the hat that Haman supposedly wore.

FILLING*

1. Place 1 package (16 ounces) **pitted prunes** in a saucepan and cover with water. Add ½ teaspoon **cinnamon**, 1 tablespoon **sugar**, and 1 tablespoon **lemon juice**. Simmer until fruit is soft and mushy. (Add more water if needed.) Let cool.

2. With an adult's help, chop 1 cup **shelled walnuts or other nuts** in a food processor or blender. Add prune mixture and mix well. Set aside.

   * Prune butter or apple butter can be substituted for prune-nut filling

DOUGH

1. With a mixing bowl, cream together 1 stick **softened butter or margarine** and ¾ cup **sugar.**

2. Beat 3 **egg yolks** in a separate bowl and add to the butter-sugar mixture. Add 1 cup **sour cream**. Mix well.

3. In a large bowl, sift together 3 cups **flour**, 2 teaspoons **baking powder**, and ¼ teaspoon **baking soda**. Add to the butter-sugar mixture. Then add 1 teaspoon **vanilla** and ½ teaspoon **grated orange rind**. Mix well.

4. On a floured board, roll out the dough about ¼-inch thick. If the dough is too sticky, cover and refrigerate for a few hours before rolling out.

5. Cut into 3-inch circles with a cookie cutter or a drinking glass turned upside down.

6. Place a teaspoon of filling in the center of each circle. Fold up two sides of the circle and pinch together. Fold up the third side and pinch together with the other two sides to form a triangle, leaving the center open.

7. Place the hamantaschen on greased baking sheets and into the oven. Bake for about 20 minutes at 350°F, until lightly browned.

Ask an adult for help using the stove, food processor, and oven.

March 31, 2024

EASTER

Easter is the most important holiday in the Christian religion. This holiday celebrates the day Christians believe Jesus Christ rose from the dead on the third day after he was crucified on Good Friday. Western churches celebrate Easter on a Sunday between March 22 and April 25. The exact date depends on the date of the first full moon after the first day of spring.

READY TO ROLL

Since Rutherford B. Hayes was president in 1878, it has been a tradition to hold the Easter Egg Roll on the White House lawn the Monday after Easter. Here are some highlights.

1974: Kids were given spoons to push the eggs along a path in the grass.

1977: President Jimmy Carter added a circus to the egg-roll fun.

1981: President Ronald Reagan replaced hard-boiled eggs with wooden eggs signed by celebrities.

1998: The roll was broadcast live over the internet for the first time.

2009: The egg roll was so popular, the White House had to give out lottery tickets to kids around the U.S. to limit participants.

A VERY YUMMY EASTER

Four cousins—Carly, Dan, Anthony, and Kiera—each made a dessert for Easter dinner. Using the clues below, can you figure out which dessert each cousin baked and what flavor it was?

	Pie	Muffins	Tart	Cupcake	Apple	Lemon	Coconut	Strawberry
Carly								
Anthony								
Kiera								
Dan								

1. Dan never bakes with coconut.
2. The girl who made muffins put strawberries in them.
3. Anthony made something with apples that was not a pie.
4. Kiera baked her favorite kind of cupcake.

Use the chart to keep track of your answers. Put an X in each box that can't be true and an O in boxes that match.

WHY ARE THESE EASTER SYMBOLS?

Rabbits: They produce so many babies, they are a symbol of new life, or resurrection.

Easter Eggs: Babies hatching from their shells are another symbol of new life.

Lamb: Lambs are also a symbol of Easter because Jesus was called the "lamb of God" and lambs were sacrificed to God in ancient Israel as a symbol of Jesus's future crucifixion.

SUNDAY

RABBIT SEARCH

The Grovers are getting ready for Easter. Can you find 10 rabbits in the scene?

GLOBAL EASTER TRADITIONS

Nine of these are real Easter traditions—but one is made up. Can you figure out which tradition is false?

1. **Australia:** Eating chocolate Easter bilbies (rabbit-eared bandicoots) instead of bunnies

2. **Florence, Italy:** Setting off a cart full of fireworks in front of a church

3. **Finland:** Children dressing up like witches

4. **Manchester, England:** Tossing hard-boiled eggs at each other on the field of Manchester United's stadium

5. **Poland:** Pouring water over each other

6. **Haux, France:** Eating a giant omelet made of 4,500 eggs in the town square

7. **Corfu, Greece:** Throwing pots and pans out their windows so they smash on the street

8. **Norway:** Reading crime novels

9. **Verges, Spain:** Walking through the streets dressed in skeleton costumes

March 3
WORLD WILDLIFE DAY

Take today to learn about amazing wild animals—like the koala! These marsupials live in Australia. They eat a diet of mainly eucalyptus leaves and sleep about 18 hours a day. The koala cuties pictured here are hanging out in their treetop home. **Look for these 22 hidden objects.**

butterfly · bat · shoe · dog bone · crown · canoe

hanger · comb · cane · pennant · cotton swab · artist's brush · funnel · teacup · sock

hourglass · heart · crescent moon · arrowhead · boomerang · mushroom · snake

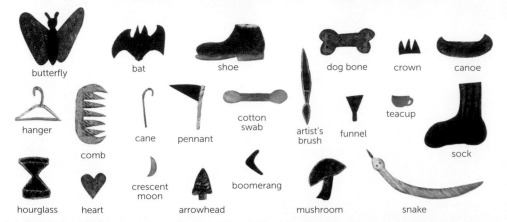

Why isn't a koala considered a bear?

It doesn't have the right koala-fications.

World Wildlife Day is meant to raise awareness of the importance of living things in our world. How does your local wildlife improve where you live?

March 30, 2024

EARTH HOUR

Earth Hour is a global environmental event that encourages people to turn off their lights for one hour. Earth Hour started in 2007 in Australia and is now celebrated in more than 180 countries and territories around the world. Famous landmarks, including **Big Ben**, the **Statue of Liberty**, the **Eiffel Tower**, and the **Sphinx and Great Pyramids of Giza,** have all participated in Earth Hour.

Earth Hour starts at 8:30 p.m. local time on the last Saturday in March.

The Statue of Liberty is modeled after the sculptor's mother.

The Eiffel Tower was built to be the centerpiece of the 1889 World Fair.

Big Ben is actually the 13-ton bell at the top of the clock tower.

The more than 4,500-year-old Sphinx was originally painted in bright colors like red, yellow, and blue.

AM   PM   PM   PM

While getting ready for Earth Hour, Bethany notices that all the country labels have fallen off the world clocks. Using the clues below, help her match each country label with the correct clock.

Mali is 8 hours behind China.
Nepal is 5 hours and 45 minutes ahead of Mali.
Ukraine is 6 hours behind China.

NEPAL

UKRAINE

MALI

CHINA

Which continent has the most time zones?   Asia (11 time zones)

International Mermaid Day

Today is all about mermaids! Andromeda is trying to get to Atlantis.
Help her swim through the maze and to the FINISH.

Where do legends of mermaids come from? Many think they were inspired centuries ago by real-life sea animals called manatees. Sailors who caught sight of these animals may have mistaken them for creatures that were part human, part fish. Tales then spread about the mythical creatures the sailors thought they saw.

FINISH

START

Seen and Heard:
Hans Christian Andersen wrote the original story of "The Little Mermaid," in which a mermaid tries to become human after falling in love with a prince.

Origin:
The first story of a beautiful mermaid may have come from a sailor or an explorer who spotted a manatee or dugong from far away.

Myth:
Mermaids and mermen have played many roles in folk stories around the world. In some stories, mermaids trick sailors into wrecking their ships or lure men to live under the sea.

BLOSSOM KITE FESTIVAL

March 2024

Kite makers and fliers from around the world come to Washington, D.C. for competitions and demonstrations

Find what's silly in the picture above. It's up to you!

March 31
NATIONAL CRAYON DAY

Do you say it "cran," "cray-ahn," "cray-awn," or "crown"?

No matter how you say it, all versions mean the same thing: a fun way to color! To celebrate this fun day honoring these beloved waxy drawing instruments, find the jigsaw puzzle pieces in this colorful crayon photo.

Take a spin around the globe to see how

March 6
INDEPENDENCE DAY

In 1957, Ghana gained its independence from the United Kingdom. Although English is Ghana's official language, about 80 languages are spoken in the country. The names of government-sponsored Ghanaian languages are listed here. Use the number of letters in each word as a clue as to where it might fit in the grid.

AKAN
DAGAARE
DAGBANI
DANGME
EWE
GA
GONJA
KASEM
MFANTSE
NZEMA

March 20, 2024
HAPPY NEW YEAR!

March 20 is Nowruz, or Iranian New Year.
To symbolize rebirth and growth, Iranians prepare *sabzeh* (sab-ZAY), sprouted seeds grown in a dish.

Happy 1,403rd! According to the Persian calendar, March 20, 2024, is the first day of the year 1403.

THE WORLD

Farion (fez) has the Greek coat of arms.

Tsarouchi (clogs) have 60 nails on the sole and weigh more than 3 pounds each!

Fustanella (kilt) has 400 pleats to represent the years of Ottoman occupation.

March 25

📍 GREEK INDEPENDENCE DAY

The Greek War of Independence started on March 25, 1821. On Greek Independence Day, the national holiday is celebrated with a military parade in Athens, the capital city. Children also march in local parades, waving Greek flags and wearing traditional costumes with symbolic significance.

March 25, 2024

📍HOLI

During Holi, people in northern India wear new white clothes. They toss colored powder called *gulal* (goo-LAHL) and colored water on one another. The streets soon fill with children and adults, their new white clothes blooming in wild bouquets of color. Can you find the jigsaw pieces below in this photo of kids holding colored powder during Holi?

Gulal colors hold special meaning. Red is for love, green is for new beginnings, and blue represents Krishna, a Hindu deity.

SUNDAY	MONDAY	TUESDAY	WEDNESDAY
	APRIL FOOLS' DAY — Be careful today—things may not be what they seem! **1**	**NATIONAL CHILDREN'S PICTURE BOOK DAY 2**	**National Find a Rainbow Day** — Rainbows may be caused by light refracting through water droplets, but that doesn't make them less magical. If there's a rain shower today, look to the skies—you just might find a rainbow. **3**
NATIONAL NO HOUSEWORK DAY — Don't touch that broom! Today's your day to take a break. **7**	*Now you see it, now you don't.* On live TV in 1983, magician David Copperfield made the Statue of Liberty disappear. **8**	**EID AL-FITR** begins at sunset. **9**	**National Siblings** — Let your siblings know how much you love them with a nice note or special treat. **10**
International Moment of Laughter Day — Here's a joke to get you started: **What color is rain?** *Watercolor* **14**	**TAKE A WILD GUESS DAY 15**	*A numbers game.* In 1929, the Cleveland Guardians became the first baseball team to put numbers on the backs of players' uniforms. **16**	**National Haiku Poetry Day** — Haiku have five beats, then count seven in line two. Finish last with fi... **17**
National Chocolate Covered Cashews Day — Did you know the cashew tree grows 32 feet tall? **21**	**PASSOVER** begins at sunset. **22**	**National Take a Chance Day** — Wanna try something new? Today's your day to give it a whirl! **23**	*Golden tickets not needed.* In 1907, Hershey Park opened for workers from Hershey's chocolate company. **24**
Pay It Forward Day — Do something kind today and start a chain reaction of good deeds! **28**	**National Zipper Day** — Three cheers for this invention: zip, zip, hooray! **29**	**National Honesty Day** — Honesty is the best policy on any day! **30**	**BIRTHSTONE** DIAMOND

THURSDAY	FRIDAY	SATURDAY

INTERNATIONAL CARROT DAY
Calling all carrot lovers: today is your day!

4

NATIONAL GO FOR BROKE DAY
It's a day to give it your all, no matter what you try!

5

NATIONAL CARAMEL POPCORN DAY

6

National Submarine Day
(The ship, not the sandwich.)

11

National Black Licorice Day
Just pick out the black sticks today, not the red!

12

Teachers' Day (Ecuador)
This day takes place on the birthday of Juan Montalvo, a popular Ecuadorian writer in the 1800s.

13

Do, re, mi wins! In 1966, *The Sound of Music* won the Academy Award for Best Picture of the Year.

18

National Hanging Out Day
Hang out your laundry on a clothesline to dry today!

19

National Look-Alike Day
"You look familiar!"

20

Great move! In 1950, Chuck Cooper became the first African American hoopster drafted into the NBA.

25

National Pretzel Day
Soft or crunchy; twisted or sticks. You choose your favorite to eat today!

26

Morse Code Day
Learning the code is as easy as
.—-. .. .

27

APRIL

These penguins look exactly the same! Who do YOU look most like?

ZODIAC SIGNS
ARIES: MARCH 21–APRIL 19

TAURUS: APRIL 20–MAY 20

FLOWERS
SWEET PEA AND DAISY

NATIONAL KITE MONTH

People have been flying kites for thousands of years. The earliest description of kite flying comes from a Chinese text from 200 BCE! Celebrate the kite during the month of April by going out and flying a kite, solving one of these kite puzzles, or telling a kite-themed joke!

FLYING NUMBERS

Each kite stands for a number. **Use the kite key to figure out the punch lines to the number jokes below.**

=0   =1   =2   =3   =4

=5   =6   =7   =8   =9

The world record for the highest altitude reached by a single kite is **4,879.54 meters** (16,009 feet).

Benjamin Franklin's famous experiment in 1752 used a kite and key to demonstrate that lightning is electricity.

Why was 6 mad at 7?
Because

What does a dollar have in common with the moon?
They both have   quarters.

Why is a circle always so hot?
Because it's   degrees

How does 10 feel without its number 1 friend? Like a

How do numbers celebrate?
With high   s

What happened when 19 and 20 got into an argument?

TIC TAC KITE

Each of these kites has something in common with the other two kites in the same row. Look at the rows across, down, and diagonally. **Can you tell what's alike in each?**

What's the best material for kites?

Flypaper

NATIONAL HUMOR MONTH

What's the funniest thing you've ever seen? For us, it might be this chicken doing stand-up. Think of your favorite jokes while you hunt through this scene for the nine hidden objects. Then perform a stand-up routine of your own!

ruler

button

slice of pizza

domino

crescent moon

magnet

golf club

lollipop

kite

During this month you can laugh, chortle, chuckle, giggle, howl, tee-hee, or LOL!

LOOK BOTH WAYS!

The chicken isn't the only one crossing the road. **Match up these riddles with their punch lines to find out why.**

1. Why did the rabbit cross the road?
2. Why did the farmer cross the road?
3. Why did the gum cross the road?
4. Why did the robot cross the road?
5. Why did the dinosaur cross the road?
6. Why did the lemur cross the road?
7. Why did the cow cross the road?
8. Why did the elephant cross the road?
9. Why did the frog cross the road?
10. Why did the dolphin cross the road?

A. Chickens weren't invented yet.
B. To get to the udder side
C. It was stuck to the chicken's foot.
D. Somebody toad him to.
E. To get to the other tide
F. It was the chicken's day off.
G. To bring back his chicken
H. To prove she could hip-hop
I. To take care of some monkey business
J. He was programmed to.

How do you fix a broken carrot?

With a carrot patch

Chomp through these questions!

4. Rate Your Plate

According to experts, how much of your plate should contain a colorful variety of fruits and veggies?

A. All of it.

B. Half of it.

C. None. Put them in a bowl.

2. Unreal!

Just two of these answers are vegetables. The other is a sweet "dough" made with almond meal. Which word is the impostor?

A. Rutabaga (ROOT-uh-BAY-guh)

B. Marzipan (MAR-tzih-pan)

C. Kohlrabi (coal-ROB-ee)

1. Market Mix-Up

Which seed packet would you buy to plant cucumbers?

3. Fifi and Fido No-Nos

These foods that many humans eat are unsafe for cats and dogs:

A. Onions and garlic

B. Chocolate

C. Both A and B

6. Rah-Rah Roots

Veggies that grow a thick, underground, edible root include:

A. Asparagus and cabbage

B. Carrots and beets

C. Sweet and hot peppers

5. Sprouter Space

Which of these has been grown in space, on the International Space Station?

A. Let us say lettuce!

B. Orange you thinking it's oranges?

C. Positive it's popcorn

7. Food Coloring

Plants get their colors from natural pigments. Chlorophyll (KLOR-oh-fill) gives vegetables:

A. The scientific name "Phil"

B. Camouflage to hide from wild rabbits

C. Green coloring

8. Dig In

Legumes (LEG-yoomz) can pack a protein punch. Some examples are peas, beans, and

A. Onions

B. Bananas

C. Peanuts

NATIONAL GUITAR MONTH

Which two guitars are exactly alike?

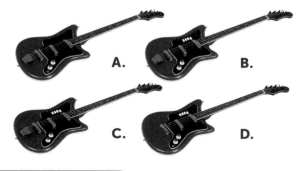

A.

B.

C.

D.

Knock, knock.
Who's there?
Guitar.
Guitar who?
Let's guitar coats — it's cold outside.

NATIONAL
MATHEMATICS AND STATISTICS
AWARENESS MONTH

POSTAGE PAW-BLEMS

Which package will cost the most to ship?

STAMPS
- 50¢
- $1
- $2

Does Purrnelope have enough money to send all four packages?

Why was the math book sad?

It had too many problems.

24 TO THE DOOR

Matt Amatics will step only on tiles with equations that equal 24. Can you help him get to his apartment door? He can move up, down, left, or right.

FINISH

9 + 12	2 x 11	15 + 9	17 + 7
7 + 15	35 – 11	8 x 3	25 – 2
3 x 4	6 x 4	20 ׀ 3	18 ׀ 7
18 + 6	40 – 16	5 x 7	33 – 10

START

SUM FUN!

Write the correct answer to each question in the blanks.

1. _____ Number of red stripes on the U.S. flag
2. _____ Number of Harry Potter movies
3. _____ Number of days in February during a leap year
4. _____ Number of squares on a chessboard
5. _____ Number of continents
6. _____ Number of seconds in an hour
7. _____ Number of U.S. states that have two words in their name

Add the above answers together to find out how many pounds the world's largest box of chocolates weighed.

North Pole

The true North Pole isn't like the South Pole. The North Pole is located in the frozen Arctic Ocean, not on land. There is a town in Alaska, though, that is called North Pole, but it is about **1,700 miles south of the real North Pole!**

55 YEARS AGO, SIR WALLY HERBERT BECAME THE FIRST PERSON TO WALK ACROSS THE FROZEN ARCTIC OCEAN AND STEP ON THE NORTH POLE.

You can reach the North Pole by completing this circular crossword puzzle. Start on the outside and work all the way until you reach the center. The first answer is done for you.

1. Activity in which you slide down a snowy hill
8. These keep your hands warm
13. An ice crystal that falls from the sky in winter
21. Santa's helpers
25. Wrap this around your neck to stay warm
29. Water _____ at 32° Fahrenheit
35. What you get when snow and ice start to melt
39. Warm chocolaty drink (2 words)
46. Where you find the South Pole
55. Where you find the North Pole
60. Heavy outer article of clothing
63. These may chatter when you're cold
67. Warms
71. You can build this "guy" outside after a winter storm
77. Cold toes sometimes feel this way
80. What winds do
83. Coldest season of the year
88. Where you ice-skate or play hockey
91. Makes hats out of wool
95. Season that marks the end of cold weather

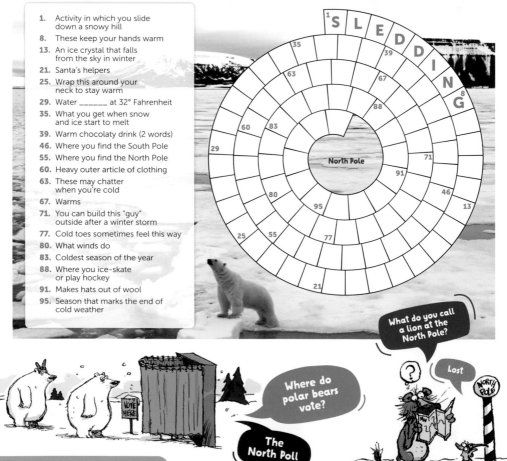

What do you call a lion at the North Pole?

Where do polar bears vote?

The North Poll

Lost

NORTH POLE

VOTE HERE

25 YEARS AGO, AMERICAN ASTRONOMERS DISCOVERED A NEW SOLAR SYSTEM WITH THREE GAS GIANT PLANETS ORBITING A SUN.

We have four gas giants orbiting our sun—Neptune, Uranus, Saturn, and Jupiter. This new solar system is located about 44 light years away from Earth.

What did one planet give to another planet for its birthday?

A ring

Can you find the hidden objects in our solar system?

boomerang

wedge of lemon

wedge of cheese

ice-cream cone

fish

mitten

yo-yo

heart

pear

button

Jupiter looks like a big marble designed with swirls and stripes. Its iconic Great Red Spot is a raging storm that's **bigger than the entire planet Earth.**

Saturn has a complex system of rings. These rings are made up of chunks of ice and rocks.

KIDS' SCIENCE QUESTION

Which planet circles the Sun the fastest?

Mercury, the planet closest to the Sun, has the fastest orbit of all the planets. It circles the Sun every 88 days. In fact, in any solar system, the closest planet must always be the fastest.

A star's pull is stronger close to the star than it is farther away. So only planets that are orbiting fast enough to resist this stronger pull of gravity will stay in orbit and not fall into the star.

Fun Fact
Our solar system's fastest planet has the same name as the messenger-god in Roman mythology.

OPENING DAY OF THE MAJOR LEAGUE BASEBALL SEASON

The first baseball game at Yankee Stadium in New York City was played on **APRIL 18, 1923– 101 YEARS AGO!**

PLAY BALL!
Use the clues to fill in the batting order on each player's card.

CLUES

A. The kids wearing glasses do not bat 1st or 9th.

B. The boy with braces bats 1st.

C. The 8th and 9th batters have the same first initial.

D. The number on the jersey of the boy batting 2nd is twice as much as the number of the kid batting 4th.

E. Batter 6, a girl, has the same color hair as batter 7.

F. The girl outfielder bats 3rd.

Lindsey — pitcher — 80
Seth — center field — 22
Cody — 3rd base — 47
Laura — 1st base — 55
Claudia — right field — 10
Hector — catcher — 44
Ariel — shortstop — 20
Jacob — 2nd base — 35
Troy — left field — 29

The first recorded baseball game took place in 1845 between teams from New York and Brooklyn.

♪ "TAKE ME OUT TO THE BALL GAME"

Write the words below in any order in the blank spaces to create silly lyrics to this famous baseball song:

house, car, pigeons, cheese, football, crayons, email, turtle, sneaker, eyeball

Take me out to the ball_____,

Take me out to the _____.

Buy me some_____ and cracker_____,

I don't care if _____ never get back.

So it's root, root, root for the _____ _____,

If they don't _____ it's a shame.

For it's one, two, three _____ you're out

At the old _____ game. ♪ ♪

HOME RUN!
Batter up! Can you find the right path to home plate? The symbols will tell you which way to move.

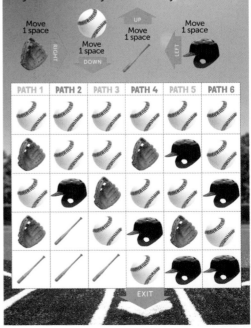

April 29
INTERNATIONAL DANCE DAY

Do a jig, tango, ballet, or waltz on this special day dedicated to all things dance. When you're done, see if you can find all 8 hidden objects in this under-the-sea scene. Even jellyfish like to make waves by doing their unique form of dance!

tennis ball

sock

hockey stick

clock

umbrella

cupcake

pineapple

scarf

START →

M T Y H F E E
C A S S A O Y U
R E S S A
O U U R
E U S R E
S T I E D

DINOSAUR DANCE-OFF

To solve the first riddle, start with the letter *M*. Then write every other letter in order on the blanks until you reach the center of the spiral, crossing out each letter once it has been used. To solve the second riddle, go back to the start and write the remaining letters in order on the blanks.

1. What do you call a dinosaur that's been dancing all night?

__ __ - __ __ __ __ - __ __ __ __

__ __ __ __ __ __ __

2. What kind of dinosaur liked to dance?

__ __ __

__ __ __ __ __ __ __ __ __ __

The Boston Marathon takes place on Patriots' Day. Only a few states celebrate this holiday, including Massachusetts. The holiday commemorates the Battles of Lexington and Concord, which were the first battles of the Revolutionary War.

April 15, 2024
THE BOSTON MARATHON

THE RUNDOWN

These five racers are poised and ready to race for their prize. Who will get the first-place trophy? Follow each runner's path to find out, and to see what the other runners place.

April 7-13, 2024
NATIONAL LIBRARY WEEK

Wally and Wendy Worm love to read. They have read all the books on these shelves, except for one. Use the clues to figure out which book they haven't read yet.

WALLY AND WENDY HAVE READ

1. All of the books with blue covers.
2. All of the books about sports.
3. All of the books with a person's name in the title.
4. All of the books on the middle shelf.

National Librarian Day is on April 16.

PUZZLING PAIRS

Add one letter to the beginning of the words in each pair to make two new words with similar meanings. **Example:** hop, tore. Add an s to the beginning to get shop and store.

1. old, hilly
2. ear, right
3. pot, peck
4. art, ash
5. late, latter
6. ring, ear
7. way, wing
8. rip, our
9. rip, rasp
10. have, hear

April 8
DRAW A BIRD DAY

This day was inspired by a little British girl who visited an uncle wounded in World War II. To cheer him up, she asked him to draw a picture of a bird. Soon after, whenever the girl visited, the uncle and other wounded soldiers competed to see who could draw the best picture of a bird.

THERE ARE ABOUT **9,000** DIFFERENT SPECIES OF BIRDS. About 1,200 of those species may become extinct by the end of the century.

JUST WING IT Fill in the squares by drawing or writing the name of each bird. Every type of bird should appear only once in each row, column, and 2 x 3 box.

April 15

WORLD ART DAY

The birthday of Leonardo da Vinci is the perfect day to celebrate art and creativity in all its forms. Da Vinci was not only a great painter but also an incredible mathematician, architect, engineer, and inventor.

CRAFT A SUPER SPACESHIP

Leonardo da Vinci designed plans for lots of different flying machines. Now it's your turn—create your own spaceship!

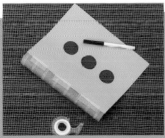

1. Decorate a **cardboard tube**. We used **paper** and a **marker**. You might use **stickers** or **paint**.

2. Cut two right **triangles** for the wings from **paper**. Cut a partial circle.

3. Fold one side of each triangle. **Tape** them to the bottom of the tube. Wrap the partial circle into a cone and tape it to the top.

4. Layer **tissue paper**. Pinch it near the top and tape it. Snip the ends, then crumple. Tape inside the tube.

NATIONAL BURRITO DAY

Made in Mexico in 2010, the world's largest burrito weighed 12,785 pounds. It was wrapped in a flour tortilla that measured nearly a mile and a half.

BOBBIE'S BURRITOS

Bobbie the Burrito Maker wanted to share the recipe for her famous fiery-hot burritos. She drew pictures of the steps involved, but as she was hanging the pictures, the wind blew them onto the floor. **Can you help Bobbie put these pictures back in order?**

The word *burrito* means "little donkey" in Spanish. Some say that long ago a food vendor carried the food on his donkey, and customers asked for his burrito, meaning the donkey holding the food. Others say it got the name because it looks like the bedrolls carried on a donkey. Either way, this sandwich of rice, vegetables, cheese, and meat wrapped in a tortilla is a popular taste sensation.

April 5

NATIONAL DEEP DISH PIZZA DAY

Deep dish pizza hails from Chicago. It's similar to a thick piece of pie with lots of tomato sauce slathered on top. *Delizioso!*

A pizza chef wants to put a total of 14 pieces of pepperoni on these two pizzas. Each numbered square tells you how many of the empty squares touching it (above, below, left, right, or diagonally) contain a pepperoni. Write an *X* on squares that can't have pepperoni. Then, write a *P* on the squares that can have pepperoni.

This grid has 4 pepperoni.

2			0
		4	
0			2

This grid has 10 pepperoni.

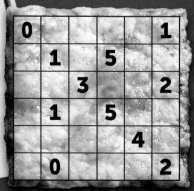

0					1
	1		5		
		3			2
	1		5		
				4	
	0				2

HINTS:
- Put an *X* on all the squares touching a zero.
- Look in the corners where a numbered square may make it more obvious where a slice of pepperoni belongs.
- Pepperoni cannot go in a square that has a number.

April 12

NATIONAL GRILLED CHEESE SANDWICH DAY

Ask for an adult's help with anything sharp or hot.

SWEET GRILLED CHEESE

1. Cut half of a peeled, baked **sweet potato** into slices.

2. **Butter** one side of two pieces of **bread**.

3. Between the two unbuttered sides, place **cheddar cheese**, sweet potato slices, and **provolone cheese**.

4. Ask an adult to heat a skillet over medium-low heat. Cook the sandwich for 5–6 minutes on one side. Flip it and cook it for 3–4 minutes. Remove from heat

April 22

NATIONAL JELLY BEAN DAY

TONGUE TWISTER
Jason enjoys sorting jelly beans into jars.

IT CAN TAKE 7 TO 21 DAYS TO MAKE ONE JELLY BEAN.

Can you find these seven jigsaw pieces in this photo of jelly beans?

April 9-10, 2024
EID AL-FITR

During the month of Ramadan, Muslims do not eat or drink from dawn to sunset. When Ramadan ends, Muslims everywhere celebrate Eid al-Fitr, the festival of fast-breaking.

They prepare special foods for friends and family. One dish common in India and Pakistan is a sweet noodle pudding called *sheer khurma*, which simply means "milk with dates." In some countries, this joyous holiday goes on for three days!

SWEET NOODLE PUDDING

1. With a parent's help, heat 3 cups **milk**, 1 cup **whipping cream,** and ½ cup **sugar** in a pan on the stove. Stir it until the mixture starts to foam.
2. Add 1 cup **uncooked vermicelli or angel-hair pasta** (broken into 3-inch pieces) and lower the heat. Stir for 15 minutes, or until the milk and cream thicken. Add ¼ cup **chopped dates**.
3. If serving warm, stir in ½ cup **nuts**, such as almonds or pistachios, and ¼ cup **raisins**.
4. If serving cold, add 1 small can **fruit cocktail**, drained, and ⅓ cup **shredded coconut**. Chill the pudding in the refrigerator.

On the Islamic calendar, a new month starts with a new moon. Every year, Eid al-Fitr falls about 11 days earlier than the previous year.

Eid al-Fitr begins when local "moon sighters" report seeing the new moon. The Judicial High Court then decides if Eid has arrived. When the sighting has been verified, Eid is declared on televisions, radio stations, and at mosques.

Children honor elderly relatives or neighbors by kissing their right hand and placing it on their forehead while greeting them.

During Eid al-Fitr, Muslim children in Egypt dance in the streets, swinging *fanous* of all sizes. Below are some countries that celebrate Eid. Read the letters in **red** from top to bottom to find out what a *fanous* is.

MALAYSIA
THAILAND
JORDAN
KUWAIT
INDONESIA
QATAR
BAHRAIN

April 22-30, 2024

PASSOVER

Every spring, a special meal called a *seder* occurs on the first night of the Jewish holiday of Passover. At the seder, everyone at the table takes part in telling the story of how the Jewish people escaped slavery, using a guide called the *Haggadah*. There is food and song. There are prayers for remembering what happened long ago and prayers that there will be no slavery anywhere at any time for any people.

In the 1930s, a rabbi lobbied Coca-Cola to make a kosher version of its soda for Passover. He was successful, and the company still makes kosher Coca-Cola today.

The youngest child traditionally asks four questions at a Passover seder. The last one is, "Why do we lean on pillows tonight during dinner?" In ancient times, only free people reclined while eating. Using pillows reminds everyone of freedom's gifts and the end of the Jews' enslavement in ancient Egypt.

1 **ROASTED EGG** The roasted egg symbolizes life.

2 **MAROR** This bitter root represents the bitterness of slavery. Horseradish is often used.

3 **ROASTED LAMB BONE** This bone symbolizes the lamb eaten quickly when the Jews fled Egypt.

4 **CHAROSET** (hah-ROH-ret) An apple-and-nut mixture represents the mortar made by the Jews when they toiled as slaves in Egypt. The sweetness of the apple symbolizes the promise of a better world.

5 **KARPAS** These greens, usually parsley, symbolize freedom. The parsley is dipped in salt water, which stands for the tears of slavery. In addition, karpas represent spring, because Passover is also a celebration of the spring harvest.

6 **PESACH** These three Hebrew letters spell *Pesach*, or *Passover*.

MAKE A MATZO PILLOW

1. Trace around a large **cereal box** twice onto **muslin fabric**. Cut out the two rectangles.

2. Thread **brown yarn** through a **large-eyed needle**. Knot the end of the yarn. Sew the two pieces of muslin together on three sides. Make a second knot. Cut off the extra yarn.

3. Fill the pocket with **polyester fiberfill**. Sew the open end closed.

4. Draw lines on the pillow with a **marker**.

April 1

APRIL FOOLS' DAY

> **Why is everyone so tired on April Fools' day?**

Here's one theory on how April 1 became April Fools' Day. New Year's Day was once celebrated on April 1 in Europe. In 1582, it was decided that New Year's would start on January 1. The people who hadn't heard about this switch continued to celebrate the holiday on April 1, which gave them the reputation of being foolish and easy to trick.

> **Because they just finished a 31-day March**

CUP O' LAUGHS

Build the perfect prank for April Fools'. If someone fills this cup too high, it will spill all over them. Whoops!

1. Use a **pushpin** to make a small hole in the bottom of a **plastic cup**.

2. Widen the hole with a **pencil** until a **bendy straw** can just fit through.

3. From the bottom, pull the straw partway through the hole. Bend the short section of the straw so it stays down.

4. Cut off the end that sticks out of the bottom of the cup.

5. To test it, fill the cup with water over a sink.

> **Why do eggs like April Fools' day?**

> **They love practical yolks.**

❶ Just right. ❷ Too much! ❸ Everything spills.

> **What monster plays the most April Fools' jokes?** **Prankenstein**

OLD-SCHOOL PRANKS

yum!

- Place vanilla pudding in an empty mayonnaise jar. Eat a big scoop in front of other people and watch their expressions of horror.

- Put a piece of plastic wrap under the lid of a saltshaker. Screw the lid back on, trim off any extra wrap, and watch your family try to shake out the salt.

- Glue a coin to the ground and grin as people try to pick it up.

- Place a leek in your sink and tell your family, "Oh, no! There's a leek in the sink."

- Call a friend and ask for Jess a few times. At the end of the day, call your friend, pretend you're Jess, and ask for messages.

April 8, 2024

TOTAL SOLAR ECLIPSE DAY

Grab your solar eclipse glasses and get ready for an event of a lifetime. The last time a total solar eclipse crossed North America was in 2017. **The 2024 eclipse will cross over 13 states and parts of Mexico and Canada.**

PATH OF TOTAL SOLAR ECLIPSE

Ancient peoples thought these heavenly spectacles spelled doom. Modern science helps us know that these are simply the result of natural occurrences.

Do not EVER look at the sun without special solar eclipse glasses. You will cause permanent damage to your eyes.

TEST YOUR ECLIPSE KNOWLEDGE

Circle a YES or NO next to each question in the chart.

People in California will get to see the eclipse in 2024.	YES	NO
A solar eclipse happens when the moon blocks the Sun's light from reaching Earth.	YES	NO
It is dangerous to look at the sun with solar eclipse glasses.	YES	NO
At the Zone of Totality, people only get to see a partial solar eclipse.	YES	NO
Total solar eclipses happen in the same place every year.	YES	NO
People long ago knew what caused solar eclipses to happen.	YES	NO

KIDS' SCIENCE QUESTIONS

What causes a solar eclipse?

Earth orbits, or moves around, the sun. The moon orbits Earth. Sometimes as the moon moves around Earth, its path puts it directly between the sun and Earth. This doesn't happen very often, but when it does, a solar eclipse occurs. That's because the moon is blocking the sun's light from reaching Earth. From Earth, it looks like the sun has gone completely dark. This happens slowly, as this image shows. The moon seems to be taking bites out of the sun until eventually there's only a ring of fire left. Then, it goes in reverse until the sun's full circle is visible again.

ZOO LOVERS' DAY

ZOOKEEPER'S BYE-BYE

When he left for home, the head zookeeper accidentally scrambled the names of the animals he said goodbye to. Help him straighten out their names. When you do, each name will rhyme with his goodbye phrase.

1. After awhile, DOCCOREIL _____
2. See you soon, you big NABBOO _____
3. Got to go, FABFULO _____
4. Time to sleep, bighorn PEESH _____
5. Cheerio, KECGO _____
6. Bye-bye, FEBLUTTRY _____
7. Toodle-oo, AKNARGOO _____
8. Take good care, RAPLO EBAR _____
9. That's all for me, PENCHEZAMI _____
10. Take a break, TRANTELSAKE _____

FIVE MOST-VISITED ZOOS IN THE U.S.

1. San Diego Zoo, San Diego, CA
2. Lincoln Park Zoo, Chicago, IL
3. Saint Louis Zoo, Saint Louis, MO
4. Columbus Zoo and Aquarium, Columbus, OH
5. Brookfield Zoo, Brookfield, IL

The oldest zoo in the world was founded in 1752 in Vienna, Austria.

April 18
NATIONAL *VELOCIRAPTOR* AWARENESS DAY
KIDS' SCIENCE QUESTIONS

Could a *Velociraptor* pack really kill a *T. rex*?

Velociraptor could not have killed *T. rex*. For one thing, the two never met. *Velociraptor* lived in Asia about 80 million years ago. *T. rex* lived in North America about 65 million years ago. But even if they had met, a *Velociraptor* pack probably couldn't have even scared a forty-foot-long *T. rex*. That carnivore could have swallowed two of those wolf-sized raptors in a single bite!

Velociraptor is Latin for "swift robber."

What do you call a sleeping dinosaur?

A dino-snore

April 26, 2024

ARBOR DAY

There weren't a lot of trees in Nebraska in the 1800s, so J. Sterling Morton proposed a holiday called Arbor Day that called for people to plant them. They would provide fuel, building material, and shade. More than one million trees were planted in Nebraska on the first Arbor Day in 1872.

Since 1972, the Arbor Day Foundation has planted more than **500 MILLION TREES** in more than 50 countries.

THAT'S ONE OLD TREE!

The oldest living organism that doesn't clone itself is a bristlecone pine located in the White Mountains of California, in Inyo National Forest. Scientists estimate that the tree is more than five thousand years old. It started growing around the time humans invented writing and the wheel! Its location is kept secret to keep people away from it. That way, it might live another five thousand years!

What did the tree wear to the pool party?

Swimming trunks

There are about **5.5 BILLION** trees in urban areas of the U.S.

TREEMONTON TOWERS

The animals of Treemonton are celebrating in their town's twin treehouses after a day of planting trees. Can you figure out how to go from the ground to the top floor without waking any bats?

NATIONAL UNICORN DAY

Take a splash at finding the pencil, pine cone, pail, paddle, pickle, pear, parasol, and paintbrush hidden in this scene.

SATURDAY, APRIL 28, 2024, is National Pool Opening Day!

April 13
NATIONAL SCRABBLE DAY

What is the highest-scoring word you can make from these Scrabble letters? Your score is the sum of the numbers on the tiles. You can use each letter only once.

10 TRICKY HIGH-SCORING SCRABBLE WORDS

1. Oxyphenbutazone
2. Muzjiks
3. Zax
4. Quetzals
5. Quixotry
6. Gherkins
7. Quartzy
8. Xu
9. Syzygy
10. Za

April 25, 2024
TAKE OUR DAUGHTERS AND SONS TO WORK DAY

Ever wonder what your parents do all day at work? On this annual holiday, you get to find out. In addition, you also get to learn more about different types of careers, and maybe think about what you'd like to do when you grow up.

At this job fair, the participants brought things to help show kids what they do at work. **Your job is to match each person to the correct object. When you're done, one object will be left. Use it to guess who hasn't arrived yet.**

April 28
NATIONAL SUPERHERO DAY

This day was created in 1995 by workers at Marvel Comics. It honors the people who protect us from the bad guys, whether comic-book superheroes or real, everyday heroes.

If you were a superhero, what would your name be?

CHOOSE YOUR BIRTHDAY MONTH

JANUARY: The Great
FEBRUARY: Captain
MARCH: The Amazing
APRIL: Doctor
MAY: The Fantastic
JUNE: Professor
JULY: The Flying
AUGUST: Commander
SEPTEMBER: The Unstoppable
OCTOBER: Agent
NOVEMBER: The Invisible
DECEMBER: The Mysterious

THEN CHOOSE THE FIRST LETTER
OF YOUR FIRST NAME

A: Guinea Pig
B: Green Bean
C: Cheese Stick
D: Marshmallow
E: Hullabaloo
F: Sandwich
G: Spinach
H: Jelly Bean
I: Sock
J: Broccoli
K: Kerfuffle
L: Puppy
M: Walrus
N: Cactus
O: Armadillo
P: Malarkey
Q: Pinecone
R: Platypus
S: Kitten
T: Waffle
U: Shenanigan
V: Scrambled Egg
W: Sloth
X: Gecko
Y: Guacamole
Z: Flapjack

Take a spin around the globe to see how

April 13-15, 2024
⊙ SONGKRAN

For three days, people in Thailand and other countries in Southeast Asia get wet to celebrate the New Year. People sprinkle water on statues of Buddha for good luck and on the hands of older relatives and friends as a sign of respect. It is a Buddhist tradition to drizzle water on people; it symbolizes rinsing away the bad luck of the old year and starting over pure for the new one.

April 23, 2024
⊙ ST. GEORGE'S DAY

Legend has it that a knight named George killed a dragon to free the city of Silene, which is in modern-day Libya. For that feat of derring-do, George was made a saint and is honored not only in England, but in parts of Italy, Portugal, and Spain.

Do You Know That Dragon?
Match the dragon to the movie or book it appears in.

1. Toothless
2. Haku
3. Smaug
4. Maleficent
5. Mushu
6. Falcor
7. Draco
8. Hungarian Horntail

a. *Sleeping Beauty*
b. *Dragonheart*
c. *Spirited Away*
d. *Mulan*
e. *The Hobbit*
f. *How to Train Your Dragon*
g. *Harry Potter and the Goblet of Fire*
h. *The Neverending Story*

These real animals may have inspired the belief in dragons:
- Dinosaur fossils
- Nile crocodile
- Goanna
- Whales

An Australian lizard

THE WORLD

April 27
⦿ KONINGSDAG

Koningsdag means "King's Day," a Netherlands' national holiday that celebrates the birthday of King Willem-Alexander. Before it was King's Day, the holiday was called Queen's Day to honor the female rulers of the Netherlands. Dutch people celebrate by wearing orange and riding through Amsterdam's canals on boats.

Somalian Flag

Gabonese Flag

Nigerian Flag

April 27
⦿ INDEPENDENCE DAY

On this day, Sierra Leone celebrates its independence from Great Britain in 1961. Back then, the new nation unveiled its own flag, and today citizens are encouraged to wave it proudly.

Fly It High
Can you figure out the three colors of the Sierra Leone flag?
Clues:

1. The top stripe of the flag has a color found in the flags of both Nigeria and Gabon, but not in Somalia's flag.

2. The middle stripe has a color found in both the Nigerian and Somalian flags, but not in the Gabonese flag.

3. The bottom stripe has a color found in the flags of both Somalia and Gabon, but not in the Nigerian flag.

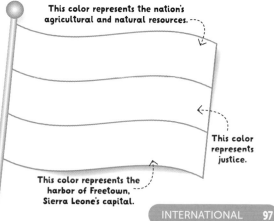

This color represents the nation's agricultural and natural resources.

This color represents justice.

This color represents the harbor of Freetown, Sierra Leone's capital.

SUNDAY	MONDAY	TUESDAY	WEDNESDAY

ZODIAC SIGNS
TAURUS:
APRIL 20–MAY 20

GEMINI:
MAY 21–JUNE 20

FLOWERS
LILY OF THE VALLEY
AND HAWTHORN

Mother Goose Da
Reread a favorite sto
then write your ow

CINCO DE MAYO

5

Mailed it! In 1840, Great Britain began to use the first adhesive postage stamp, called the Penny Black. **6**

NATIONAL TOURISM DAY
Take time today to plan a vacation with your family! **7**

No Socks Day
Free your toes!

8

MOTHER'S DAY

12

One of the greats. The Great Comet of 1861 was first spotted by amateur Australian astronomer John Tebbutt. It was visible around the world for three months. **13**

National Dance Like a Chicken Day

14

International Day of Families
Learn about families that may be differe than yours.

15

Commemoration of Atatürk, Youth and Sports Day (Turkey)
This national holiday celebrates Turkey's youth and the republic's founder. **19**

WORLD BEE DAY

20

National Strawberries and Cream Day

21

National Buy a Musical Instrume Day

2

The last Model T. In 1927, the Ford Motor Company made the 15 millionth— and last— Model T. **26**

MEMORIAL DAY

27

National Brisket Day
Grab the barbecue sauce and dig in!

28

National Paper C Day
Keep it all togethe

29

THURSDAY	FRIDAY	SATURDAY
NATIONAL BABY DAY heir first year, babies ep 5,400 hours on age and use roughly 360 diapers. **2**	**Święto Konstytucji 3 Maja (Poland)** The Polish Parliament passed the country's Constitution on May 3, 1791. Today, Poles celebrate with parades, concerts, and speeches. **3**	**International Firefighters' Day** Thank a brave firefighter today for their service. **4**
National Sleepover Day eak out the sleeping bags! **9**	*All aboard!* In 1869, a golden spike was driven into the track at Promontory Summit, Utah, to complete the first coast-to-coast railroad in the United States. **10**	*Compute this!* In 1997, IBM's Deep Blue became the first computer to win a match against a world chess champion. **11**
"I'd like to thank the Academy . . . ." this day in 1929, the st Academy Awards mony (also known as e Oscars) was held. **16**	*Off to see the Wizard!* In 1900, the first copy of *The Wonderful Wizard of Oz*, by L. Frank Baum, was printed. **17**	**National Visit Your Relatives Day** **18**
World Turtle Day **23**	**National Scavenger Hunt Day** **24**	**National Brown-Bag-It Day** What's your favorite packed lunch? Make it and take it. **25**
National Water a Flower Day Drink up! **30**	**World Parrot Day** **31**	**BIRTHSTONE** EMERALD

MAY

A visit doesn't have to be in person. You can also visit your relatives virtually by:

- **Calling on the phone**

- **Scheduling a video call**

- **Setting up a group text**

Kalpana Chawla

ASIAN/PACIFIC AMERICAN HERITAGE MONTH

George Takei

Pay tribute to the generations of Asian/Pacific Americans who have uplifted American history, society, and culture. Match each person to their historic accomplishment.

1. At 17, she was the youngest woman to win a snowboarding gold medal, at the 2018 Winter Olympics in PyeongChang.

2. At the age of 21, this architect and sculptor designed the Vietnam Veterans Memorial in Washington, D.C.

3. This actor was the first Asian American to play a major character on an American TV show, as the original Mr. Sulu on *Star Trek*.

4. This two-time Olympian is a Chinese-American figure skater who grew up in Salt Lake City and is a 2022 Winter Olympics Gold Medalist.

5. This Pulitzer Prize–winning journalist, filmmaker, and immigration activist was born in the Philippines and raised in the U.S.

6. This Olympic gold medalist, who was considered the greatest freestyle swimmer in the world, helped popularize surfing.

7. An advocate for equal rights, this lawyer and politician was the first woman of color and the first Asian American elected to Congress.

8. This astronaut was the first Indian American woman to go into space.

Duke Kahanamoku

Nathen Chen

Jose Antonio Vargas

Patsy Mink

Maya Lin

Chloe Kim

The U.S. Pacific Islands region includes our 50th state, Hawaii, as well as the territories of Guam, the Commonwealth of the Northern Mariana Islands, the Republic of the Marshall Islands, the Federated States of Micronesia, the Republic of Palau, and American Samoa.

NATIONAL STRAWBERRY MONTH

SWEET STRAWBERRY PIZZA

1. Line a large baking sheet with parchment paper.

2. Have an adult preheat the oven to 375°F.

3. Stretch or roll 12 ounces of fresh **pizza dough** into a large oval and place it on the baking sheet.

4. Brush the dough with 2 tablespoons of unsalted, melted **butter**.

5. Slice 10–12 **strawberries** and arrange them on top. Combine 2 tablespoons **sugar** and 1/8 teaspoon **cinnamon** and sprinkle it over the pizza.

6. Bake the pizza for 20–25 minutes or until the dough is golden and the strawberries begin to bubble.

Ask for an adult's help with anything sharp or hot.

STRAWBERRY WORDS

The letters in **STRAWBERRY** can be used to make many other words. Use the clues below to come up with some of them. A beam of sunshine, for example, might make you think of the word RAY. **See how many of the others you can guess.**

1. A beam of sunshine — R A Y
2. Not dry — _ _ _
3. A large rodent — _ _ _
4. Grizzly or polar — _ _ _ _
5. Where the sun rises — _ _ _ _
6. The sun is one — _ _ _ _
7. The opposite of 5's answer — _ _ _ _
8. Spiders spin them — _ _ _ _
9. Term for meat cooked just a little — _ _ _ _
10. A command to a dog — _ _ _ _
11. H_2O — _ _ _ _ _
12. A dog without a home — _ _ _ _ _
13. Perspire — _ _ _ _ _
14. It makes bread rise — _ _ _ _ _
15. Huck Finn's friend Tom — _ _ _ _ _ _

INTERNATIONAL
DRUM MONTH

Drums have been played for centuries all over the world. Early drums were sections of hollowed tree trunks covered at one end with reptile, fish, or other animal skins. Today, drum "skins" are usually made of a plastic called *Mylar*.

The oldest drum was found in China. Made from clay and alligator hides, it dates back as early as **5500 BCE**.

The largest drum—**18 feet 2 inches** in diameter, **19½ feet** tall, and weighing **15,432 pounds**—was created in South Korea in 2011. The drum is a traditional Korean CheonGo drum.

crash cymbal

ride cymbal

snare drum

hi-hat cymbals

high tom

mid tom

floor tom

bass drum

drum throne (seat)

DRUM MATCH

Match each of these drums to its region of origin.

1. **Adufe**
2. **Bodhrán**
3. **Conga**
4. **Djembe**
5. **Pandeiro**
6. **Steel Pan**
7. **Taiko**

A. **Brazil**
B. **Cuba**
C. **Ireland**
D. **Japan**
E. **Portugal**
F. **Trinidad and Tobago**
G. **West Africa**

ANIMAL ACTS

- **Rabbits, kangaroo rats, and other rodents** use their paws to drum the ground, warning others of approaching predators.

- **Palm cockatoos** of Australia break off a stick or seedpod, hold it in their feet, and rap against a hollow tree branch to attract a mate.

- **Macaque monkeys** drum objects to show strength. The louder the drumming, the bigger and stronger the macaque probably is.

NATIONAL PET MONTH

What odd, weird, or wacky things can you find in this pet shop?

More than 63 million households own dogs. More than 42 million have cats. And 6 out of 10 households have more than one pet. Circle sets of four emojis together that have two cats and two dogs. One side of each square must touch a side of another square in the same set. You are done when all the squares are circled.

Dogs keep cool by panting. They also sweat through their foot pads.

Cats can spend up to half their awake time grooming themselves.

A goldfish named Tish lived 43 years. It was won at a fair in 1956.

Underwater, iguanas can hold their breath for up to a half hour.

A group of ferrets is called a *business*.

Christopher Columbus brought back two parrots as pets for Queen Isabella when he returned from his journey to the Americas.

Pigs are really clean animals and only roll in the mud to cool off. They're also smarter than other pets.

What did the cat say when the dog ran away from home?

"This is the best dog-gone day ever!"

Where do cats and dogs go on vacation?

Pets-ylvania

140 YEARS AGO, CONSTRUCTION ON THE FIRST SKYSCRAPER BEGAN.

The 10-story, 138-foot-tall Home Insurance Company building was located in Chicago, Illinois. It was completed the following year and stood until 1931 when it was demolished to make room for an even taller 45-story, 535-foot-tall building.

The tallest skyscraper in the world is the Burj Khalifa in Dubai, United Arab Emirates. It is 162 floors and 2,717 feet tall. It was designed by an architectural firm from Chicago.

Welding the Details

Skyscrapers have a steel frame or skeleton. This welder is securing the steel pieces together to form the framework. **See if you can find all the hidden objects in the picture.**

lemon

drinking straw

pennant

toothbrush

ruler

horseshoe

seashell

belt

HOW DO THE WORLD'S TALLEST STRUCTURES MEASURE UP?

What is the tallest building in the world?

The library. It has many stories.

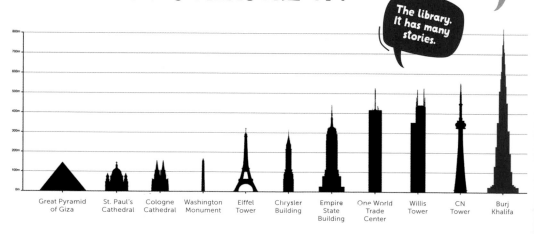

| Great Pyramid of Giza | St. Paul's Cathedral | Cologne Cathedral | Washington Monument | Eiffel Tower | Chrysler Building | Empire State Building | One World Trade Center | Willis Tower | CN Tower | Burj Khalifa |

May 6, 1994
30 YEARS AGO, THE CHANNEL TUNNEL, OR "CHUNNEL," OFFICIALLY OPENED.

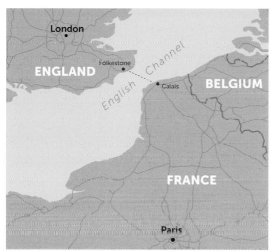

The Chunnel is an undersea railway link between England and France that stretches under the English Channel. Thanks to the Chunnel, people don't need to take ferries or planes to get from England to Europe. They can now take a high-speed train.

The Chunnel is 246 feet (75 meters) deep. **That's as deep as a Giant Sequoia is tall!**

ALL ABOARD!

You're about to climb aboard the train to zip across the Chunnel from England to France. But before you leave, scan your surroundings. There are some things in this picture that could happen in real life and there are some that are so silly that they're only make-believe. Cross out everything that is make-believe before you hop on board.

TRAIN HUMOR

To solve each riddle, start at the arrow and write every other letter in order in the center spaces. Cross out each letter once it's been used. Keep going around the circle until you've landed on each letter exactly once.

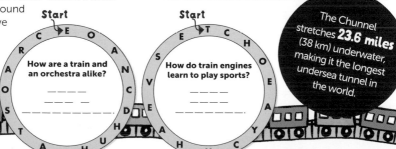

Start

R C E O
R A
A N
O C
S D
T H
A C H U

How are a train and an orchestra alike?

_ _ _ _
_ _ _ _
_ _ _ _ _ _ _ _

Start

E T C H
S O
V E
E A
A Y
H H C

How do train engines learn to play sports?

_ _ _ _
_ _ _ _ _ _ _

The Chunnel stretches **23.6 miles** (38 km) underwater, making it the longest undersea tunnel in the world.

May 4, 2024
KENTUCKY DERBY

Every first Saturday in May since 1875, the Churchill Downs racetrack in Lexington, Kentucky, has hosted a special Thoroughbred-horse race, the Kentucky Derby. The Derby is the first of three races known as the Triple Crown of Racing, which also includes the Preakness Stakes race and the Belmont Stakes race. Before the horses can go to the starting, you'll need to help solve this word search.

Can you find all 27 words and phrases? When you're all done, the uncircled letters will help you solve a horsey riddle.

We've replaced **HORSE** in the crossword with 🐴

RIDDLE: Why did the pony have to gargle?

Put the uncircled letters in order on the blanks.

ANSWER: ___ ___ ___ ___ ___ ___ ___ ___ ___ ___ ___ ___

___ ___ ___ ___ ___ ___ ___ ___ ___ ___ ___ .

WORD LIST

CLOTHESHORSE	HORSEHAIR	HORSETAIL	SAWHORSE
DARK HORSE	HORSELAUGH	HORSEWHIP	SEAHORSE
EAT LIKE A HORSE	HORSEMANSHIP	HORSE RACE	STRONG AS A HORSE
HOBBYHORSE	HORSEPLAY	ONE HORSE TOWN	TROJAN HORSE
HOLD YOUR HORSES	HORSEPOWER	PACKHORSE	WARHORSE
HORSEBACK	HORSERADISH	RACE HORSE	WORKHORSE
HORSEFLY	HORSESHOE	ROCKING HORSE	

May 26, 2024

INDY 500

Called the "Greatest Spectacle in Racing," this competition at the Indianapolis Motor Speedway takes place on the last Sunday of May. Thirty-three drivers zoom 200 laps around a 2½-mile track for a total of 500 miles.

Which things in this picture are silly? It's up to you!

In 2013, Tony Kanaan had the fastest average winning speed: **187.433 MPH.** He had the fastest time, too: 2 hours, 40 minutes, and 3.4181 seconds.

INDY TRADITIONS

Drink the Milk: Three-time Indianapolis 500 winner Louis Meyer drank a glass of buttermilk after winning the 1936 race. Except for the years between 1947 and 1955, a bottle of milk has been presented to the winner ever since.

The first Indy 500, in 1911, took winner Ray Harroun **6 HOURS, 42 MINUTES.**

Kiss the Bricks: The Speedway became known as "the Brickyard" after it was paved with 3.2 million paving bricks in 1909. Later, asphalt was laid over the track, except for one yard of brick at the start-finish line. After NASCAR champion Dale Jarrett won a race in 1996, he knelt down and kissed the Yard of Bricks. Now other winners do it, too.

NATIONAL CARTOONISTS DAY

Today marks the first appearance of a newspaper comic strip: *Hogan's Alley*, created by Richard Felton Outcault in 1895. This Sunday comic featured Mickey Dugan, known as the Yellow Kid, who starred in various versions of the strip until January 1898.

Find the funny! Write a caption for each cartoon.

How to Draw a Grumpy Cartoon Bear

1. Start with a circle for the skull. Draw a large oval behind it for the jaw. Add the nose.

2. Define the snout by drawing a circle around the nose. Add eyes.

3. Draw a downturned mouth and slanting eyebrows. Don't forget ears!

4. Flatten the top of the head a little bit. Finish up with a furry coat and other details. Ta-da!

Do cartoons make you laugh? Good news— **WORLD LAUGHTER DAY** is the first Sunday in May. Try laughing in a different language. Instead of texting *hahaha*, type *55555* (Thai, because 5 is pronounced "ha"), *jajaja* (Spanish), or *MDR* (French for *mort de rire*—"dying of laughter").

May 4 is **FREE COMIC BOOK DAY!** On the first Saturday in May, participating comics stores around the world give away at least one FREE book to anyone who visits.

The longest-running newspaper comic in history is *The Katzenjammer Kids*. The main characters, Hans and Fritz, have been getting into cartoon trouble since 1897.

Bake a giant chocolate chip cookie.
Roll out cookie dough into one pizza-sized cookie!

Create doodles from ink fingerprints.

May 30

NATIONAL CREATIVITY DAY

Do stuff with tiny stones.
Pile them high, paint them, create a drawing around them, or use them as the pieces in a game of jacks.

Today is the day to try something new. Tap into your creative side and create something special. Here are some ideas to get you started!

Draw a chameleon!
What color will you make it?

Vtrsyr s vpfr
That's "Create a code" in code (if you shift your hands to the right on a keyboard to type it).

What kind of code will you make up?

Dance it out!
Make up a dance move that uses only your legs. Then make up one that uses only your arms. What do they look like when you put them together?

Do a new hairdo.
With permission, use gel or a styling tool to give yourself a different hairstyle. Then name it.

May 11
EAT
WHAT YOU
WANT DAY

Grab your favorite snack to celebrate today. Then solve this food puzzle! These food phrases and pictures are all mixed up. **Can you match each food with the correct phrase?**

1. **The**  **of my eye.**

2. **A couch** .

3. **Like two** **in a pod.**

4. **As cool as a** .

5. **Don't cry over spilled** .

6. **One smart** .

7. **Don't put all your** **in one basket.**

8. **Spill the** .

9. **Bigger** **to fry.**

10. **The big** .

May 17
WORLD
BAKING
DAY

HOMEMADE BROWNIES

1. Have an adult preheat the oven to 350°F. Spray a 9-inch baking pan with nonstick cooking spray.

2. In a large bowl, mix together 1 cup **sugar**, 1/3 cup **unsweetened cocoa powder**, 1/2 cup **flour**, 1/4 teaspoon **baking powder**, and 1/4 teaspoon **salt**.

3. Add 1/2 cup melted **butter**, 2 **eggs**, and 1 teaspoon **vanilla extract**. Stir until well blended. *Optional:* Fold in 1/4 cup **mini chocolate chips**, 1/4 cup **mini marshmallows**, and 1/4 cup finely chopped **pecans**.

4. Spread the mixture in the prepared pan.

5. Bake 20–25 minutes, or until a toothpick put in the center comes out clean.

6. Cool in the pan on a wire rack, then cut into squares. Recipe makes 16 brownies.

Ask for an adult's help with anything sharp or hot.

NATIONAL HAMBURGER DAY

Ground-beef-and-onion patties cooked up by immigrants in the U.S. were named after the German city of Hamburg. "Hamburg steak" was served in New York restaurants as early as 1837.

On this day dedicated to this tasty sandwich, can you spot the 17 differences between these two photos?

Can't get enough beef on a bun? May is also National Hamburger Month!

Americans eat about **13 BILLION BURGERS** each year—enough to circle Earth 32 times!

Do you know how to make a hamburger laugh?

You pickle it.

We're having burgers on the grill?

No, I think they would be better on plates.

The record for the largest hamburger weighs in at more than **2,566 POUNDS**, set in Pilsting, Germany, in 2017.

May 5

CINCO DE MAYO

Today marks Mexico's victory over an invading French army in the Battle of Puebla in 1862. In the U.S., Cinco de Mayo (*Fifth of May*) spotlights Mexican heritage and culture with parties, parades, piñatas, and plenty of *deliciosa* food. Although it's a pretty minor holiday in Mexico, it became an official U.S. holiday in 2005, to celebrate Mexican culture and heritage.

MOLE POBLANO, a sauce containing chili pepper, chocolate, and spices, is the official dish of Cinco de Mayo.

Cinco de Mayo is NOT Mexico's Independence Day. That's September 16.

Match these Spanish words with their English translations.

1. La familia   A. Friend
2. El amigo   B. Country
3. La fiesta   C. Food
4. El país   D. Family
5. El desfile   E. Parade
6. La comida   F. Party

MINI PIÑATAS

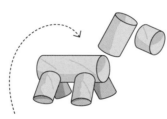

1. For each piñata, collect four short **paper tubes**. For legs, cut two of the tubes in half. **Tape** the legs to a full-sized tube. If you like, fill the tubes with **wrapped candy** (or leave them empty and use the mini piñata as a table decoration). Tape over the ends.

2. For the head, cut off the end of the fourth tube and tape it back on sideways, as shown. Tape the head to the body.

3. Wrap the piñata with **masking tape**. Shape ears from the tape.

4. Cover the piñata with **crepe-paper strips**. Add **wiggle eyes**.

Although piñatas are most commonly associated with Mexico, they may be Chinese in origin. In the 14th century, the tradition of smashing clay pots came to Europe. The Italians called it *pignatta*, meaning "earthenware cooking pot." In the 16th century, Europeans brought the tradition to Mexico, although Mayans and Aztecs had previously decorated clay pots with feathers to be broken. Today, piñatas are made from paper and cardboard rather than clay pots, for safety.

May 12, 2024

MOTHER'S DAY

In 1868, Ann Jarvis tried to establish "Mother's Friendship Day" between mothers on both sides of the Civil War. But it was her daughter, Anna Jarvis, who was able to convince President Woodrow Wilson to sign a bill in 1914 recognizing Mother's Day as a national holiday, celebrated on the second Sunday in May.

Grapes, chicken nugget, and syrup

Nutella, strawberry, and whipped cream

Mint, cantaloupe, and ham

Pear, bacon, and honey

Peanut butter, banana, and blueberries

Apple and cheddar cheese

MAMA WAFFLES

Surprise Mom with breakfast in bed. Make up some toaster waffles and then crown them with any of these tasty toppings.

What other topping creations can you come up with?

MOM MATCH

Every year, about 113 million Mother's Day cards are sent. Match each card to the baby animal that sent it.

Anna Jarvis hated how commercialized Mother's Day had become by the 1920s, and she tried to get people to stop buying flowers, cards, and other gifts.

Mother's Day is celebrated in nearly 50 countries, though some on different days. The United States, Italy, Australia, Belgium, Denmark, Finland, and Turkey all celebrate it on the second Sunday of May.

I really look up to you, Mama!

Mommy, you really bring me out of my shell!

To my mother, who makes our den such a cozy place!

Ewe really raise the baaaa, Maaaa!

Even though I'm in a great school now, I'll always be your small fry, Mom!

May 1
MAY DAY

People have celebrated May Day for thousands of years. Giving bouquets of wildflowers (often anonymously) and dancing around a maypole decorated with streamers are two May Day traditions. The celebration welcomes spring and new life. Get in the May Day spirit with these flower puzzles. Then go outside and enjoy real-life flowers.

FLOWER **OR NOT**?

Each pair of words has one flower and one faker. **Circle the flowers.**

Bluebell **or** Barbell?

Snapdragon **or** Snickerdoodle?

Chrysalis **or** Chrysanthemum?

Rhododendron **or** Rapscallion?

Gladiolus **or** Gondola?

Clementine **or** Clematis?

Hydra **or** Hydrangea?

Foxglove **or** Bearclaw?

JUMBLED FLOWERS

Unscramble each set of letters to get the name of a flower.

YILL _____ _____ _____ _____

LITUP _____ _____ _____ _____ _____

ICALL _____ _____ _____ _____ _____

LOVEIT _____ _____ _____ _____ _____ _____

FADIFOLD _____ _____ _____ _____ _____ _____ _____ _____

Scotland's national flower is the thistle. Legend says it became the national flower after saving the lives of an army of Scots. Invading Vikings stepped on the poky plants and yelled in pain, waking the Scottish warriors and giving them time to escape.

COUNT THE CODE

Count the number of petals on a flower. Then write the matching code letter in the center of the flower. Fill in the rest of the flowers to find the answer to this riddle.

WHAT DID THE DOG DO AFTER HE SWALLOWED A FIREFLY?

KEY

3 - E	9 - K
4 - D	10 - A
5 - I	11 - T
6 - R	12 - B
7 - H	13 - W
8 - G	14 - L

In Hawaii, May 1 is called **LEI DAY**. On this day, people honor the custom of weaving and wearing flower leis.

HIDDEN FLOWERS

A flower is hidden in the letters of each sentence. Find **ASTER** in the first one. Then find a different flower in each of the others.

1. As Terry says, vanilla is better than chocolate.
2. A superhero seldom fails.
3. Ms. Gorda is your new teacher.
4. This fir is taller than it was last year.
5. On the porch, I don't get sunburned.

MEMORIAL DAY

Originally called Decoration Day, Memorial Day is a day to remember soldiers and their sacrifices. The first national celebration took place in 1868 at Arlington National Cemetery. Today, many towns celebrate with a parade to honor and remember soldiers.

START

Help Connor find his way through the crowd to meet his friends at the Memorial Day parade.

FINISH

POPPY POWER

*In Flanders fields the **poppies** blow*
Between the crosses, row on row,
That mark our place; and in the sky
The larks, still bravely singing, fly
Scarce heard amid the guns below.

—FROM "IN FLANDERS FIELDS"

Lieutenant Colonel John McCrae, a Canadian doctor, wrote the poem quoted above on May 3, 1915, while treating soldiers on the battlefields of Flanders in Belgium during World War I. His poem inspired a Georgia schoolteacher, Moina Belle Michael, in 1919 to wear and hand out red silk poppies in soldiers' honor. Today, American Legion volunteers distribute more than 2.5 million red crepe-paper poppies each year, with donations used to assist veterans and military families.

MAKE A POPPY BOUQUET

Cut a flower from **red craft foam**. Hold a **black button** to the flower's center. Poke a **green fuzzy stick** through the back of the flower and thread it through the buttonholes. Poke it back through the flower. Twist the end around the stem. Fill a vase with your poppies.

May 3, 2024

SPACE DAY

The first Friday in May is all about future astronomers, astronauts, and out-of-this-world explorers. This day encourages kids to study science, technology, engineering, and math, so you can reach for the stars—and the planets!

ASTRONOMY is the study of space, the universe, and all the objects in them. Which three celestial objects can you spell from the letters in ASTRONOMY? What other words can you find?

PLANETARIUM FIELD TRIP

Planetariums are a place to learn more about the night sky. **Can you find all of the hidden objects in the picture?**

airplane

taco

pizza

banana

cane

balloon

candle

artist's brush

KIDS' SCIENCE QUESTIONS

How do astronomers discover other galaxies?

Astronomer Dr. Ken Croswell says the trick is to find the galaxies among the many objects in the sky. If an object shows as a point of light, it's probably a star, not a galaxy. If the object looks like a pinwheel, it's a galaxy. Each galaxy is made up of many stars swirling around, so only a galaxy can take this swirly shape. If the object is a fuzzy patch whose light is moving faster than 500 kilometers per second, then it's probably a galaxy. It can't be part of our galaxy because it's moving too fast for our galaxy to hold it. So, if it's that far away and still bright enough to see, it's probably another galaxy. But astronomers still make mistakes. If the galaxy is compact, they may think, at first, that it's a star!

Halley's Comet passes by Earth only every 75 to 76 years. The last time was 38 years ago. So, get ready for the next sighting—in **2062!**

NATIONAL PAPER AIRPLANE DAY

Test out the aerodynamic skills of this aerobatic airplane.

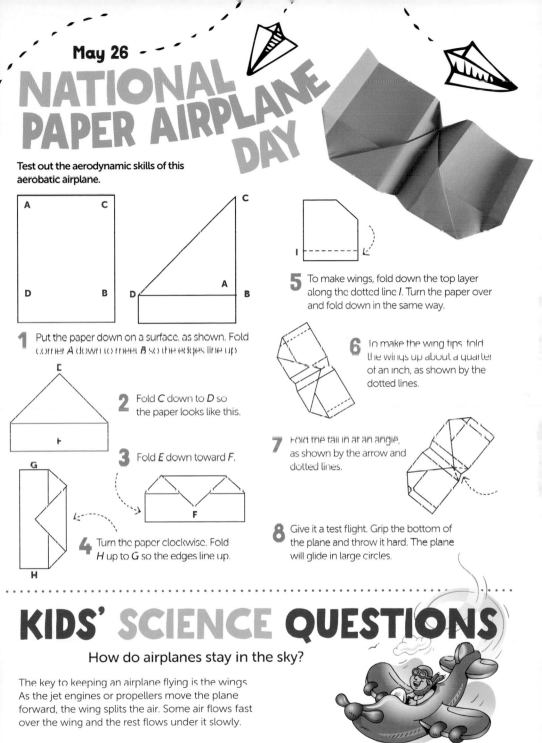

1 Put the paper down on a surface, as shown. Fold corner *A* down to meet *B* so the edges line up.

2 Fold *C* down to *D* so the paper looks like this.

3 Fold *E* down toward *F*.

4 Turn the paper clockwise. Fold *H* up to *G* so the edges line up.

5 To make wings, fold down the top layer along the dotted line *I*. Turn the paper over and fold down in the same way.

6 To make the wing tips, fold the wings up about a quarter of an inch, as shown by the dotted lines.

7 Fold the tail in at an angle, as shown by the arrow and dotted lines.

8 Give it a test flight. Grip the bottom of the plane and throw it hard. The plane will glide in large circles.

KIDS' SCIENCE QUESTIONS

How do airplanes stay in the sky?

The key to keeping an airplane flying is the wings. As the jet engines or propellers move the plane forward, the wing splits the air. Some air flows fast over the wing and the rest flows under it slowly.

Here is where the experts disagree. Some say that the faster flow of air over the wing lowers the air pressure above it. Then the higher pressure of the slow-moving air underneath pushes upward on the wing.

But other scientists say the explanation is simpler than that: The plane flies because the wing is set at an angle that pushes downward on the air.

May 8
NO SOCKS DAY

Why don't grizzlies wear socks?

They prefer to go bear-foot.

Finding matching socks can be hard! Going sockless not only avoids this mind-bending activity, but also frees up toes and laundry loads. But at the end of the day, these socks still need to find their match. **Can you find them all?**

BONUS! Which objects start with the letter *P*?

May 13
NATIONAL FROG JUMPING DAY

START

BONUS! Find the two matching frogs.

Mark Twain's famous short story "The Celebrated Jumping Frog of Calaveras County," published in 1865, inspired this special day. Complete this leapfrog puzzle by finding a path from **START** to **FINISH** by hopping from frog to frog. The correct path uses frogs that are juggling an even number of objects.

Want to play a game of leap frog?

BONUS! How many objects are being juggled along the right path? Add 'em up!

FINISH

INTERNATIONAL MUSEUM DAY

There are many different types of museums: life science, history, technology, engineering, earth and space science, and fine art. **What kind of museum would you like to visit today?**

Can you make your way through the paintings on this wall? Enter the maze at the **START** and exit at the **END**.

MUSEUM LOGIC

Using the clues, can you figure out who went to which museum on which day?

Use the chart to keep track of your answers. Put an **X** in each box that can't be true and an **O** in boxes that match.

- Lawrence went on a field trip to the art museum last month. He went to a different museum on Saturday with his parents.
- Kelsey went to a museum on a weekday. Her favorite exhibit was of a red locomotive.
- Sofia wants to be a fashion designer.
- Sean didn't go to a museum on Sunday or Monday.

	Sean	Sofia	Lawrence	Kelsey
Space				
Art				
Railroad				
Fashion				
Friday				
Saturday				
Sunday				
Monday				

May 1

LABOR DAY

Many countries celebrate Labor Day with parades like this one, held in Belgium.

In the United States and Canada, Labor Day falls in September. But for roughly 90 other countries, the day to celebrate workers is May 1. Several Asian, European, South American, and African countries remember their workers on this day and celebrate the rights that they have.

May 5

KODOMO NO HI

In Japan, *Kodomo no Hi,* or Children's Day, is all about wishing kids health and happiness. Carp streamers made from brightly colored paper or cloth, called *koinobori*, are hung from the rooftops and public buildings as a symbol of children's determination and strength.

Carp, or koi fish, are thought to be strong and spirited, overcoming all obstacles to swim upstream.

Japanese Carp Kite

1. For the body, cut a vase shape from a **paper bag**. Tape a **fuzzy stick** to the body's widest part. Leave 1 inch of the fuzzy stick hanging off each edge.

2. For scales, cut up **cupcake liners** and glue them to the narrow part of the body. Use pieces of **coffee filters** for the tail and fins.

3. Decorate the head with **colored paper**.

4. Punch two holes in the head and tie **yarn** through them for a hanger. Twist the ends of the fuzzy stick together.

THE WORLD

eople around the world celebrate in May.

May 9
⚲ VICTORY DAY

This Russian holiday marks Nazi Germany's surrender to the Soviet Union in 1945. It honors the millions of people who lost their lives in World War II, known in Russia as the Great Patriotic War. Military parades are held in major cities, with the largest one in Moscow's Red Square. It ends with fireworks displays set off in 15 parks around the city. **Can you find where the three jigsaw pieces fit into this photo of the Red Square fireworks?**

May 17
⚲ CONSTITUTION DAY

Norway's celebration of its independence in 1814 is known as *syttende mai* (seventeenth of May). But kids know it as a day when they can have as many *pølser med lompe* (hot dogs in a potato tortilla) and as much *is krem* (ice cream) as they like!

Norwegians eat as much as 10 times more ice cream on May 17 than on any other spring day.

ZODIAC SIGNS

GEMINI:
MAY 21–JUNE 20

CANCER:
JUNE 21–JULY 22

BIRTHSTONES

PEARL, ALEXANDRITE,
AND MOONSTONE

National Rotisserie Chicken Day

Drumstick or white meat?

2

He really was walking on air.

In 1965, Edward Higgins White II became the first American astronaut to walk in space.

3

NATIONAL HUG YOUR CAT DAY

4

Hot-Air Balloon Day

The highest hot-air balloon flight reached 68,986 feet.

5

Oh boy, oh boy, oh boy.

On this day in 1934, Donald Duck appeared for the first time.

9

National Ballpoint Pen Day

Jot down a note, story, or letter with your favorite pen.

10

A wonder of the world. In 1770, explorer Captain James Cook discovered the Great Barrier Reef off the coast of Australia. His studies of the reef introduced the scientific community to this living marvel.

11

NATIONAL RE ROSE DAY

12

FATHER'S DAY

EID AL-ADHA
begins at sunset.

16

Welcome home! In 1885, the Statue of Liberty arrived at New York Harbor after a long boat journey from France, where it was made.

17

International Picnic Day

18

National Watch D

Got the time?

19

23

National Pink Flamingo Day

National Water Gun Fight Day

30

Swim a Lap Day

Dive in!

24

NATIONAL CATFISH DAY

25

National Canoe Day

Grab a paddle.

26

THURSDAY	FRIDAY	SATURDAY

FLOWERS
HONEYSUCKLE AND ROSE

Say Something Nice Day

"You're the best!"

"I love your style!"

"I'm glad you're my friend!"

"You're hilarious!"

1

National Day (Sweden)

...des celebrate this day ...h special ceremonies ...coming new Swedish citizens.

6

National Chocolate Ice Cream Day

Eat it before it melts!

7

WORLD OCEANS DAY

8

National Sewing Machine Day

A stitch in time

13

FLAG DAY

14

Fasten your seatbelts! In 1921, Bessie Coleman was the first African American to receive a pilot's license

15

- Rainforests only make up about 3 percent of our planet, but they are home to more than half of the world's land animals.

- Some rainforests are hot and near the equator. Some are cool and farther from the equator.

- Rainforests are important for the earth's water cycle.

FIRST DAY OF SUMMER

20

Go Skateboarding Day

Don't forget your pads and helmet!

21

WORLD RAINFOREST DAY

22

NATIONAL ICE-CREAM CAKE DAY

27

NATIONAL ALASKA DAY

28

International Mud Day

Make some mud pies to celebrate.

29

NATIONAL ACCORDION AWARENESS MONTH

The accordion was invented in Germany in 1822 by Friedrich Buschmann. This instrument is like a piano that you can carry around with you. As you play the notes on the keyboard, you squeeze or expand the box so air can make the reeds inside the instrument vibrate and make sound.

Campfire Joe is playing the accordion out on the range. Examine the picture. Can you find all the hidden objects?

magnet

clothespin

straw

banana

comb

glove

bell

leaf

canoe

candle

candy cane

cookie

sock

pizza

Knock, knock.
Who's there?
Accordion.
Accordion who?
Accordion to the weather report, it's going to rain tomorrow.

The word accordion comes from the German word *akkord*, which means **"agreement or harmony."** When the accordion is played, the notes are definitely in harmony with each other!

AFRICAN AMERICAN MUSIC APPRECIATION MONTH

African American musicians have created some of the most innovative music styles, such as jazz. Unscramble the names of musical instruments used in a New Orleans jazz band. Then copy the circled letters in order onto the blanks at the bottom of the page to answer the riddle.

1. JORAN: _ _ _ _ (O) _
2. BOMTRONE: _ _ _ _ _ _ (O) _ _
3. BUTA: (O) _ _ _ _
4. XOOPHENSA: _ _ _ _ (O) _ _ _
5. TUPTREM: _ _ _ _ (O) _ _
6. CARLNITE: _ _ _ _ _ _ (O) _
7. IPNOA: _ (O) _ _ _
8. SURMD: _ (O) _ _ _
9. SABS: _ _ _ (O)
10. ATGUIR: _ _ _ _ _ _

Why do farmers play soft jazz for their corn stalks?

It's easy _ _ _   _ _ _ _   _ _ _ _ _ _

NATIONAL CANDY MONTH

CANDY COUNTER

As you're deciding what candy you want to eat this month, count out these sweet treats. Write a **>** or **<** to show which group in each row has more and which group has fewer. Then, circle the row that has exactly 10 pieces of candy.

What kind of bunny doesn't hop?

A chocolate bunny

What is a rabbit's favorite candy?

Lolli-hops

NATIONAL FRESH FRUIT AND VEGETABLE MONTH

Can you spot a fruit or vegetable hiding in each sentence?
Example: The shi**p eas**ed into port.

1. In the showroom, a car rotated on a platform.
2. Maya looked up each book Liam recommended.
3. The dog's bark alerted the cat.
4. "I'm getting a new bicycle Monday," said Darnell.
5. Adrianna gets up early every morning.
6. I bought a teapot at Oscar's sale.
7. Pete and his mom baked his teacher rye bread.
8. That clown can spin a chair on his hand.

GREAT OUTDOORS MONTH

To celebrate the great outdoors, why don't you, well, go out into the great outdoors! Before you do, though, make these trusty binoculars so you can better explore the world around you.

Did you know that if you hiked all the trails in Switzerland you would walk around the world ONE AND A HALF TIMES?

MAKE YOUR OWN BINOCULARS

1. Decorate **two short cardboard tubes** with **stickers** and **markers**.
2. **Tape** the tubes together.
3. Use a **hole punch** to punch a hole in each tube.
4. Thread a piece of **yarn** through each hole and tie a knot.

SENSING THE OUTDOORS

It makes sense to use your senses while you're in the outdoors! Read the ideas for hearing, feeling, seeing, and smelling. Which sense is missing? How could you use that sense in the outdoors?

*About **3 MILLION** people hike on the Appalachian Trail (the AT) every year.*

HEAR...
- [ ] wind in the trees
- [ ] moving water
- [ ] birdsongs

FEEL...
- [ ] the sun on your face
- [ ] smooth and rough bark
- [ ] a smooth rock
- [ ] a pine cone

SEE...
- [ ] birds flying
- [ ] treetops swaying
- [ ] clouds moving
- [ ] different types of leaves
- [ ] an insect

SMELL...
- [ ] the air
- [ ] grass
- [ ] a flower

June 6, 1944

80 YEARS AGO, THE ALLIED FORCES IN WORLD WAR II INVADED NORMANDY, FRANCE.

Codenamed Operation Overlord, D-Day was an effort to liberate France from Nazi Germany. More than 156,000 American, British, and Canadian forces were involved in D-Day by sea and by air.

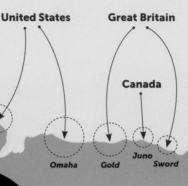

United States   **Great Britain**

Canada

Utah   Omaha   Gold   Juno   Sword

This invasion took years of planning. It was the largest amphibious invasion in military history. Amphibious refers to a military invasion of land by sea.

D-Day marked a major turning point in the war, in favor of the Allied forces.

The soldiers landed on five beaches: Utah, Omaha, Gold, Juno, and Sword. These are not the beaches' actual names, but rather their code names for the D-Day invasion.

During the rest of the war, these beaches were used as temporary harbors. It was from here that the Allied forces unloaded 2,500,000 soldiers, 500,000 vehicles, and 4,000,000 tons of supplies needed to fight the war.

The cipher disk was invented by Leon Battista Alberti in the 15th century. A version of the cipher disk was used by soldiers in the American Civil War.

SECRET CIPHER DISK

1. With a **paper fastener**, attach a **9-inch paper plate** to a **6-inch paper plate**, as shown.
2. Cut 52 half-inch squares of **colored paper**.
3. Arrange 26 squares along the edge of the 6-inch plate, evenly spaced. **Glue** them in place.
4. Repeat step three with the 9-inch plate.
5. Write one letter of the alphabet on each square around the larger plate. Write the numbers 1 to 26 on the squares around the smaller plate.
6. To use the cipher disk, choose a key by lining up *A* with any number. Using numbers in place of letters, write a secret message. Send the cipher disk and the message to a friend. Be sure to tell your friend the key so that he or she can decipher the message!

Crack this code!
Key: A = 9
7-23-3 26-23-11-19!

165 YEARS AGO TODAY, THE MELODY FOR "HAPPY BIRTHDAY TO YOU" WAS COMPOSED BY MILDRED J. HILL.

The Guinness World Records noted in 1998 that this was one of the **MOST RECOGNIZED SONGS IN THE ENGLISH LANGUAGE.**

SAME AND DIFFERENT

While you sing the "Happy Birthday to You" song three times, can you find all the ways these pictures are alike and different?

CAKE
MATCHES

Each slice of cake has a match. Find all 10 matching pairs.

Which friends did the baby deer invite to her birthday party?

Her nearest and deer-est friends

June 21

INTERNATIONAL DAY OF YOGA

Breathe in . . . breathe out. Take a few moments today to try some yoga stretches. Then look for the 16 hidden objects in this yoga studio.

Although we don't know exactly when yoga was invented, we do know its origin was in **NORTHERN INDIA AT LEAST 5,000 YEARS AGO.** Its purpose was to encourage physical, mental, and spiritual discipline.

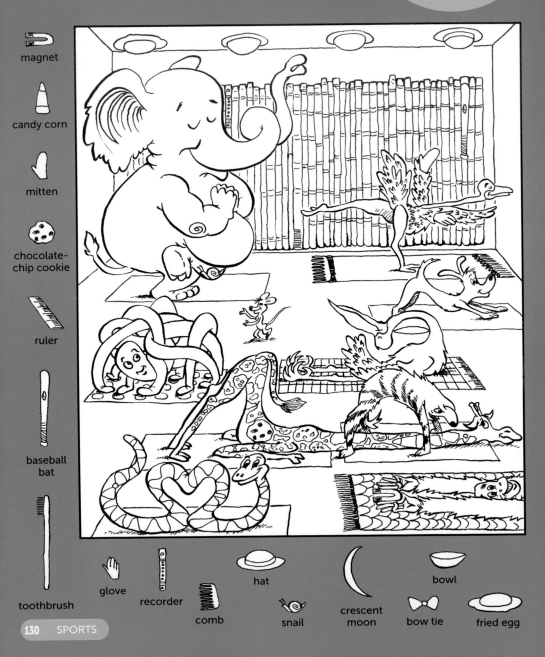

magnet

candy corn

mitten

chocolate-chip cookie

ruler

baseball bat

toothbrush

glove

recorder

comb

hat

snail

crescent moon

bow tie

bowl

fried egg

NATIONAL HOCKEY LEAGUE
STANLEY CUP FINAL

It's that time of year again for the top NHL teams to battle it out on the ice to see who will win the coveted Stanley Cup.

The Stanley Cup is named after Lord Stanley of Preston, the governor general of Canada in 1892. He bought the first cup for the league.

HOCKEY STICK CHALLENGE

In the spirit of the game, these kids have hit the rink.
How many hockey sticks can you find in the picture?

A new Stanley Cup isn't made every year. The same cup is given to the championship's winning team for 100 days during the off-season.

Why did the hockey rink melt after the game?

Because all the fans left

Why do hockey players make the best birthday cakes?

Because they know all about icing

What did the hockey goalie say to the puck?

"Catch you later."

HOCKEY MATH

Brush up on your math skills. Can you solve both problems?

There are 20 minutes 🕐 in each period. After 15 minutes 🕐 of the first period, how many minutes are left in the period?

☐ − ☐ = ☐

There are 60 fans 🚩 GO TEAM watching the game today. In between periods, 20 fans 🚩 GO TEAM get up to get snacks. How many fans are left in their seats?

☐ − ☐ = ☐

June 15
NATURE PHOTOGRAPHY DAY

Focus in on the 18 hidden objects in and under this tree.

ghost · fish · hanger · candy corn · artist's brush · slice of pizza · umbrella · bell · bowling ball

necktie · bat · shuttlecock · tooth · ice-cream cone · heart · cane · crown · pointy hat

PICTURE THIS!

Here are some tips for taking photos of animals.

- **Wait It Out:** Animals won't follow directions. You'll have to wait patiently to get a good shot.

- **Focus on the Eyes:** Humans often connect with others through eye contact, so focus on the animal's eyes or head.

- **Get Low:** Instead of pointing your camera downwards, kneel or lie down (from a safe distance) so you're on the animal's level.

- **Zoom In:** Close-up photos show a lot of detail about an animal's face, eyes, or fur. Use the camera's zoom feature to get a detailed photo.

- **Snap, Snap, Snap:** Don't expect every photo to be perfect. Photographers often take 100 pictures to end up with one they really like.

- **Practice!** To practice your skills, take plenty of pictures of pets, birds, or insects, or visit a zoo or aquarium.

National Camera Day is June 29!

WORLD MUSIC DAY

In honor of World Music Day and the start of summer, it's the perfect time to enjoy some outdoor music, Have a picnic   grab some lawn chairs and this book, because you need to help find all the hidden objects before the music ends!

mop

envelope

nail

hamburger

domino

turtle

necktie

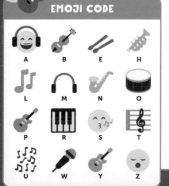

What is a bunny's favorite kind of music?

Hip-hop

MUSIC MADNESS

Use the music code to fill in the letters to complete the jokes.

EMOJI CODE

A	B	E	H
L	M	N	O
P	R	S	T
U	W	Y	Z

What kind of music do mummies like? _ _ _ _ _

What is a bubble's least favorite type of music? _ _ _ !

What do you get when a musician loses their beat?

_ _ _ _ _ _ _ _ _ _ _ _ _ _ _

June 10

NATIONAL
HERBS AND
SPICES DAY

Spice up your day with this word search. **Can you find all 18 of these popular herbs and spices?**

WORD LIST

ALLSPICE	NUTMEG
ANISE	OREGANO
BASIL	PAPRIKA
CARDAMOM	PARSLEY
CAYENNE PEPPER	SAFFRON
CHIVES	SAGE
CINNAMON	THYME
CURRY	TURMERIC
DILL	
FENNEL	

```
R E P P E P E N N E Y A C P E
A U N H K L S Q A G X Y S C A
B N L S E K M E H D Y O I N K
X A A N I S E Y V R T P G O I
C G S D I L L F R I S K R M R
E M E I T X U U E L H B V A P
S C E G L C C V L N D C O N A
A I B R C J A A N H N Q N N P
F R V Z A P L C U K C E J I V
F E E R R V Y S T T V T L C X
R M U M D Y U R M Q B F W S U
U R I P A R S L E Y T X Z H T
N U Y Y M O N A G E R O J Q G
N T B L O Y J K P Y E M Y H T
S Q U J M F T O B D W I N H U
```

Celebrate more delicious foods with these four holidays.

June 11

NATIONAL
CORN
ON THE COB
DAY

A typical ear of corn has about 800 kernels.

June 21

NATIONAL
SMOOTHIE
DAY

Mashed beans will make a smoothie thicker without adding any bean flavor.

June 22

NATIONAL
ONION
RING
DAY

Americans eat an average of 22 pounds of onions per person per year.

June 26

NATIONAL
CHOCOLATE
PUDDING
DAY

The first known recipe for chocolate pudding appears in a cookbook from 1730.

June 16, 2024

FATHER'S DAY

Honor Pops this year by decorating something he'll love to use—a brush for the grill!
We've painted a dotted pattern—what designs will you come up with?

1. Cover the bristles of a **basting brush** with **foil** and secure with **masking tape**.

2. Put some **dot stickers** on one side of the basting brush's wooden handle. Then **paint** that side of the handle and the dots. Allow the paint to dry overnight. Carefully remove the dots.

3. Repeat step 2 on the other side of the handle.

This one-of-a-kind brush makes a lovely and useful gift.

Knock, knock.
Who's there?
Wheelbarrow.
Wheelbarrow who?
Wheelbarrow some money from Mom and Dad.

Knock, knock.
Who's there?
Kentucky.
Kentucky who?
Dad Kentucky you in at night.

June 14
FLAG DAY

Flag Day celebrates the official adoption of the stars and stripes by the Second Continental Congress on June 14, 1777. Flag Day was first celebrated in 1885 at the Stony Hill School, a one-room school in Waubeka, Wisconsin.

MAKE RED, WHITE, AND BLUE NACHOS

Before you begin, ask an adult to set the oven to broil.

1. Open and spread a 6-ounce bag of **blue tortilla chips** evenly on a 9-by-13-inch pan.

2. Spoon 1 cup **salsa** over the chips.

3. Sprinkle 1 cup shredded **white cheddar cheese** on top. Add toppings, such as **chopped tomatoes, sliced olives**, and **black beans**, if you'd like.

4. Ask an adult to broil the nachos for 3 minutes. Let stand for 3 minutes before eating.

ON JUNE 14, 1777, Congress decided the U.S. flag would have 13 stripes, alternating in red and white, plus 13 white stars in a blue field. The number 13 was chosen because there were 13 colonies.

After Vermont and Kentucky became the 14th and 15th states, the flag was changed to 15 stars and 15 stripes in 1795.

As new states joined the country, there wasn't enough room to keep adding stripes. So in 1818, Congress decided the flag would go back to 13 stripes and have one star for every state.

The arrangement of the 50 stars on today's flag was created by a high school student. Robert Heft of Ohio created the flag for a class project when Alaska and Hawaii were about to become states. He also sent his design to the White House. Heft got a B- on the project, but the teacher changed it to an A after President Eisenhower chose Heft's design as our new flag.

June 20, 2024

FIRST DAY

Kick off summer with these fun activities!

3 SUNNY-DAY CRAFTS

- **Create a suncatcher** using colored paper, yarn, and tissue paper.
- **Build a sculpture** using objects from nature.
- **Make your own bubble wands** from fuzzy sticks. Dip them in some bubble solution, and blow!

3 WAYS TO USE SIDEWALK CHALK

- **Create a story** just by drawing pictures.
- **Create a life-sized board game,** drawing the game spaces with chalk.
- **Write funny jokes** or cheerful messages on your sidewalk.

3 WATER BALLOON GAMES

- **Yard Toss.** Place four rulers (or other markers) at varying distances. See who can toss a water balloon the farthest without bursting it.
- **Exploding Tag.** Fill a few water balloons and set them aside. Instead of tagging another player, *It* lightly tosses a water balloon at that person (below the neck). If it doesn't pop, that person becomes *It*!
- **Balloon Bowling.** Use empty cans and plastic bottles as pins and a water balloon as the ball. Set the pins on a flat surface outdoors and see how many you can knock down.

For people in Australia, Argentina, and the rest of the Southern Hemisphere, today is the first day of winter.

The first day of summer is also called the summer solstice. It's the day with the most daylight hours in the Northern Hemisphere.

In northern Alaska, the sun never fully sets today, and in 1906, locals began celebrating by playing baseball in the midnight sun. The Alaska Goldpanners baseball team took over the tradition in 1960. Their annual summer solstice game starts at 10:30 p.m. and finishes by 2 a.m.—in the sunlight.

Be sure to throw away the pieces after the balloons pop!

Summertime is beach time! Rey wants to buy one pair of sandals and one pair of sunglasses at Sally's Sea Store. Can you help her find the best deal?

NATIONAL TURTLE RACES DAY

On your mark, get set, go! On the first Saturday of June every year, turtles can strut their stuff and see who is the fastest shelled reptile in the land and sea. The competing turtles are placed inside of a circle, and the first to cross out of the circle's borders is the winner!

What do you get when you cross a turtle with a porcupine?

A slowpoke

COME OUT OF YOUR SHELL

Stick your neck out—like this box turtle—and learn about these reptilian creatures. Then find the objects hidden in this scene.

handbag · polar bear · seahorse · slice of pizza · kite · duck · dog bone · skateboard · peanut · mushroom · rabbit · horn · soccer ball · apple · wedge of cheese

TURTLE MATCH UP

Draw a line to connect each turtle to its exact match.

ASTEROID DAY

Asteroid Day marks the anniversary of the 1908 Tunguska impact, in which an asteroid hit the earth in Siberia, destroying 800 square miles of forest. The goal of Asteroid Day is education and awareness.

ORBITING A SPACE POTATO

Planets aren't the only bodies in space that can have moons orbiting them. The potato-shaped asteroid shown here, which is named **Ida** (EYE-duh), is just one of many asteroids massive enough to have their own moons. Gravity keeps Ida's moon, Dactyl (DACK-tull), going around the asteroid, just as Earth's gravity keeps our moon in orbit around us.

Dactyl is just 1 mile wide. Our moon is 2,160 miles wide!

Dactyl orbits Ida the long way.

Like most asteroids, Ida isn't round. It contains so little material that its gravity isn't strong enough to pull it into a sphere shape.

Craters on Ida and Dactyl were caused by smaller asteroids that hit their surfaces over time.

Ida and Dactyl are in the asteroid belt, between the orbits of Mars and Jupiter.

KIDS' SCIENCE QUESTIONS

What is the difference between an asteroid and a meteor?

Asteroids are sometimes called *minor planets*. They are fairly small, rocky worlds. Like Earth and the other planets, asteroids orbit around the sun. Most asteroids are in a "belt"—a group of orbiting paths that lie between Mars and Jupiter.

A *meteor* is a streak of light we see in the sky when a much smaller bit of rock enters Earth's atmosphere and burns from the heat of friction as it falls through the air.

Two other important terms are *meteoroid* and *meteorite*. A meteoroid is a bit of rock that could burn up to create a meteor—before it enters the atmosphere. Meteorites are much more unusual. A meteorite is any part of a meteoroid that hits Earth's surface because it has not been completely burned up during its fall.

Meteorite

June 8
NATIONAL BEST FRIENDS DAY

How much do you know about your best friend?
How much do they know about you?

Answer these questions about yourself, then guess how a friend might answer them.
Have your friend do the same—then compare your answers!

1. How I'd spend the day if the power went out
2. What I'd like to become famous for doing
3. The nickname I'd choose
4. My middle name
5. My favorite singer
6. How my friends would describe me
7. A place I'd like to visit
8. My favorite team
9. My favorite foods
10. My favorite thing to wear
11. Something I do to make my friends laugh
12. Something I'm really good at
13. My favorite book
14. Something that scares other people but not me
15. My favorite outdoor thing to do
16. My favorite color
17. Where I go when I want to be alone
18. What I'm afraid of
19. The superpower I wish I had
20. Something I've always wanted

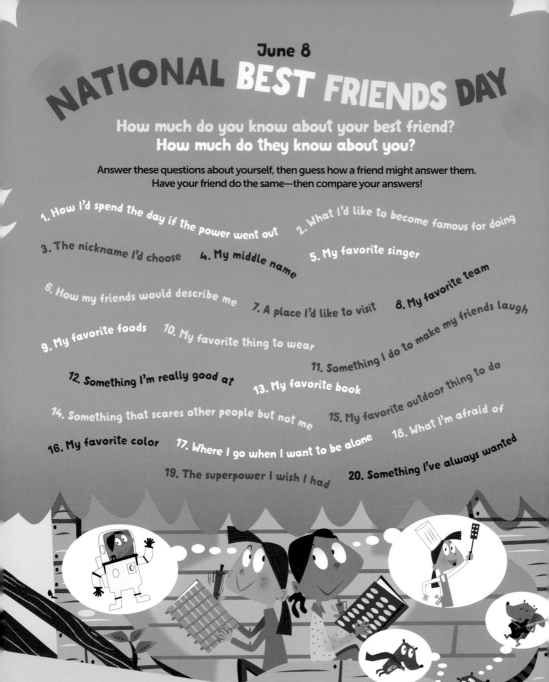

FUNNY FACE-OFF
Challenge one or more friends to this game of giggles!

IN ROUND ONE, take turns making funny faces.

IN ROUND TWO, take turns telling jokes or riddles.

IN ROUND THREE, take turns doing silly dances.

THE GOAL? Lots of laughs all around!

June 19
JUNETEENTH

On this day in 1865, a Union general announced to the people of Galveston, Texas, that slavery had been abolished in the United States, more than two-and-a-half years after the Emancipation Proclamation. The newly freed slaves in Texas erupted in a joyous celebration, and the event became known as Juneteenth.

Today people around the country celebrate this anniversary of the freedom from slavery with parades, festivals, and barbecues.

STRAWBERRY
BUBBLE LEMONADE

Put 1 cup **strawberries** into a blender. Blend until thick and smooth. Add 3 cups **lemonade** and 2 cups **seltzer.** Blend together and chill. Pour ¼ cup **maple syrup** onto one plate and 2 packs of **Pop Rocks** onto another. Dip the rims of 6 glasses into the maple syrup and then into the Pop Rocks. Add a few **ice cubes** to each glass and pour in the strawberry lemonade.

The color red is an important part of Juneteenth, and people eat and drink red foods, such as strawberry soda, hot sauce on barbecue, and red velvet cake.

June 27
NATIONAL
SUNGLASSES DAY

There are five pairs of sunglasses that match exactly in this beach scene. **Can you find them all?**

Reports suggest that someone in the U.S. loses, breaks, or sits on a pair of sunglasses every 14 minutes!

Take a spin around the globe to see ho

June 12
◉ DIA DOS NAMORADOS

Valentine's Day falls in February, but in Brazil the holiday honoring love is in June. *Dia dos Namorados* means "Boyfriend and Girlfriend's Day." Couples celebrate with cards, candy, and dinner.

These kids tangled up their balloon strings. Can you figure out whose is whose?

June 16
◉ YOUTH DAY

Youth Day commemorates a protest by black students in South Africa in 1976.
At the time, the government discriminated against people who weren't white, and the students were peacefully protesting an unfair law. The police fired on the protesters and many students lost their lives. This terrible event eventually led to a change in the government. Today, South Africans honor those students on Youth Day by visiting museums, attending events about history, and by helping their communities.

South Africa's flag is unique in that it uses six main colors in the design.

THE WORLD

eople around the world celebrate in June.

June 17
○ NATIONAL DAY

National Day in Iceland celebrates the country's independence from Denmark in 1944. In every town, a woman is chosen to read a poem or give a speech. She wears the national costume of Iceland, and many other people do, too. The whole country celebrates with parades, marching bands, carnivals, and concerts.

June 20
○ FLAG DAY

Día de la Bandera Nacional honors the flag of Argentina and the man who created it, Manuel Belgrano, a military leader who helped the country become independent from Spain. Every June 20, Argentina's president gives a speech and a big parade is held in the town where the flag was first flown.

The "Sun of May" was added to the flag in 1818, inspired by the sun on the first Argentine coin. It also honors an Incan sun deity, Inti.

The blue stripes are known as *celeste,* which means "sky blue."

Although Belgrano first raised the flag in 1812, it went through many variations until this official version was approved in 1861.

SUNDAY	MONDAY	TUESDAY	WEDNESDAY
BIRTHSTONE RUBY	**National Postal Workers Day** Deliver your thanks to your mail carrier. **1**	**World UFO Day** Keep your eyes on the skies. **2**	*"We are the keepers of the flame of liberty."* In 1986, after a two-year restoration, President Reagan lit the Statue of Liberty's torch in honor of its 100th anniversary.
Charge! For one week, starting today, Pamplona, Spain, holds the Running of the Bulls as part of the San Fermín Festival (which begins on July 6). **7**	**National Video Game Day** Get your thumbs in shape. **8**	**National Sugar Cookie Day** Frosting, sprinkles, and lots of sugar— the recipe for a delicious cookie. **9**	**DON'T STEP ON A BEE DAY** **10**
Far out! In 2015, NASA's New Horizons probe became the first spacecraft to fly near Pluto. **14**	**NATIONAL I LOVE HORSES DAY** **15**	**NATIONAL ARTIFICIAL INTELLIGENCE APPRECIATION DAY** Thanks! **16**	*There's a mouse in the house.* In 1955, Disneyland opened in Anaheim, California. **1**
Liberation Day (Guam) People celebrate with a carnival and parade with giant floats. **21**	**NATIONAL HAMMOCK DAY** **22**	**GORGEOUS GRANDMA DAY** **23**	**NATIONAL DRIVE-THRU DAY** **24**
NATIONAL SOCCER DAY **28**	**Global Tiger Day** Wear stripes today! **29**	**PAPERBACK BOOK DAY** **30**	**INTERNATIONAL LIFEGUARD APPRECIATION DAY** **3**

THURSDAY	FRIDAY	SATURDAY
INDEPENDENCE DAY **4**	*From books to billions.* In 1994, Amazon.com was founded. It started as an online bookstore and has expanded into one of the most profitable businesses in the world. **5**	*Play ball!* In 1933, the first Major League Baseball All-Star Game was played. **6**
NATIONAL BLUEBERRY MUFFIN DAY **11**	**NATIONAL EAT YOUR JELL-O DAY** **12**	**INTERNATIONAL DAY OF ROCK 'N' ROLL** **13**
NATIONAL SOUR CANDY DAY **18**	*Giving women a voice.* In 1848, the first women's rights convention began in Seneca Falls, New York. One of their main goals was to get women the right to vote. **19**	**NATIONAL MOON DAY** **20**
National Hot Fudge Sundae Day **25**	**NATIONAL AUNT AND UNCLE'S DAY** **26**	**What's Up, Doc?** On this day in 1940, Bugs Bunny was born! **27**

If you could go to the moon, what would be the top five things you would bring?

1. _____

2. _____

3. _____

4. _____

5. _____

ZODIAC SIGNS
CANCER:
JUNE 21–JULY 22

LEO:
JULY 23–AUGUST 22

FLOWERS
LARKSPUR AND
WATER LILY

ICE CREAM MONTH

CRISS-CROSS ICE CREAM

Ike's Ice-Cream Shop has the best ice cream in town! The Word List names the most popular flavors and toppings at the shop. Fill in the cone puzzle with the words in the list. One is already done for you.

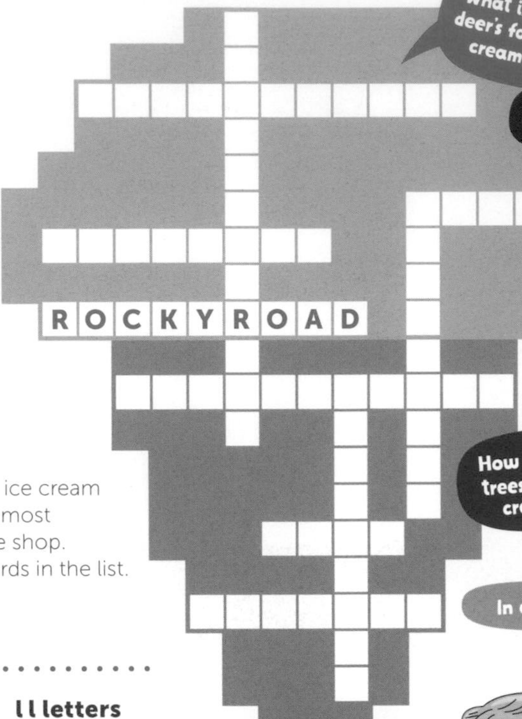

What is a female deer's favorite ice-cream flavor?

Cookie doe

R O C K Y R O A D

How do evergreen trees like their ice cream served?

In a pine cone

WORD LIST

4 letters
mint

6 letters
cherry

7 letters
vanilla

8 letters
hot fudge

9 letters
chocolate
~~rocky road~~
sprinkles

11 letters
banana split
cookie dough

12 letters
whipped cream

SCOOPIN' IT UP

This picture graph shows the number of ice-cream cones Ike's Ice-Cream Shop sold on Thursday, Friday, and Saturday. Use the picture graph to find out how many ice-cream cones were sold on each day.

What is an herbivore's favorite type of ice cream?

Mint chocolate chip, because they only eat greens.

KEY: Each 🍦 = 4 ice-cream cones sold.

Thursday	🍦	🍦	🍦		
Friday	🍦	🍦	🍦	🍦	🍦
Saturday	🍦	🍦	🍦	🍦	

1. How many cones did the shop sell on Thursday? **12**

    4 + **4** + **4** = **12**

2. How many cones did the shop sell on Friday? ☐

    ☐ + ☐ + ☐ + ☐ + ☐ = ☐

3. How many cones did the shop sell on Saturday? ☐

    ☐ + ☐ + ☐ + ☐ = ☐

NATIONAL BERRY MONTH

July is also National Blueberry Month, National Blackberry Month, and National Raspberry Month. If you love berries, this is a great month for you!

Can you find the 22 hearts hiding in the fruit below?

The bumps on blackberries and raspberries are called *drupelets.*

BERRY ICE POP

On a hot summer day, nothing tastes better than a fruity ice pop, especially one loaded with berries. Follow these instructions, and tips, to make your own! Then, experiment with other types of berries. What is your favorite?

BANANAS 'N' BERRIES

1. Put 1 cup of frozen or fresh **strawberries** (green tops removed) into a blender. Add ½ cup of **milk** and 2 tablespoons of **honey**. Put on the blender lid. Ask an adult to blend until creamy.

2. Cut a **banana** into chunks. Place one on the stick of each ice-pop form.

3. Pour the strawberry mixture into each form, leaving room for the stick and banana. Put the stick into the form.

4. Place the pops in the freezer. When they're frozen solid, remove them from the forms (or tear away the paper cups) and enjoy!

ICE-POP TIPS

- Wash your hands and any fresh fruit before you begin.

- Ask an adult to help with anything sharp.

- You can make the pops in purchased ice-pop forms, 3-ounce paper cups, or even ice-cube trays. With paper cups or trays, use aluminum foil to cover them. Poke a clean treat stick into each pop through the foil.

WILD ABOUT WILDLIFE MONTH

With over 8.7 million wildlife species in the world, there's a lot to celebrate this month. Take some time to learn about a new animal or find out what animals live in your area.

JUMBLED ANIMALS

Unscramble each set of letters to get the name of a wild animal.

BRAZE   __ __ __ __ __

MELAC   __ __ __ __ __

ADNAP   __ __ __ __ __

TEACHHE   __ __ __ __ __ __ __

RAPLO RABE __ __ __ __ __ __   __ __ __ __ __

GUESS WHO?

Can you figure out what these animals are?

LAND OR SEA?

Do you know which of these animals live on the land and which live in the water?

KOMODO DRAGON
BRITTLESTAR
ALPACA
MANATEE

STINGRAY
CHINCHILLA
BONGO
BARRACUDA

PENGUIN POSES

Most of the seventeen or so species of penguins live in the Southern Hemisphere. This group of emperor penguins is one of the seven or eight penguin species that make Antarctica their home.

Can you find at least 20 differences between these two photos?

NATIONAL PARK AND RECREATION MONTH

This month was first celebrated in 1985!

It's a beautiful day at the park! But it looks as if there are some silly shenanigans going down. **Can you spot what's silly?**

PLASTIC-FREE JULY

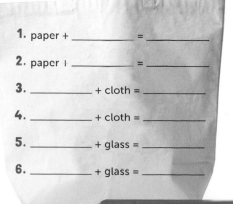

Water bottles, grocery bags, straws—too many plastic items are used only once and then thrown away. Plastic garbage is polluting the ground and turning up in rivers and oceans, where it's harming birds and fish.

Give the environment a break this month and stick with reusable water bottles, cloth tote bags, and paper straws. Try making it a habit that lasts past July.

Paper, cloth, and glass are reusable materials that are also reusable in this puzzle. Combine each word with one from the Word List to form a new word.

WORD LIST

back
dish
eye
hour
table
weight

1. paper + _____ = _____

2. paper + _____ = _____

3. _____ + cloth = _____

4. _____ + cloth = _____

5. _____ + glass = _____

6. _____ + glass = _____

July 1, 1874

150 YEARS AGO, PHILADELPHIA BECAME THE HOME OF THE FIRST ZOO IN THE UNITED STATES.

It's feeding time at the zoo. Follow each zookeeper's path to see what the animals are having for dinner.

There were 1,000 animals in the Philadelphia Zoo on opening day. **TODAY, THERE ARE 1,300.**

On opening day, people traveled to the Philadelphia Zoo by **FOOT, HORSE AND CARRIAGE, AND STEAMBOAT.**

Knock, knock.
Who's there?
Zoo.
Zoo who?
Zoo think you can come out and play?

TICKET PRICES WERE STEEP IN 1874: 25 CENTS FOR ADULTS AND 10 CENTS FOR KIDS. Today it costs $24 for adults and $19 for kids.

Ha ha!
Ha ha!

A police officer stopped a woman who was driving with a penguin in the back seat of her car.
"This is illegal. You need to take the animal to the zoo," said the officer.
The next day he saw her with the penguin again.
"I thought I told you to take him to the zoo," he said.
"I did," replied the woman. "Today I'm taking him to the beach."

55 YEARS AGO TODAY, MANKIND LANDED ON THE MOON AS PART OF THE UNITED STATES' APOLLO 11 MISSION.

Can you find at least 15 differences between these two photos?

Since 1969, a total of **SIX** NASA missions have landed on the Moon.

Neil Armstrong was the first person to step on the Moon. He said, **"THAT'S ONE SMALL STEP FOR MAN, ONE GIANT LEAP FOR MANKIND."**

ALL TWISTED UP

Try to say these tongue twisters three times fast.

The moon's magnificence moved Maggie.

Lana and Luna had lunch before launch.

Shane stares at shining stars.

2024 SUMMER OLYMPIC

Twenty-five Summer Olympic sports are hiding in this grid. Look for them up, down, across, backward, and diagonally. **Be a good sport and find as many as you can.**

WORD LIST

- ~~ARCHERY~~
- BADMINTON
- BASKETBALL
- BEACH VOLLEYBALL
- CANOEING
- CYCLING
- DECATHLON
- DISCUS
- DIVING
- FENCING
- GYMNASTICS
- HANDBALL
- HIGH JUMP
- JUDO
- LONG JUMP
- MARATHON
- PENTATHLON
- SAILING
- SHOT PUT
- SOCCER
- SPRINTING
- SWIMMING
- TENNIS
- TRIATHLON
- WRESTLING

J	B	L	B	G	H	B	B	O	B	S	L	E	D	V
K	N	L	H	W	R	E	S	T	L	I	N	G	E	D
O	B	A	F	I	Q	A	R	E	C	C	O	S	X	D
N	A	B	G	N	G	C	A	N	O	E	I	N	G	I
E	D	T	N	H	Y	H	A	N	D	B	A	L	L	V
G	M	E	I	Q	M	V	J	T	E	N	N	I	S	I
N	I	K	M	P	N	O	F	U	O	Q	U	J	U	N
I	N	S	M	M	A	L	M	O	M	T	O	T	C	G
T	T	A	I	U	S	L	A	F	O	P	R	O	S	S
N	O	B	W	J	T	E	R	I	E	I	A	X	I	N
I	N	L	S	G	I	Y	A	N	A	H	G	Y	D	O
R	V	U	G	N	C	B	T	T	T	O	Y	R	E	W
P	F	G	J	O	S	A	H	I	M	C	S	E	C	B
S	E	E	I	L	T	L	O	S	K	K	H	H	A	O
A	N	Q	J	H	O	L	N	D	C	E	O	C	T	A
I	C	U	L	N	A	Q	O	A	U	Y	T	R	H	R
L	I	O	C	Y	C	L	I	N	G	J	P	A	L	D
I	N	C	S	P	O	R	T	S	G	I	U	M	O	I
N	G	N	G	O	L	S	T	A	I	V	T	O	N	N
G	F	I	G	U	R	E	S	K	A	T	I	N	G	G

BONUS PUZZLE

We've also hidden five Winter Olympic sports in the grid. Can you find them?

GAMES—PARIS, FRANCE

Even animals like to get in on Olympic action. These otters are trying to win the gold medal in synchronized swimming. **You can go for the gold by searching for all 20 hidden objects in the scene.**

BONUS
Can you find 5 ladybugs in this scene?

adhesive bandage

kite

ruler

arrowhead

megaphone

slice of bread

candle

paper clip

slice of pizza

domino

party hat

tea bag

heart

drumstick

paw print

tennis ball

envelope

pencil

worm

question mark

July 10

DON'T STEP ON A BEE DAY

Spend the day making a bee-utiful craft!

You Need
* Egg carton
* Scissors
* Glue
* Paint
* Paintbrush
* Pencil
* Twist tie
* Bubble wrapping

Before you begin *Adult: Cut the **egg carton** into sections. Glue two cups together.*

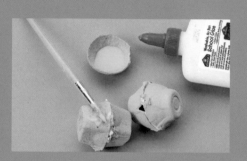

1 Paint.

Paint the bee's body yellow. Let dry.

2 Paint.

Paint stripes on the body. Paint eyes and a mouth. Let dry.

3 Poke.

Use a **pencil** to poke a hole above the bee's face. Bend a **twist tie** into a V. Stick the pointed end of the V into the hole.

4 Cut.

Cut four teardrop shapes from **bubble wrapping**. **Glue** two on each side of the bee. Where will your bee fly?

July 12
PAPER BAG DAY

TAKE A FOX TO LUNCH!

Update your paper lunch bag with this cute fox.

1. To make the fox's ears, cut the corners of a **paper bag** as shown. Set the ears aside.

2. Fold down the top of the bag. **Tape** a **coffee filter** under the fold. Trim the coffee filter so it's the same width as the bag.

3. Tape the ears to the back of the bag.

4. Use **markers** to draw eyes, a nose, a mouth, and the inside of the ears.

July 31
UNCOMMON MUSICAL INSTRUMENT AWARENESS DAY

Check out how each of these one-of-a-kind instruments makes its unique sound.

The Great Stalacpipe Organ at Luray Caverns in Virginia is the world's largest musical instrument. It produces sound by gently tapping stalactites that hang from the ceiling of the caves.

The Sea Organ in Zadar, Croatia, is a series of 35 pipes of different sizes and lengths that are hidden in a series of stairs. The Adriatic Sea produces sound as the tide pushes water and air into the echoing chambers under the steps.

The Singing Ringing Tree in Burnley, England, is a swirling, 9.8-foot-tall sculpture made out of more than three hundred steel pipes. As the wind blows on the hill, the pipes make a beautiful and eerie sound.

NATIONAL MAC AND CHEESE DAY

For lunch today, why not make your own mac and cheese in a mug?

You Need

- ½ cup uncooked elbow macaroni or small shell pasta
- 1 large ovenproof mug or jar
- ¼ cup shredded cheddar cheese
- 1 tablespoon flour • ½ cup milk • ¼ teaspoon salt

Topping:
- 1 tablespoon butter • 1 tablespoon bread crumbs

1. Place the **macaroni** in the mug. Add the **cheese**, **flour**, **milk**, and **salt**. Stir lightly with a spoon.

2. Mix together the **melted butter** and **bread crumbs** in a small dish.

Adult: Place the mug on a baking pan. Bake for 25–30 minutes or until the mixture is bubbling on top. Remove the mug and top the macaroni with the bread-crumb mix. Bake for another 3–5 minutes or until the bread crumbs start to brown. Remove from the oven. Let cool for 5–10 minutes. Makes one serving.

Before You Begin

Adult: Preheat the oven to 375°F. Melt the butter.

MAKE TWO!
Eat one now, refrigerate the other. When ready to eat, microwave until warm.

These four holidays give you a chance to celebrate even more delicious foods.

July 12
NATIONAL PECAN PIE DAY

The pecans float to the top of the pie by themselves while the pie is baking.

July 13
NATIONAL FRENCH FRY DAY

Belgium is the world's top french-fry eater. Belgians eat about 165 pounds of fries per person in a year.

July 15
NATIONAL GUMMY WORM DAY

Gummy worms were invented as a way to get kids' attention and gross out their parents.

July 22
NATIONAL MANGO DAY

Mangoes, cashews, and pistachios are all part of the Anacardiaceae family, which also includes poison ivy!

· ·

July 31
NATIONAL AVOCADO DAY

Plant what you eat!

1. Wash the pit and remove any bits of avocado. Then poke three toothpicks into the sides of the pit, and place it on the top of a glass filled with water. The round end of the pit should be down, and the pointed end should be faceup. Keep it out of direct sunlight, but in a warm place.

2. Be sure there is always some water covering the bottom of the pit. It will take two to six weeks to sprout. As the roots and stem begin to grow, the pit will split. When the stem is about six inches long, cut it in half, to about three inches tall.

3. When the roots are thick and new leaves have formed on the stem, plant it in a large pot (about 10 inches across) filled with rich soil. The pit should be a bit exposed above the soil. Keep it watered so the soil is moist, and put it in a place that gets plenty of sunlight.

One avocado tree can grow around **150** avocados!

CALIFORNIA grows more avocados than any other state.

Knock, knock.
Who's there?
Avocado.
Avocado who?
Avocado an awful cold. Ah-choo!

INDEPENDENCE

GET THE FACTS BEHIND THIS STAR-SPANGLED CELEBRATION.

EPIC FIREWORKS

There are over

16,000

fireworks displays around the country to celebrate the Fourth of July.

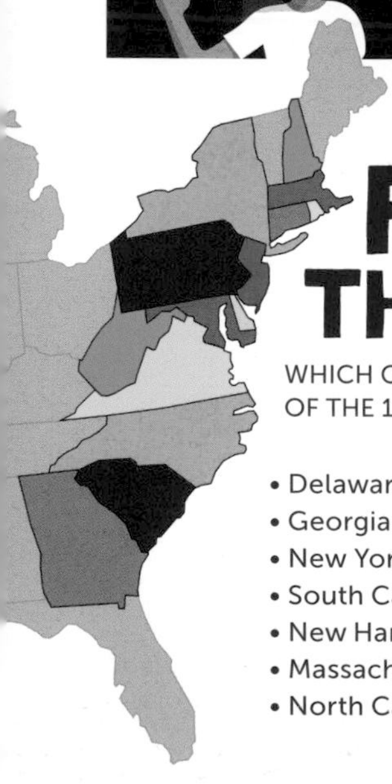

THE FIRST THIRTEEN

WHICH OF THESE WAS NOT ONE OF THE 13 ORIGINAL COLONIES?

- Delaware
- Georgia
- New York
- South Carolina
- New Hampshire
- Massachusetts
- North Carolina
- Rhode Island
- New Jersey
- Virginia
- Pennsylvania
- Maryland
- Vermont
- Connecticut

PATRIOTIC TOWN NAMES

EAGLE COLORADO

Patriot INDIANA

Equality ILLINOIS

Liberty Kentucky

FREEDOM CALIFORNIA

INDEPENDENCE MISSOURI

DAY

PICNIC PREP

TOP SELLERS FOR JULY 4

MEAT	PRODUCE	SAUCE
Beef	**Berries**	**Barbecue**

Life, liberty, and what else?

The pursuit of happiness!

WHAT'S IT ALL ABOUT?

The Revolutionary War (1775–1783) was the 13 American colonies' fight for independence from England.

On July 4, 1776, the Second Continental Congress adopted the Declaration of Independence, officially cutting ties with the British.

STILL GOING!

OLDEST FOURTH OF JULY FESTIVITIES
Bristol, Rhode Island

Bristol had its first celebration in 1785. (July 4 wasn't a holiday until 1870!)

How come there's no knock-knock joke about America?

Because freedom rings

HISTORIC FLAG

A Revolutionary War battle flag from 1776 sold for

$12,336,000

at an auction in 2006.

HOW MANY PEOPLE?

ESTIMATED U.S. POPULATION

JULY 1776

2.5
MILLION

JULY 2024

336
MILLION

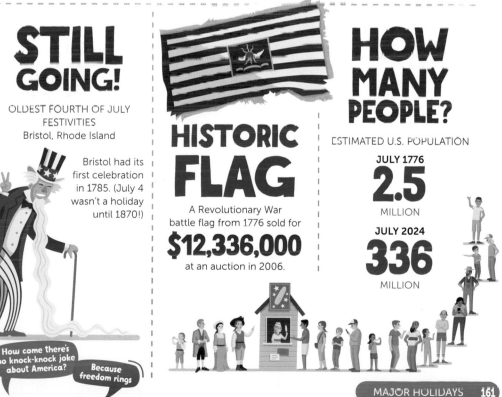

SHARK AWARENESS DAY

This day celebrates these fascinating and diverse creatures and their important role in keeping oceans healthy. Started by the Shark Trust, Shark Awareness Day seeks to create positive attitudes toward sharks. **Celebrate by making this shark treasure box!**

1. Cut six fins and two tails from **thin cardboard.** Bend a ½-inch flap on the bottom of each piece.

2. **Glue** the pieces together in pairs, leaving the flaps unglued. Glue the fin and tail flaps to an empty **tissue box.** Hold them in place with **masking tape** while the glue dries.

3. **Paint** the shark or cover it with **paper.** Let it dry.

4. Cut teeth, eyes, and a mouth from **felt.** Glue them on.

5. Store treasures inside. To retrieve them, stick your hand in the shark's mouth!

What sharks would you find at a construction site?

Hammerhead sharks

Sharks existed about **450 million** years ago, well before the dinosaurs.

Sharks don't have bones. Their skeletons are made of cartilage, the same stuff that makes up your ears or the tip of your nose.

Shark skin feels like sandpaper. It's covered with tiny teeth-like scales.

When you flip a shark over on its back, it goes into a trancelike state. Scientists use this trick to study or help sharks.

WORLD SNAKE DAY

Snakes are reptiles, just like turtles, alligators, lizards, and crocodiles. Like these other reptiles, they have scales, are cold-blooded, and have a three-chambered heart. Snakes are unique, though, because they are the only reptiles that don't have legs. **This snake's all twisted around the trunk of this tree. Search carefully and see if you can find all of the objects hidden in this scene.**

banana

paper clip

gingerbread man

camel

star

duck

bell

crown

egg

bowl

BONUS!
Can you find the crescent moon, spoon, and horn?

What did the snake say to his little sister?

Stop being such a rattle-tail!

Snakes are able to smell with their **TONGUES**.

What is a snake's favorite state?

Hiss-issippi

What kind of snake likes dessert?

Snakes can go **MONTHS** without eating.

BZZZZ!!!

A pie-thon

NATIONAL WALK ON STILTS DAY

In the year 1411, stilts were banned in the medieval city of Namur, Belgium.

In 1980, Joe Bowen walked more than **3,000 MILES** across the country on stilts!

In 1891, Sylvain Dornon walked from **PARIS TO MOSCOW** in 58 days on stilts.

STILTS CAN BE A HELPFUL TOOL. Need to reach the apples on the top of a tree? Need to string some lights? Stilts may be the solution.

Can you spot the kid walking on stilts? After you find him, see how many other silly things can you find.

SNACK SHACK

NO PARKING

July 28
NATIONAL WATERPARK DAY

Today is a *grrrr-8 day* to visit the waterpark! Figure out which path gets you from START to FINISH.

BONUS: See how many 8s you can find in the scene.

How many other words can you make out of the letters in **WATERPARK?** We found a fruit, a martial art, and a warm jacket.

START

OPEN 7:30 am to 10:00 pm DAILY

SNACKS

Hot Dogs $8.00 · Soda, Pizza $4.00

Max 8 People

Min. 28 lbs old

Min. 68 lbs old

Parking $4/hr

ABB · 123

Buy 8 Tickets get 1 Free!

Splash Zone!

Hard Turn 10 ft. Ahead

Splash Zone!

Ice Cream 8 flavors

Splash Zone!

08

4:83:8

The Figure Eight

FINISH

Next Show 8:00

HATS: 2 for $8.00

T-SHIRTS $4.98

BACKYARD WATERPARK

Even if you can't celebrate at a waterpark, have a splashing good time at home playing these water games.

With a parent's permission, set up plastic chairs in a circle around a sprinkler. Play **"musical" chairs** with water instead of music! Have someone in charge of turning the **sprinkler** on and off. Walk around the chairs when the water is on, and try to take a seat as soon as the water turns off.

Play **spray-bottle freeze tag**. To "freeze" the other players, *It* must squirt them using a small plastic spray bottle filled with water.

Instead of Duck, Duck, Goose, play **Duck, Duck, Drench**. Fill a cup with water. Walk around your friends in a circle. Choose your "goose," and dump the water on him or her.

July 1
CANADA DAY

This holiday celebrates the anniversary of July 1, 1867, on which the British government combined three North American colonies into one area called Canada. People celebrate with parades, barbecues, and fireworks.

Take a spin around the globe to see ho

July 14
LA FÊTE NATIONALE

Known as Bastille Day outside of France, this celebration commemorates the beginning of the French Revolution. On July 14, 1789, an angry group of Parisians stormed a prison called the Bastille. The French Revolution sparked the abolishment of the French monarchy. French people spend the day with family and friends and watch fireworks at night.

Can you find at least 15 differences between these two pictures?

THE WORLD

people around the world celebrate in July.

July 26

📍 INDEPENDENCE DAY

On July 26, 1847, the Republic of Liberia declared independence, making it the first democratic republic in Africa. Liberia, which means *land of freedom*, was a colony first settled by freed American slaves in 1822. Each year, a National Orator is selected to give a speech.

Fill in the grid with these 14 popular Liberian ingredients and dishes.

BONUS: Read the highlighted letters in order, left to right, top to bottom, to find out the capital of Liberia.

CASSAVA
COCONUT
DUMBOY
FISH
FUFU
JOLLOF RICE
KANYAH
OKRA
PALAVA
PALM OIL
PEPPERS
PLANTAINS
POTATO GREENS
YAMS

July 28-29

📍 FIESTAS PATRIAS

Peru's biggest holiday spans two days. July 28 marks the date Peru declared its independence from Spain in 1821. And on July 29 people honor Peru's armed forces and police. Peruvians around the country celebrate with parades, concerts, food fairs, and fireworks.

SUNDAY	MONDAY	TUESDAY	WEDNESDAY

ZODIAC SIGNS
LEO: JULY 23—AUGUST 22
VIRGO: AUGUST 23—SEPTEMBER 22

BIRTHSTONES
PERIDOT AND SPINEL

FLOWERS
GLADIOLUS AND POPPY

NATIONAL CHOCOLATE CHIP COOKIE DAY
4

Abracadabra! In 1926, Houdini spent 91 minutes underwater in a sealed tank before escaping.
5

Far out! In 2012, NASA's Curiosity rover landed on Mars.
6

NATIONAL LIGHTHOUSE DAY
7

NATIONAL PLAY IN THE SAND DAY
11

NATIONAL MIDDLE CHILD DAY
12

What goes up, must come down. In 1961, Communist East Germany began building the Berlin Wall. The wall separated Germany until 1989 when it was torn down.
13

WORLD CALLIGRAPHY DAY
14

Going up. In 1868, helium was discovered by French astronomer Pierre Janssen.
18

National Potato Day
Mashed, fried, baked—potatoes are good no matter how you slice 'em!
19

World Mosquito Day
This day commemorates the 1897 discovery that mosquitoes transmit malaria.
20

Aloha! In 1959, Hawaii became the 50th U.S. state.
21

Kiss and Make Up Day
Arguments happen—but at the end of the day, it's important to forgive one another.
25

WOMEN'S EQUALITY DAY
This day celebrates the adoption of the Nineteenth Amendment in 1920, which gave women the right to vote.
26

National Banana Lovers' Day
What an a-peel-ing day!
27

La Tomatina (Spain)
During this festival in Buñol, Valencia, participants throw tomatoes at each other.
28

AUGUST

THURSDAY	FRIDAY	SATURDAY
National Alpaca Day (Peru) This day celebrates the important Andean animal and the hard work of alpaca breeders. **1**	**NATIONAL ICE CREAM SANDWICH DAY** **2**	*Go for the gold!* In 1936, Jesse Owens won his first of four gold medals at the Berlin Olympics. **3**
National Zucchini Day Zucchinis aren't only green. They can also be yellow! **8**	**NATIONAL BILLIARDS AND POOL DAY** **9**	**Qixi Festival (China)** Also known as Chinese Valentine's Day, this festival celebrates the romantic legend of the cowherd and the weaver girl. **10**
National Relaxation Day What do you think is the best way to relax? **15**	*Game on!* In 1954, the first issue of *Sports Illustrated* was released. **16**	**National Thrift Shop Day** Buying used clothes doesn't just save money— it's good for Earth, too! **17**
WORLD FOLKLORE DAY **22**	**National Sponge Cake Day** Do you prefer chocolate or vanilla sponge cake? **23**	*Vesuvius erupts.* In 79 AD, Mount Vesuvius erupted, burying Pompeii in volcanic rock and mud. The city was untouched until it was excavated in the 18th century. **24**
Movie time! In 1997, Netflix was founded, initially as an online DVD rental service. **29**	**National Beach Day** Go have some fun in the sun before summer is over! **30**	**National Trail Mix Day** Take a hike with a tasty treat! **31**

FAMILY FUN MONTH

CANOEING CREW

Canoe believe how much fun this family is having on their paddling trip? **There are 12 hidden objects in this scene. How many can you spot?**

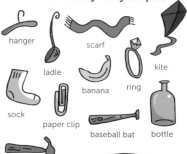

hanger

scarf

kite

ladle

banana

ring

sock

paper clip

baseball bat

bottle

hammer

glove

The Asian short-clawed otter is the smallest otter in Asia, but it comes from a large family. There are often as many as 15 children. In this clan, the older siblings help out Mama and Papa by watching out for the young ones.

MY FAMILY

_____
NOUN

Ask a family member for words or phrases to fill in the blanks. Then read the story out loud!

Dear _____,
       FRIEND'S FIRST NAME

We just had the best family vacation!

Everyone came along except _____, whom we
     SIBLING'S/ COUSIN'S NAME

had to put in a kennel. First, we went all the way to _____
     NEARBY STREET

to visit the Museum of the American _____. It was
     BODY PART

_____! Did you know that humans used to have three
  ADJECTIVE

_____? Then we went to _____
  SAME BODY PART (PLURAL)   **FRIEND'S LAST NAME**

World. We had to wait _____ hours in line to get on the
     HIGH NUMBER

"Rocket to _____ City" ride, but it was so worth it! I hurt
    APPLIANCE

my left _____ on the way down the last drop, but
    NOUN

was OK after Mom rubbed _____ on it. Then I got the
     FOOD YOU DON'T LIKE

chance to _____ a giant _____! That was
    VERB   **TYPE OF INSECT**

awesome, but its breath smelled like deep-fried, _____
     LARGE NUMBER

-year-old _____. And that was just Monday! I'll write
  NOUN (PLURAL)

again soon to tell you about the rest of the trip. Bye!

NATIONAL EYE EXAM MONTH

Did you know that your eyes move about 100,000 times a day? Or that many experts think the eyes can detect millions of different colors? Human eyes are pretty special. And they need to be taken care of! A regular eye exam is a great way to make sure your eyes are healthy and working their best.

This eye doctor's office is bustling with kids and critters looking for some new glasses. What silly things can you see in the scene?

5 TIPS FOR HEALTHY EYES

Why did the dalmatian go to the eye doctor?
Because he was seeing spots

1. Wear sunglasses when it's sunny outside.

2. Take a break every 20 minutes when you're staring at a screen to look 20 feet away for 20 seconds. (This is called the 20-20-20 rule!)

3. Get plenty of exercise. Healthy eyes start with a healthy body!

4. Speaking of healthy, be sure to eat plenty of fresh fruits and veggies.

5. If you notice any changes in your eyes, let an adult know and make an appointment to see the eye doctor.

110 YEARS AGO, THE PANAMA CANAL OFFICIALLY OPENED.

The canal drastically reduced the amount of time that ships needed to travel from coast to coast in North America. Instead of having to go all the way around the tip of South America, they could cut through the new canal instead. This saved about 8,000 miles and five months of travel.

The canal is still used today. About **12,000** ships travel through it every year.

It cost about **$375 MILLION** to dig and build the canal. How much is that in today's money? About **$8 BILLION**.

As many as **45,000** people worked on the construction of the canal.

IN THE WHEELHOUSE

These folks are in the wheelhouse of their ship getting ready to pass through the canal. As the captain makes his way into line, see if you can spot all of the hidden objects in the scene.

2 drumsticks
light bulb
crescent moon
scarf
chick
croquet mallet
arrow
egg
eyeglasses
lightning bolt
potato
muffin
exclamation point
wedge of lemon
pear

85 YEARS AGO, PRESIDENT FRANKLIN DELANO ROOSEVELT (FDR) CREATED NATIONAL AVIATION DAY IN HONOR OF ALL THINGS AVIATION.

Today especially celebrates the contributions of Orville and Wilbur Wright, since August 19 is also Orville's birth date. FDR likely chose this date because Orville was the first person to fly in an airplane.

The Wright brothers built the world's first powered airplane in **1903.**

The Wright brothers owned a bicycle sales and repair shop in **DAYTON, OHIO.**

back

front

craft stick

ENGINEER A FLYER

Put your engineering and aviation skills to the test with this project inspired by one of the Wright brothers' designs.

You Need

- Poster board
- Ruler
- Pencil
- Scissors
- Glue
- Large craft stick
- 2 large paper clips

1. Cut out five rectangles from **poster board** in the sizes shown.

2. **Glue** the largest rectangle across the middle of a nine-inch rectangle for the wings. Glue a four-inch rectangle across the front end. Let dry.

3. Glue the second nine-inch rectangle on top of the first, with the wings sandwiched between. Glue the **craft stick** at the front end of the body. Slide a **paper clip** over the front end. Then add a second clip over the first. Let dry.

4. Make a half-inch cut in the back end. Glue the second four-inch rectangle into the slot, as shown. Let dry.

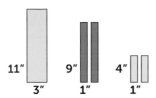

11"   9"   4"
3"   1"   1"

How to Launch

Test your thumb on the craft stick, with your pointer and middle fingers on either side of the body, behind the wings. Throw it straight—and not too hard.

Controlling Your Flyer

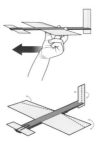

Try folding at the dotted lines to change the way it flies.

NATIONAL

Don't let summer pass you by without making it out to the course. At the very least, help Garin the Goat find his lost golf ball. **Begin at START and keep your eyes peeled as you move along the path to FINISH.**

1. Where did the modern game of golf originate in the 1400s?

a. Germany b. England c. Scotland

2. The dimples on a golf ball help with the control, lift, and smoothness of the ball's flight. How many dimples are typically on a golf ball?

a. 100–300 b. 300–500 c. 500–700

3. Which astronaut took this sport to space?

a. Alan Shepard
b. Neil Armstrong
c. Buzz Aldrin

GOLF MONTH

Ready to take a swing on this one? Which things are silly in this puzzle? It's up to you!

August 12-18, 2024
U.S. AMATEUR CHAMPIONSHIP

The U.S. Amateur Championship, created in 1895, **is the oldest United States Golf Association (USGA) championship**. This year, it will be held at Hazeltine National Golf Club in Chaska, Minnesota.

August 13
LEFT-HANDERS DAY

Here are the left-handed champions of the USGA Amateurs:

Erica Shepherd
2017 Girls' Junior

Julia Potter
2013, 2016
Women's
Mid-Amateur

Brad Benjamin
2009 Amateur
Public Links

Cory Whitsett
2007 Junior Amateur

Brian Harman
2003 Junior Amateur

Phil Mickelson
1990 Amateur

Ralph Howe III
1988 Amateur
Public Links

NATIONAL CLOWN WEEK!

August 1–7

Can you tell what's alike in each row of clowns, across, down, and diagonally?

"Bump a nose!" is how clowns wish each other good luck before a show.

CIRCUS LINGO

Step right up and try to match each of these slang terms for circus workers to their meaning.

1. candy butcher
2. funambulist
3. icarist
4. joey
5. mitt reader
6. roustabout
7. rubberman
8. slanger

A. acrobat who juggles another acrobat with their feet
B. balloon vendor
C. big-cat trainer
D. circus laborer
E. clown
F. concession vendor
G. fortune teller
H. tightrope walker

NATIONAL
TELL A JOKE DAY

These pups are learning how to tell great jokes. Can you help them figure out the punch lines? To solve these riddles, use the fractions of the words given below.

Why was the dog excited to go to school?

Last ⅓ of BUS
First ½ of MEOW
Last ½ of PULL
Last ⅗ of SWING
First ¼ of BALL
Last ½ of TREE

Why did the dog study before class?

First ⅓ of PURPLE
Last ¼ of JUMP
First ⅖ of QUEEN
Last ⅓ of SKI
First ⅕ of ZEBRA

The class was having a

☐☐☐☐☐☐☐☐
☐☐☐☐

In case the teacher gave a

☐☐☐☐☐☐

BONUS: How many bones can you find in this scene?

Rats and monkeys actually laugh! Rats even have **TICKLISH NECKS.**

BALL

August 3, 2024

CAMPFIRE DAY AND NIGHT

Solve the riddle, then celebrate Campfire Day and Night (the first Saturday in August) and Toasted Marshmallow Day (August 30) by finding 12 differences between the two pictures above.

I'm squishy and sweet and airy and light.
I'm brown when I'm roasted. Inside, I'm still white.
Need s'more hints? This might do the trick:
I'll be at the campfire stuck on your stick.

August 10
NATIONAL S'MORES DAY

Don't forget about National S'mores Day on August 10! Try these tasty twists on the classic treat!

Stuffed Apple

With a spoon, scoop out the core of a small **apple**. (Leave some apple at the bottom.) Combine **melted butter**, crushed **graham crackers**, **brown sugar**, **mini marshmallows**, **chocolate chips**, and **butterscotch chips**. Fill the center of the apple. Bake in a small baking dish until the apple is soft.

Banana Sandwich

Graham cracker

Marshmallow creme

Chocolate syrup and peanut butter

Banana

August 31
EAT OUTSIDE DAY

Celebrate Eat Outside Day by finding things that rhyme with *grill* or *eat* in this scene.

BONUS! Find 9 grill spatulas in the scene.

The largest hamburger ever made weighed 2,566 lb. 9 oz.!

What's the best side of the house to put the grill on?

The outside

August 3

NAVAJO CODE TALKERS DAY

During World War II, the Navajo Code Talkers were U.S. Marines who were able to send secret messages across radio and telephone, and the enemy could never break the code. That's because the code talkers were speaking in their native Navajo language. Since that language was an oral language, and not a written one, it was impossible for the enemy to figure out the code.

NAVAJO CODE NAMES FOR SHIPS

Military Word	Navajo Word	Translation
Ships	Toh-Dineh-Ih	Sea Force
Battleship	Lo-Tso	Whale
Aircraft	Tsidi-Moffa-Ye-Hi	Bird Carrier
Submarine	Besh-Lo	Iron Fish
Minesweeper	Cha	Beaver
Destroyer	Ca-Lo	Shark
Transport	Dineh-Nay-Ye-Hi	Man Carrier

MANY NATIONS SEARCH

Other Native nations also assisted the U.S. military as code talkers. Look up, down, diagonally, backward, and across to find each nation's name in the word search.

Assiniboine	Kiowa
Cherokee	Lakota
Cheyenne	Menominee
Chippewa	Meskwaki
Choctaw	Mississauga
Comanche	Muscogee
Cree	Osage
Crow	Pawnee
Hopi	Seminole

```
V  I  Z  Z  M  N  E  T  S  B  W  M  L  C  E
C  G  E  E  E  E  S  X  O  C  F  W  G  O  E
R  D  A  E  N  N  E  C  I  U  F  V  M  M  K
I  O  L  W  G  G  I  M  H  Q  O  U  Q  A  O
B  P  A  F  P  O  E  O  I  O  T  Y  N  N  R
A  P  O  V  C  S  C  H  B  E  C  H  D  C  E
W  Z  A  H  K  R  A  S  N  I  E  T  P  H  H
O  C  R  W  E  T  F  N  U  L  N  U  A  E  C
I  S  A  E  O  T  E  W  Z  M  L  I  H  W  D
K  K  K  K  S  Y  W  O  R  C  R  C  S  J  D
I  Q  A  M  E  N  O  M  I  N  E  E  Q  S  L
K  L  I  H  W  D  N  S  V  T  L  G  U  A  A
B  P  C  H  I  P  P  E  W  A  V  A  T  H  A
A  G  U  A  S  S  I  S  S  I  M  S  Q  A  G
B  S  E  M  I  N  O  L  E  S  Y  O  H  H  S
```

180 MAJOR HOLIDAYS

YOUR OWN CODE

There are many ways to make up secret codes. You can write words in reverse, mix up letters, or use numbers or symbols (emojis, pictures, or drawings) to represent letters. Here are a couple fun examples.

CAR CODE

A   C   D   E

G   H   I   L

N   O   P   R

S   T

Make up your own code and then write a letter to a friend using that code. You'll want to provide a "key" in a separate letter so they can decipher your note! Otherwise, it will remain a mystery forever.

During one important battle, six code talkers sent **800 MESSAGES WITHOUT ONE ERROR!**

The first group of 29 code talkers were so successful that **A TOTAL OF 400** were eventually recruited.

President Ronald Reagan named August 14 as **NATIONAL CODE TALKERS DAY** in 1982.

SHOOTING STAR DAY

There are 30 different star words and phrases hidden in this grid. For each one, the word STAR has been replaced with ★. Look up, down, across, backward, and diagonally.

WORD LIST

CORNSTARCH
CUSTARD
DASTARDLY
KICK-START
LODESTAR
LUCKY STARS
MEGASTAR
MOVIE STAR
MUSTARD
POLESTAR
ROCK STAR
STAR ANISE
STAR MAP
STAR FRUIT
STAR POWER
STAR-STUDDED
STARBOARD
STARBURST
STARDOM
STARDUST
STARFISH
STARGAZE
STARLIGHT
STARLING
STARSHIP
STARSTRUCK
STARTUP
STARVE
SUPERSTAR
WISH UPON A STAR

```
★ B O A R D I D A ★ D L Y
E T H G I L ★ ★ S H I P P
D T S N S U P E R ★ O A T
O ★ L U C K Y ★ S L M A R
L K A ★ A N I S E ★ D O ★
T C K N S T A ★ R E C F D
R I C T O A T A D K I ★ H
E K U S S P E D ★ S U L C
W ★ R R L U U Z H M I M ★
O L T U F T D H A T E S N
P I S B S ★ A ★ S G V M R
★ N ★ ★ ★ D O M A I ★ E O
T G M O V I E ★ E O W R C
```

THE PERSEID METEOR SHOWER

streaks across the sky every summer. Stargaze on a cloudless night and you might just spot a shooting star.

TRIVIA QUESTION:

What is a shooting star?

Put the uncircled letters in order on the blanks.

It _ _ _ ' _ _ _ _ _ _ _ _
_ _ _ . _ _ ' _ _ _ _ _ _ _ _ .

What wears a coat in the winter and pants in the summer?

A dog

August 26

NATIONAL DOG DAY

What could be better than a yard full of dogs?
There are **32 objects** hidden in this puppy patch.
Can you find them all?

banana	caterpillar	funnel	mushroom	ring
bean	cotton candy	glove	nail	sailboat
bowl	crescent moon	golf tee	needle	slice of pie
bowling ball	crown	heart	oilcan	wedge of lemon
butter knife	fishhook	ice-cream cone	peanut	
can	four-leaf clover	lollipop	pencil	
carrot	frying pan	magnet	piece of popcorn	

August 16
NATIONAL ROLLER COASTER DAY

Take this stomach-dropping coaster all the way from **START** to **FINISH**.

START

Formula Rossa in Abu Dhabi, the fastest roller coaster in the world, reaches a top speed of 149 miles per hour!

Kingda Ka in New Jersey, the tallest roller coaster in the world, soars to 456 feet high!

Leap-The-Dips in Pennsylvania, the oldest roller coaster in the world, opened to the public in 1902!

The Steel Dragon in Japan, the longest roller coaster in the world, is 8,133 feet long!

FINISH

NATIONAL BEACH DAY

Today is the day to slather on the sunscreen, put on your bathing suit, and hit the waves. Gullbert had a busy Beach Day. **Can you figure out the order in which these scenes occurred?**

F

A

B

C

G

D

E

H

TONGUE TWISTER
BRIA BROUGHT BRIGHT BEACH BLANKETS.

DON'T LIVE NEAR A BEACH?
Here are some ways you can bring the beach to you.

1. Put on your bathing suit and sunglasses.

2. Lay a beach towel down in your living room or backyard.

3. Play relaxing sounds of the ocean waves on an electronic device.

4. Pour yourself a refreshing drink, like lemonade.

5. Relax while reading a book or make a sandcastle out of moldable sand.

Take a spin around the globe to see how

August 15

⊙ THE DAY THE LIGHT RETURNED

On August 15, South Koreans celebrate the National Liberation Day of Korea, or *Gwangbokjeol*, which literally means "the day the light returned." The holiday commemorates when Korea was liberated from Japanese occupation in 1945. Koreans take the day off from work and school to attend parades and celebrations. The national flag, called *Taegukgi*, is proudly displayed everywhere.

⊙ ROYAL EDINBURGH MILITARY TATTOO

Every August at Edinburgh Castle, more than 1,200 performers from around the world put on a spectacular show of music, dance, and military marches called a tattoo. Since the first Edinburgh Tattoo in 1950, more than 14 million people have attended. Each year, around 100 million people in 30 countries also watch on television.

Can you find 16 differences between these two pictures?

THE WORLD

August 20
HAPPY 1,024th BIRTHDAY, HUNGARY!

Known as both Az államalapítás ünnepe (State Foundation Day) and Szent István ünnepe (Saint Stephen's Day), there are lots of reasons for celebration on August 20. Hungarians celebrate the foundation of the Kingdom of Hungary in the year 1000; the name day of the first king of Hungary, Stephen I; and the Day of the New Bread, which marks the traditional end of the grain harvest. Throughout the country on this national holiday, there are festivals, parades, and fireworks. The largest fireworks display is in the capital city, Budapest, over the Danube River in front of Parliament. Since 2007, there has also been a competition to find "The Birthday Cake of Hungary," with the winning cake announced (and eaten) on August 20.

> A rakhi is a bracelet made of red and gold thread, like these here.

August 19, 2024
RAKSHA BANDHAN

Raksha Bandhan is an Indian festival that celebrates the loving and caring bond between sisters and brothers. This year, it falls on August 19. A sister ties a *rakhi* to her brother's wrist, and her brother responds with a gift. It is a special day when sisters and brothers think fondly of each other and pray for each others' blessings.

SUNDAY	MONDAY	TUESDAY	WEDNESDAY

No Rhyme or Reason Day

This day celebrates words that don't rhyme and silly idioms.

1

LABOR DAY

2

U.S. BOWLING LEAGUE DAY

3

NATIONAL WILDLIFE DAY

4

International Literacy Day

You read it here first!

8

NATIONAL TEDDY BEAR DAY

9

St. George's Caye Day (Belize)

This holiday marks the defeat of the Spanish navy in 1798.

10

PATRIOT DAY

11

Cheese it up!
National Cheese Toast Day
National Double Cheeseburger Day

GOUDA

15

Malaysia Day (Malaysia)

This patriotic holiday commemorates the formation of the Federation of Malaysia on this day in 1963.

16

The beginning of a legacy. On this day in 1849, Harriet Tubman escaped from slavery. She went on to help free dozens of enslaved people with the help of the Underground Railroad.

17

Fly, fight, and win. On this day in 1947, the U.S. Air Force was created.

18

FIRST DAY OF FALL

22

National Volleyball Day

Set, spike, score!

23

WORLD GORILLA DAY

24

World Dream Day

What do you dream of How can you make yo dreams come true?

25

BROADWAY MUSICALS DAY

29

Independence Day (Botswana)

Africa's oldest democracy, Botswana, became independent in 1966.

30

BIRTHSTONE
SAPPHIRE

ZODIAC SIGNS
VIRGO: AUGUST 23– SEPTEMBER 22

LIBRA: SEPTEMBER 23– OCTOBER 22

THURSDAY	FRIDAY	SATURDAY
International Day of Charity ...ok for ways to give ...our community, ...ether it's a service, ...nations, or ...en just a smile. **5**	*Out to sea.* In 1620, the Pilgrims set out on the *Mayflower*, looking for a place to live where they could have religious freedom. **6**	**National Salami Day** It's a good day, any way you slice it. **7**
National Day of Encouragement You can do it!  **12**	*On your mark, get set, GO!* In 1970, the first New York City Marathon was held. **13**	**National Cream Filled Doughnut Day** Doughnut make you smile?  **14**
:-) In 1982, the first ...emoticon a typed, ...deways smiley face— was created **19**	**NATIONAL FRIED RICE DAY** **20**	**International Day of Peace** How can you keep the peace in your family? **21**
National Lumberjack Day What's a lumberjack's favorite month? Sep-TIMBER! **26**	**NATIONAL SCARF DAY**  **27**	**National Good Neighbor Day** Be a good neighbor today and every day. **28**

FLOWERS
ASTER AND
MORNING GLORY

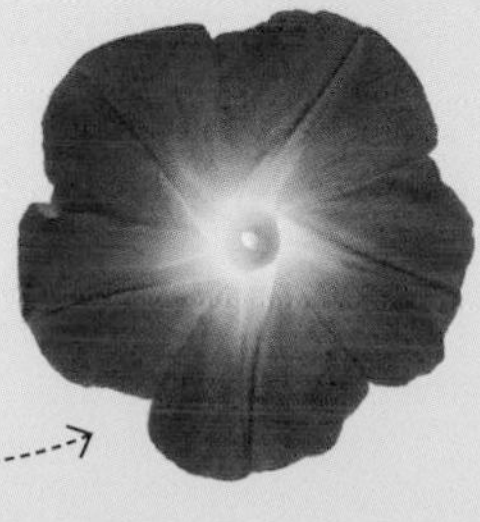

SEPTEMBER

NATIONAL HISPANIC HERITAGE MONTH

Franklin Chang-Diaz

Sonia Sotomayor

This month-long celebration (September 15–October 15) recognizes the contributions of Hispanic Americans and honors their history and culture. Match each pioneering Hispanic American with his or her historic achievement.

1. Who was the first Hispanic American to serve in the U.S. Senate (1928)?

2. Who was the first Hispanic American MLB Hall of Fame inductee (1973)?

3. Who was the first Hispanic American to earn an EGOT, winning an Emmy, Grammy, Oscar, and Tony award (1977)?

4. Who was the first Hispanic American astronaut (1980)?

5. Who was the first Hispanic American doctor—and the first woman—to become U.S. surgeon general (1990)?

6. Who was the first Hispanic American activist inducted into the National Women's Hall of Fame (1993)?

7. Who was the first Hispanic American musician inducted into the Rock & Roll Hall of Fame (1998)?

8. Who was the first Hispanic American U.S. Supreme Court justice (2009)?

Octaviano Ambrosio Larrazolo

Rita Moreno

Dr. Antonia Novello

Carlos Santana

Hispanic and **Latinx** don't mean the same thing. **Latinx** means that someone is from Latin America (nearly every country south of the U.S., including the Caribbean). **Hispanic** means from a Spanish-speaking country, and not all Latin American countries speak Spanish.

Roberto Clemente

Dolores Huerta

NATIONAL CHICKEN MONTH

What time is it? Time to celebrate chickens! Say "Hooray!" for these important birds, then find the **8 objects** hidden in this chicken clock shop.

cookie

orange

ring

basketball

coin

ball of yarn

button

sun

BETTER BREAKFAST MONTH

SUNNYSIDEUP

Use the clues below to fill in the boxes of this spiral—but there's a twist! The last letter of each word is also the first letter of the next word. Use the linking letters to help you spin all the way to the center.

1. One way to serve fried eggs

11. People eat these by the stack

18. Fresh-____ orange juice

25. Small, sweet fried cake, usually with a hole in the center

32. Machine used to heat slices of bread

38. Dried fruit topping for oatmeal

44. Popular flavor of jam

53. Color of butter

58. Type of dark-colored bread, heated up

67. This pouch sits in a mug of hot water to make a common breakfast drink

72. What you pour over biscuits

76. Yellow parts of eggs

80. What you pour over waffles

84. Containers of yogurt are made of this

90. ____ cheese is typically spread on a bagel

94. Liquid poured over cereal

97. Utensil used to spread butter or jelly

According to a 2019 survey, America's top 5 breakfast foods are eggs, sausage, bacon, pancakes, and toast. What's your favorite way to start the day?

NATIONAL HONEY MONTH

Since we wouldn't have honey without bees, this month is a bee-fitting time to honor these fuzzy insects, too. **To find the answer to the riddle, first cross out all the pairs of matching letters.** Then write the remaining letters in order in the spaces beneath the riddle.

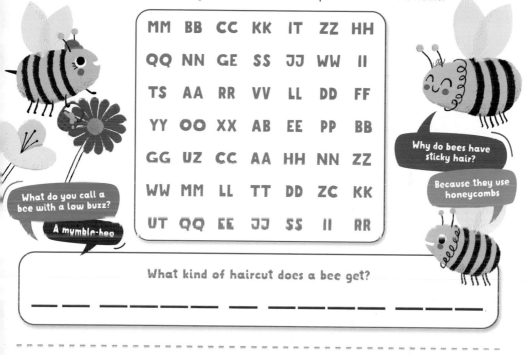

MM	BB	CC	KK	IT	ZZ	HH
QQ	NN	GE	SS	JJ	WW	II
TS	AA	RR	VV	LL	DD	FF
YY	OO	XX	AB	EE	PP	BB
GG	UZ	CC	AA	HH	NN	ZZ
WW	MM	LL	TT	DD	ZC	KK
UT	QQ	EE	JJ	SS	II	RR

Why do bees have sticky hair?

Because they use honeycombs

What do you call a bee with a low buzz?

A mumble-bee

What kind of haircut does a bee get?

__ __ __ __ __ __ __ __ __ __ __ __ __ __ __ __

Great Shakes

NATIONAL
SHAKE
MONTH

Come with these animal friends to check out Ellie's Great Shake Food Truck. **But before you leave the scene, don't forget to find all the hidden objects.**

necktie

guitar

sock

purse

tomato

pie

potato

star

September 14, 1814

210 YEARS AGO TODAY, AMERICAN FRANCIS SCOTT KEY PENNED THE WORDS TO A POEM THAT WOULD EVENTUALLY BECOME THE U.S. NATIONAL ANTHEM, "THE STAR-SPANGLED BANNER."

Key wrote this poem after listening to a long night of fighting during the War of 1812. Things did not look good for the Americans, and Key feared the British would be victorious. However, when he awoke, he saw the Stars and Stripes still flying over an American fort while the British were retreating. America had won the battle!

"THE STAR-SPANGLED BANNER"

Read the words of Key's poem. Then use these words to draw a picture of what you imagine Key saw on the morning of September 14, 1814.

O say can you see, by the dawn's early light,
What so proudly we hail'd at the twilight's last gleaming,
Whose broad stripes and bright stars through the perilous fight
O'er the ramparts we watch'd were so gallantly streaming?
And the rocket's red glare, the bomb bursting in air,
Gave proof through the night that our flag was still there,
O say does that star-spangled banner yet wave
O'er the land of the free and the home of the brave?

250 YEARS AGO, MANY BELIEVE JOHNNY APPLESEED WAS BORN.

His real name was John Chapman, but he is known as Johnny Appleseed because he introduced apple trees to large portions of the Midwest. He often walked barefoot, wore very simple clothing, and carried with him a bag of apple seeds— which is what gave him his famous nickname.

The story goes that he also wore a **COOKING POT** as a cap!

During his lifetime, he took apple seeds to nearly **100,000 SQUARE MILES** of the American frontier.

TRAVELING ALONG WITH JOHNNY

As Johnny Appleseed carries forth his apples, scan the scene. **Find the following 16 hidden objects:** needle, candle, fountain pen, spoon, golf club, closed umbrella, pennant, sailboat, arrow, banana, wishbone, question mark, nail, crown, tack, and heart.

Ask an adult to help with anything sharp or hot!

September 21, 2024
INTERNATIONAL EAT AN APPLE DAY

Celebrate Johnny Appleseed and this holiday by making these apple snacks:

APPLE SANDWICHES
Core and slice an apple. Use two slices for "bread." Possible fillings: cheese, peanut butter, or chocolate spread.

SWEET APPLE YOGURT
Chop up an apple. Put it in a bowl. Stir in honey and yogurt. Sprinkle cinnamon on top.

CARAMEL APPLE ON A STICK
Soften caramel dip in a microwave. Skewer an apple chunk and dip it in the caramel. Sprinkle it with chopped nuts, mini chocolate chips, or sprinkles. Let it set in the fridge.

September 21, 2024

NATIONAL GYMNASTICS DAY

While these cat gymnasts practice *purr*-fect form, you can solve this puzzle. First use the clues below to figure out the words. Each word is a hidden object to look for in the big scene. Once you've found the **13 hidden objects**, transfer the letters with numbers into the correct spaces to learn the punch line to the joke.

September is also
HAPPY CAT MONTH!

1. A salmon or a trout. _ _ _ _
                         1

2. There are 50 stars on the U.S. _ _ _ _ _ .
                                        2

3. Twirl spaghetti with this. _ _ _ _
                              3

4. "And a partridge in a _ _ _ _ tree."
                         4

5. A king's headwear. _ _ _ _ _
                      5

6. A monkey's favorite fruit. _ _ _ _ _ _
                                        6

7. Put it on a one-year-old's birthday cake. _ _ _ _ _ _ _
                                                         7

8. A long orange vegetable. _ _ _ _ _ _
                                  8

9. Pound nails with this. _ _ _ _ _ _
                            9

10. Write with this at school. _ _ _ _ _ _ _
                                  10

11. A "sunny-side-up" breakfast food. _ _ _ _ _   _ _ _
                                         11

12. Put this up when it rains. _ _ _ _ _ _ _ _
                              12

13. Use this to hit a puck. _ _ _ _ _ _   _ _ _ _ _
                                    13

HOW DO YOU GET A CAT TO DO TRICKS?

__ __ __
4 12 8

__
6

__ __ __
11 3 2

__ __
13 10

__
6

__ __ __
5 6 8

__ __ __ __ __ __ __
5 3 1 8 12 9 7

INTERNATIONAL MINIATURE GOLF DAY

What silly things can you spot in this scene? **Circle them all!**

What did the astronaut get when he went mini-golfing?

A black hole in one

There are **9 objects** hidden in this mini golf course. **Can you find them all?**

waffle	toothbrush	pizza	pencil	crown	banana	ruler	sailboat	bat

September 16
COLLECT ROCKS DAY

Rocks rock! And collecting rocks can be a lot of fun. There are so many different kinds to find on walks, at the beach, or even in your own backyard. Here's a craft you can do with some of the rocks you collect.

We need to keep Earth and its plants, soil, and animals safe. So be sure to use nontoxic paint in this project!

CREATE YOUR OWN CONSTELLATION

1. Wash and dry your **rocks**.

2. Use **white paint** to create stars. Let dry. Paint the stars with **glow-in-the-dark paint**. Let dry.

3. Optional: Use **black paint** in the area around the stars. Let dry.

4. Place your rocks in a sunny spot, inside or outside, such as a windowsill or backyard. Arrange the rocks to make your constellation. The stars will soak up the light during the day and glow at night.

September 17
INTERNATIONAL
COUNTRY MUSIC DAY

International Country Music Day is celebrated on September 17, the birthday of Hank Williams, one of the most influential singer-songwriters in 20th century America. Williams was rejected by the *Grand Ole Opry* show after his first audition in 1946, but he didn't give up and finally made his debut in 1949.

Take a trip to the Opry House in Nashville and find at least 15 differences between these two pictures.

The Grand Ole Opry is a live country music concert and radio show held a few times a week in Nashville, Tennessee. The show has been broadcast since 1925, making it one of the world's longest-running radio shows.

The best-selling country music artists of all time are Garth Brooks, George Strait, and Shania Twain.

The birthplace of country music is Bristol, Tennessee.

Nashville, Tennessee, is called the Music City because it's the home of the country music industry.

This photo of Hank Williams is a publicity photo from 1951. Radio stations used photos like this one to make listeners familiar with the voices they heard on the radio.

APPLE NACHOS

1. Place **apple slices** on a plate.
2. Drizzle **caramel** and **chocolate sauce** toppings over the apple slices.
3. Spoon **granola** over the slices.
4. Sprinkle on your favorite toppings, such as **chocolate chips, raisins,** or **sliced almonds**.

September 13

KIDS TAKE OVER THE KITCHEN DAY

Treat your family to these delicious desserts!

FRUIT KEBABS

1. Drain a can of **pineapple chunks**. Put the chunks into a bowl.
2. Wash some fresh **raspberries** and **blueberries**. Pat them dry.
3. Peel and slice a **kiwi**.
4. Peel an **orange** and a **grapefruit**. Cut them into bite-sized pieces.
5. Carefully poke **wooden skewers** through the fruit.
6. To eat the kebabs, remove the fruit with your fingers.

NATIONAL FORTUNE COOKIE DAY

Your fortune cookie has a coded message in it!
Follow the directions below to crack the code and read your fortune.

1. Change each **B** to the letter that comes before it in the alphabet.

2. Change the **X** to the letter that comes after **K** in the alphabet.

3. Each time you see a **Y**, change it to a letter that sounds like a part of the face.

4. Change each **Q** to a letter that sounds like the word are.

5. Change the **H** to the next-to-last letter of the alphabet.

6. Find a **T**. Change it to the letter that comes two letters before **P** in the alphabet.

7. Change each **D** to the letter that comes after **R** in the alphabet.

8. Change the **K** to a letter that sounds like the word you.

9. Change each **J** to the letter that comes three letters after it in the alphabet.

10. Change the **F** to a letter that sounds like the word sea.

11. Change the **V** to a letter that sounds like a hot drink.

12. Change the **W** to one of the letters in the word **OK**.

13. Change each **G** to the second vowel in the alphabet.

14. There should be four **P**s remaining. Change each to a perfectly round letter to finish the message.

```
   __ __ __ __ __ !           __ A            __ __ __ __ __ __ __ __ __
   D  J  Y  X  G!   H  P  K  B̶  Q  G    P  T  G

   __ __ A __ __ __           __ __ __ __ __ __ !
   D  J  B̶  Q  V    F  P  P  W  Y  G!
```

*Just be yourself;
you are wonderful.*

September 9 is International Sudoku Day!

About
3 BILLION
fortune cookies are eaten every year!

COOKIE SUDOKU

Fill in the blanks by drawing each missing cookie. When you are done, each row, column, and little grid must contain one of each kind of cookie.

A "shear" pleasure.

I'm drawn to it.

It's a piece of cake!

Out of this world!

I get a kick out of it!

Moving right along.

An apple a day couldn't keep me away!

September 2, 2024

LABOR DAY

Labor Day honors the contributions of American workers. The first U.S. Labor Day was celebrated in 1882 as part of the labor union movement. Today, it's unofficially the end of summer. **"How's your job?"** Match each silly answer above to the worker.

DOCTOR

BAKER

SOCCER PLAYER

ASTRONAUT

ARTIST

HAIRDRESSER

TRAFFIC OFFICER

Think of other jobs, and create your own answers!

THE EIGHT-HOUR WORK DAY was established by the Adamson Act, which was passed on September 3, 1916. In the 19th century, Americans worked twelve hours a day, seven days a week!

At least **20,000 PEOPLE** showed support for unions by attending the first Labor Day parade in New York City in 1882.

Women ride on a float in the 1909 Labor Day parade in New York City.

Grover Cleveland signed an act in 1894 to make **LABOR DAY** a national holiday.

September 8, 2024

NATIONAL GRANDPARENTS DAY

This holiday to honor grandparents is celebrated on the second Sunday in September. The 24 grandparent names below are hidden in this word search. Search up, down, across, backward, and diagonally to find them all. Only the words in CAPITAL LETTERS are hidden.

GRANDMOTHER WORD LIST

ABUELA (Spanish)
BABCIA (Polish)
BIBI (Swahili)
GRAMMY
GRANDMA
HALMONI (Korean)
LOLA (Filipino)
MAWMAW
NANA
NONNA (Italian)
OMA (German)
YIAYIA (Greek)

GRANDFATHER WORD LIST

ABUELO (Spanish)
BABU (Swahili)
DZIADZIU (Polish)
GRAMPS
GRANDPA
HALABEOJI (Korean)

LOLO (Filipino)
NONNO (Italian)
OPA (German)
PAPPOÚS (Greek)
PAWPAW
POP

The number of grandparents you have doubles with each generation: 4 grandparents, 8 great-grandparents, and 16 great-great-grandparents. How many grandparents do you have 10 generations back?

What do you call your grandparents?

```
M A Y S I W U A G N F P K I
F M U O A B P I O B V L N N
G D F M P D I N Z P W G O N
X N W S N A N B B D K G N R
W A W A X O P A W P A W N K
M R R R V P C P T I F I A E
P G B X L K Y Q O H A A Z B
I J O E B A L A H Ú Q B L D
U B A B O K Y N J A S U S O
Z H A L M O N I B F C E P P
T Q O T P C Y U A Q B L M A
O L N A N A E M C Y R A A L
V M R R W L B T M T I B R O
Z A A U O K T O P A W A G L
N X G G B M J V Z D R C V T
P O P O Ú A I C B A B G N W
```

5 WAYS TO HAVE FUN WITH YOUR GRANDPARENTS

1. Have a picnic together.

2. Build a zany sculpture.

3. Send each other postcards.

4. Play a board game or a video game.

5. Read stories aloud to each other.

September 17
CONSTITUTION DAY

The United States Constitution was written during the summer of 1787 at Independence Hall, Philadelphia. On September 17, it was signed by state delegates at the Constitutional Convention and then sent on for ratification, or approval, by the states.

CONSTITUTION CRISSCROSS

Use the clues to fill in the answers.

ACROSS

4. Delegate from New York, and the name of a hit Broadway musical

5. Smallest state, and the only state who refused to send delegates

7. President of the Convention, and Father of our Country

DOWN

1. Country's second president. He was not at the Convention. He was in London as an Ambassador of the U.S.

2. Oldest delegate, and a kite flyer in lightning storms

3. Author of the Declaration of Independence, but not at the Convention. He was in Paris as an Ambassador of the U.S.

6. Virginia delegate and author of the Constitution

Even though it was a hot summer, all the doors and windows were kept closed during the Constitutional Convention. This was to keep the public from listening in on what was happening inside. The delegates needed to debate issues freely, without any interference from the public.

September 22, 2024

THE FIRST DAY OF ~~FALL~~ ~~AUTUMN~~ FALL

Wait a minute, is it *fall* or *autumn*? Why do the other three seasons only have one name? A long time ago, this season was called *harvest* because farmers gathered their crops between August and November for winter storage; however, as more and more people moved to cities in the 16th century, new names popped up.

Autumn comes from *autumnus*, a Latin word that means "drying-up season." Fall comes from *fiaell*, an Old English word that means "falls from a height," like the leaves that fall . . . in fall. Today, *autumn* is used more commonly in British English and *fall* is used more commonly in American English, but they're interchangeable.

So, whatever you call it, here are some ways to celebrate the season!

AUTUMN

Weaving Through Autumn Leaves

Help these kids find a clear path to the hot cider.

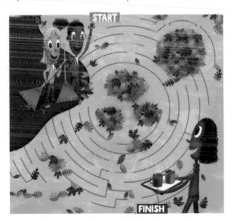

4 Ways to Have Fun with Autumn Leaves

1. Cut out a bird shape from **poster board**. Glue on colorful leaves as feathers.

2. Write a message on two small pieces of **brown paper**. Fill two buckets with leaves, and hide a message in each. Give the buckets to two friends. Whoever finds the message first wins!

3. Make a mobile! Use **string** to hang leaves from a **stick**.

4. Cut out the inside circle from a **paper plate**. Glue leaves around the outer rim to make a festive wreath.

FALL

Leafy Fall Maze

Help these kids find a clear path to their house.

4 Ways to Celebrate Fall

1. Make leaf-creature place mats! Use colorful **leaves**, clear **self-adhesive paper**, and **construction paper**.

2. Sip a warm autumn drink. Heat up some **apple juice**, stir it with a **cinnamon stick**, and toss in a few **cranberries**.

3. Pumpkin greetings! Instead of making a card, paint a small **pumpkin** for someone special.

4. In a nearby park, your backyard, or on a hike with your family, collect **leaves** and match them to the tree they fell from. For an added challenge, identify the tree.

Its tongue has a forked tip that grabs more nectar with each lick than an unforked tongue could get.

Each wing moves in a figure 8, beating 70 to 80 times a second.

NATIONAL HUMMINGBIRD DAY

A hummingbird's long tongue can reach nectar that is deep within a flower.

Its tiny feet grip branches as it rests, but it doesn't walk much.

A hummingbird's iridescent colors can vary because tiny structures on the feathers reflect light differently at different angles.

On the first Saturday of September every year, we get to celebrate these minuscule winged friends. Check out the science behind their speedy flight.

KIDS' SCIENCE QUESTION

How fast can hummingbirds fly?

The tiny hummingbird is a giant among fliers. With wings that move so fast they hum and blur, it zips from one food source to another to fuel its speed.

It can fly in all directions, even backward and upside down. It can also hover like a helicopter. Considering the bird's size, its large brain and heart and impressive speed outshine those of many other birds and mammals.

In just one second, it can fly a few hundred times the length of its body. That would be like you running a few football fields in one second. On average, hummingbirds can fly about 30 mph. Speedy, right?

September 22–28, 2024

SEA OTTER AWARENESS WEEK

The last full week in September recognizes the important role that sea otters play in the ecosystem where they live.

Where do otters go to watch movies?

What is an otter's favorite book series?

What did the otter say to the rock star?

An otter-torium

Harry Otter

"Can I have your otter-graph?"

Otters are one of the few mammals to use **tools**. They use rocks to break open clams and other shellfish.

Otters have the **thickest fur** of any mammal. They don't have blubber like other sea mammals, so the fur helps keep them warm.

September 22

NATIONAL ELEPHANT APPRECIATION DAY

An elephant's trunk is an amazing thing. It can be used as a snorkel, to store water, or even to shell a peanut!

To get the answer to the riddle below, first cross out all the pairs of matching letters. Then write the remaining letters in order in the space below the riddle.

QQ	BE	EE	NN	MM	OO	WW
LL	CA	SS	VV	YY	US	ZZ
ET	AA	RR	NN	HE	EE	YY
HH	XX	YL	DD	PP	UU	OV
GG	OO	ET	SS	CC	QQ	II
CC	RA	EE	MM	AA	TT	VE
LI	BB	KK	VV	ZZ	NG	TT

Why do elephants have trunks?

___ ___ ___ ___

___ ___ ___ ___ ___

There are lots of holidays to celebrate animals in September. Here are just a few:

September 21, 2024

INTERNATIONAL RED PANDA DAY

Red pandas like to munch on bamboo, but they are not related to pandas. They are related to raccoons, weasels, and skunks.

September 28, 2024

INTERNATIONAL RABBIT DAY

Rabbits can turn their ears 180 degrees to listen for predators.

September 25

NATIONAL LOBSTER DAY

In the wild, most lobsters are greenish blue to blackish brown, but about one out of every two million lobsters is blue!

September 3
NATIONAL SKYSCRAPER DAY

Soar to the top with this skyscraper quiz.

1. **Completed in 1885, the world's first skyscraper was the Home Insurance Building in Chicago, Illinois. How tall was it?**
   a. 10 stories
   b. 20 stories
   c. 30 stories

2. **Where is the Jeddah Tower, which started construction in 2013, located?**
   a. Antarctica
   b. Batuu
   c. Saudi Arabia

3. **When it was completed in 2010, the Burj Khalifa in Dubai, United Arab Emirates, was the world's tallest building. How many floors does it have?**
   a. 16 floors with really high ceilings
   b. 163
   c. 1,630

4. **Which New York City skyscraper was the tallest building in the world from 1931 to 1972?**
   a. Chrysler Building
   b. Empire State Building
   c. Woolworth Building

5. **The tallest building in the U.S. is the One World Trade Center in New York City. How tall is it?**
   a. 1,001 feet
   b. 1,555 feet
   c. 1,776 feet

6. **The Shanghai Tower in China has the world's tallest elevator, at 2,074 feet tall. How fast can it travel?**
   a. 45.8 mph
   b. Mach 5
   c. Warp speed

September 9
INTERNATIONAL SUDOKU DAY

September 9 is the perfect day to celebrate Sudoku. This logic number puzzle challenges puzzle lovers to fill a 9 x 9 grid with numbers from 1 to 9. The name is Japanese for "single number," but the first modern appearance of the puzzle, called "Number Place," was in an American magazine in 1979.

This Riddle Sudoku puzzle uses letters instead of numbers. **Fill in the squares so that the six letters appear once in each row, column, and 2 x 3 box.** Then read the orange squares to find out the answer to the riddle.

Riddle: What did the nut say when it sneezed?

"___ ___ ___ ___ ___ ___!"

Letters: **A C E H S W**

	W		S	A	
S			E		
H			W		
		A			
		W			S
E	S	C		H	

1. Tear a page of newspaper in half.

2. Fold one of the pieces in half.

MAKE A HAT DAY

3. Fold the top corners down.

Today's your day to explore your creativity by making something you can actually wear.

4. Fold the bottom bands up.

5. Tape the corners of the band.

6. Decorate your hat.

Can you make a pirate's hat for Talk Like a Pirate Day?

Why couldn't the pirate play cards?

Because he was sitting on the deck

September 19
INTERNATIONAL TALK LIKE A PIRATE DAY

Ahoy, maties! *Aaaaarrr* you ready to get into the spirit of this silly holiday? **Celebrate by finding the hidden objects in this scene.** Because after all, if anyone can talk like a pirate, a pirate's parrot can!

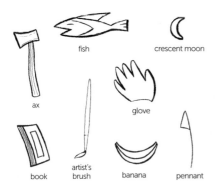

fish

crescent moon

ax

glove

book

artist's brush

banana

pennant

spool of thread

pencil

dish

heart

crown

The lotus flower is a symbol of hope and purity.

Take a spin around the globe to see ho

September 2

NATIONAL DAY

On September 2, 1945, Ho Chi Minh declared Vietnam's independence from France. Today, Vietnamese people commemorate this holiday by decorating streets and buildings with the country's flag to display patriotism.

Make a lotus, the national flower of Vietnam.

1. Cut a lily-pad shape from **green cardstock**.

2. For petals, cut out ten 4-inch raindrop shapes from **pink cardstock**. Cut a 1-inch slit in the rounded end of each petal to create two flaps. Glue one flap over the other so the petal creates a cupped shape. Repeat this with the remaining nine petals.

3. Glue the cupped ends of five petals in a circle on the lily pad. Glue a second circle inside the first with the remaining petals.

4. Cut two squares from **yellow cardstock**. Crumple one into a ball. Wrap the other around the ball. Flatten the wrapped ball and glue it to the center of the flower.

September 11

ENKUTATASH

These flowers are also known as adey abeba.

Happy Ethiopian New Year! Enkutatash marks the first day of the first month of the Ethiopian calendar. People celebrate Enkutatash by eating a traditional meal with their families and giving gifts to children. Children sing, dance, pick flowers, and paint pictures to give to their families and neighbors.

Children pick yellow daisies called meskel flowers, which only bloom during this season. Can you find the three puzzle pieces in this photo?

THE WORLD

September 18
📍 FIESTAS PATRIAS

On this day in 1810, Chile decided to establish a Congress, a step which eventually led to the country becoming independent from Spain. Today, the September 18 anniversary is celebrated with "patriotic parties." Every town throws a large party with live music, dancing, and barbecues.

The national dance of Chile is called the *cueca*. During independence day celebrations, dancers will wear traditional clothing to perform the dance. Unscramble the names of five musical instruments that are traditionally used to accompany the cueca.

ARTIGU _____

PRAH _____

ANOPI _____

COCODRAIN _____

MEANITURBO _____

September 23
📍 SAUDI NATIONAL DAY

On this day in 1932, two kingdoms were unified by King Abdulaziz ibn Saud, who changed the name to the Kingdom of Saudi Arabia to honor his family, the House of Saud. Today, people commemorate this occasion with all kinds of cultural events and celebrations. The people wear green, and everywhere they go, the country is decorated with Saudi Arabia's green flag.

Green represents Islam, as it is believed to be the prophet Muhammad's favorite color.

The Arabic inscription is the *shahāda*, the Islamic declaration of faith. The words are written in an artistic form of Islamic calligraphy called *Thuluth*.

The sword symbolizes how strictly the nation will uphold justice.

SUNDAY	MONDAY	TUESDAY	WEDNESDAY
BIRTHSTONES OPAL / TOURMALINE **ZODIAC SIGNS** ♎ ♏ **SCORPIO:** OCTOBER 23–NOVEMBER 21 **LIBRA:** SEPTEMBER 23–OCTOBER 22		**National Pumpkin Spice Day** It's fall, so get your pumpkin everything going on! **1**	**ROSH HASHANAH** begins at sunset. **2**
National Coaches Day Give 'em a high five! **6**	**NATIONAL LED LIGHT DAY** **7**	**National Fluffernutter Day** Peanut butter and marshmallow: sticky, but satisfying. **8**	*Power up!* In 1936, the Hoover D near Las Vegas bega producing hydroelec power. Its electricit was sent to Los Ange 266 miles away. **9**
NATIONAL TRAIN YOUR BRAIN DAY **13**	**INDIGENOUS PEOPLES' DAY** **14**	**Global Handwashing Day** And NO, this is not the only day of the year you should wash your hands! **15**	*Talk about a wordsm* Today is the birthday Noah Webster, the au of the first America dictionary. **16**
NATIONAL SUSPENDERS DAY **20**	*Let there be light!* In 1879, Thomas Edison's light bulb stayed lit for thirteen and a half hours, becoming the first light bulb to work for longer than a few minutes. **21**	**International Caps Lock Day** IT'S LIKE YELLING BUT ON PAPER. **22**	**NATIONAL BOSTON CREAM PIE DA 23**
City of Brotherly Love. In 1682, Philadelphia was founded. **27**	**National First Responders Day** Celebrate the helpers who take immediate action in emergency situations. **28**	**International Internet Day** How has the internet made your life easier? **29**	**National Candy Corn Da** Get a head start fo tomorrow's festiviti **30**

THURSDAY	FRIDAY	SATURDAY
Soldiers' Day (Honduras) ...s holiday takes ...ce on the birthday ...Francisco Morazán, ...amous Honduran ...tary leader. **3**	**National Taco Day** Taco 'bout awesome!  **4**	**NATIONAL DO SOMETHING NICE DAY** **5**
...rld Porridge Day Watch out for Goldilocks! **10**	**YOM KIPPUR** begins at sunset. **11**	*Table for six billion?* On this day in 1999, the six billionth living human was born. **12**
...salines Day (Haiti) ...national holiday ...brates the founding ...r of Haiti, ...-Jacques Dessalines, ...was killed ...his day ...06. **17**	**National No Beard Day** Celebrate the clean shaven among us! **18**	**National New Friends Day** Make new friends, but keep the old! **19**
...ited Nations Day ...United Nations was ...ed on this day in 1945. ...d War II had just ended, ...51 countries joined ...her to try to ...tain ...e ...nd ...world. **24**	**WORLD PASTA DAY** **25**	**National Mule Day** A mule is a cross between a male donkey and a female horse. **26**
HALLOWEEN **31**	**FLOWERS** MARIGOLD COSMOS	

GLOBAL DIVERSITY AWARENESS MONTH

The world is full of many different cultures, and this month we get to celebrate them! You probably have friends who have different traditions than you. Many of these traditions have come from other cultures.

The diversity we can find in the United States is one of the things that make it such a great country. We celebrate our differences and learn from each other.

What goes around the world but doesn't move?

The equator

Birthday Traditions Around the World

On birthdays in **MEXICO**, it's traditional for someone to shove the birthday boy or girl's face into their cake after they take their first bite.

AUSTRALIANS celebrate their birthday by eating fairy bread—buttered bread with rainbow sprinkles.

In **THE NETHERLANDS**, everyone in the family gets birthday wishes, not just the birthday person.

JAMAICAN birthday boys or girls get flour thrown at them!

In **VIETNAM**, everyone celebrates their birthday on the same day of the year, called Tet, which is also the beginning of the new year. Children get red envelopes filled with money as presents.

Can you match the cultural tradition with the country that practices it?

China   Greece   Norway
Iceland   Japan

1. In the most populated country in Asia, it isn't rude to slurp noodles—it just means you're enjoying the food!

2. On Christmas Eve in this country, everyone gives books as gifts, followed by an evening of reading together.

3. In homes in this large island country, you always remove your shoes before entering.

4. Even when eating a sandwich, the people in this country are big on using silverware. Table manners are very important to them.

5. Instead of putting their baby teeth under a pillow, kids in this European country throw their teeth onto their roofs.

NATIONAL BULLYING PREVENTION MONTH

If you've ever wondered if you have been a bully, this quiz could help you find out.

The sad truth is, bullying is pretty common. Without realizing it, even you could have been a bully to someone in your life. This month, make an extra effort to be kind to everyone you meet. The bullying can stop with you!

1. You hear your best friend teasing a kid about being overweight. You:

a. Laugh. Your friend said it in a funny way.

b. Leave. You don't want any part of your friend's behavior.

c. Quietly urge your friend to leave the kid alone.

2. A really embarrassing picture of a kid you know is being sent around. You:

a. Show it to everyone around you and then forward it to someone else.

b. Refuse to accept it, or if it's electronic, delete it from your phone or email.

c. Tell an adult you trust and ask him or her what to do.

3. When your teacher tells you to form groups, you notice that the same kids are excluded every time. This time, you:

a. Hurry to form your group so that you won't get stuck with those kids.

b. Don't worry about those kids. Someone else will choose them.

c. Invite them into your group. No one wants to be left out.

4. A popular group of kids you really want to be friends with asks you to help play a mean trick on someone. You:

a. Play along. They are going to do it with or without you, and this might make you friends with the popular kids.

b. Pretend you are not going to be in school the day of the trick so you can't be part of it.

c. Tell them you think it sounds mean and they shouldn't do it.

5. You see your friend pushing around a kid at recess. You:

a. Watch. The kid probably had it coming, and no one else who's watching is stopping the fight.

b. Leave. It isn't your fight.

c. Get a teacher. Your friend may not like it, but at least no one will get hurt.

RESULTS

If you answered mostly a:
Careful! You could be a bit of a bully. Before you act, think about how your actions might make others feel.

If you answered mostly b:
You don't bully others, but you don't stick up for kids who are being bullied, either. Ask yourself, "How can I help?"

If you answered mostly c:
You stick up for kids who are being bullied. Good for you! Soon, others may follow your lead.

35 YEARS AGO, A MASSIVE EARTHQUAKE MEASURING APPROXIMATELY 6.9 ON THE RICHTER SCALE SHOOK THE SAN FRANCISCO BAY AREA.

This earthquake was a particularly noteworthy quake considering it hit just as the 1989 World Series was beginning at the Giants' Candlestick Park. Because of that, many people saw the shaking take place in real time on national television.

9 and over
8-8.9
7-7.9
6-6.9
5-5.9
4-4.9
3-3.9
2-2.9
0-1.9

The Richter Scale measures energy waves emitted by earthquakes

0-1.9
Can be detected only by seismograph

2-2.9
Hanging objects may swing

3-3.9
Comparable to vibrations of a passing truck

4-4.9
May break windows, cause small or unstable objects to fall

5-5.9
Furniture moves, chunks of plaster may fall from walls

6-6.9
Damage to well-built structures, severe damage to poorly built ones

7-7.9
Buildings displaced from foundations, cracks in the earth; underground pipes broken

8-8.9
Bridges destroyed, few structures left standing

9 and over
Near-total destruction, waves moving through the earth visible to the naked eye

STRONG STRUCTURES

Architects and engineers try to build structures that can withstand an earthquake. These are some of the design elements that help protect San Francisco's Golden Gate Bridge from natural forces: winds, waves, and earthquakes.

The cables absorb up-and-down and side-to-side movement caused by traffic, weather, and earthquakes.

The towers and concrete blocks transfer the weight of the cables (and all they hold up) into the ground.

Hundreds of steel ropes suspend the deck and trusses from the two main cables.

Each main cable is three feet thick.

The ends of the cables are anchored to each shore by huge blocks of reinforced concrete.

Steel-beam trusses support the deck.

The state of Nevada is an intriguing place with vast deserts throughout the state and a snow-capped mountain range (the Sierra Nevadas) on its western border. This is where Lake Tahoe is located: a beautiful alpine resort destination that straddles the Nevada and California border.

These adventurous tourists are testing their balance on paddle boards on Lake Tahoe's crystal waters. While they try to stay afloat, scan the scene and see if you can find all of the hidden objects.

loaf of bread

envelope

pickax

hat

magnet

mushroom

pea pod

handbell

flowerpot

ear of corn

dog bone

broom

artist's brush

muffin

NATIONAL ROLLER-SKATING MONTH

Examine the roller derby participants in these two illustrations carefully.
Can you spot what is the same and what is different?

Kelly: You're back from your roller-skating lesson. How did it go?

Michael: OK, I guess.

Kelly: What was the hardest part?

Michael: The pavement.

ON A ROLL

Follow the paths to match each kid to his or her shoes.

WORLD SERIES CHAMPIONSHIP

The American League champion team faces off against the National League champion team in a best-of-seven-games series every year. But why is it called the World Series if only North American teams are eligible to play? One legend is that the New York World newspaper was the series's original sponsor; however, that's incorrect. When the World Series was first created at the turn of the century, baseball was the quintessential all-American game, and it wasn't played in many other countries around the world. The organizers claimed that their championship series was showcasing the best baseball players in the world as a way to draw a bigger crowd. And the name stuck, even as baseball has gained popularity in many countries around the globe.

SS	BB	NN	VV	RR	TT	PP
EE	OO	TH	HH	MM	LL	KK
WW	QQ	XX	CC	DD	EN	FF
BB	EW	SS	KK	PP	HH	GG
RR	UU	TT	DD	YO	VV	BB
EE	RK	HH	NN	MM	SS	PR
	AN	AA	BB	KF	RR	
	EE	DD	GG	DD	SS	
		PP	KK	ES		
		NN				

To solve this puzzle, cross out all the pairs of matching letters. Then write the remaining letters in order from left to right and top to bottom in the spaces beneath the riddle.

What baseball team does a joker like best?

FLY CATCHER

Can you help this outfielder catch the fly ball before it hits the ground?

START

FINISH

How is a baseball team similar to a pancake?

They both need a good batter.

How do baseball players stay cool?

By sitting next to the fans

Why are baseball players so rich?

Because they play on diamonds

October 2, 2024
RANDOM ACTS OF POETRY DAY

What kind of tree has poems on it?

A poetry

What hand is best to write poetry with?

Neither—you should use a pencil!

4 Random Ways to Celebrate Poetry

1. Make up a tune and turn your favorite poem into a song. Perform it for your family.

2. Write a poem from an interesting point of view. For example, imagine what a fork would say about being in the dishwasher.

3. Research some poets and read their poems. Try to memorize a poem you like.

4. Challenge yourself to write a short poem and share it with a friend.

October 5, 2024
WORLD CARD MAKING DAY

Celebrate the day by making these Halloween-inspired cards to give to a friend!

Spooky Eyeball Card

1. Fold a piece of **cardstock** in half.

2. On the front, use a **white paint pen** to write: *"Eye" hope you have a "ball" this Halloween!*

3. For eyes, glue **cotton balls** onto the card. Cut out irises from cardstock and draw pupils on them with a black **marker**. Glue the irises to the cotton balls.

4. Write a message inside.

Drizzle Art Card

1. Drizzle **gel glue** in a fun design onto **craft foam**. Let the glue dry overnight.

2. Paint over the craft foam and dried glue using no more than two coats of **acrylic paint**. Let it dry.

3. Carefully peel off the glue. Glue the drizzle art to a folded piece of **cardstock** to make a card.

70% of people include their pet's name when signing greeting cards.

October 16
DICTIONARY DAY

There are tons of fun words hidden in the dictionary. Take a moment to find a new word to add to your vocabulary. Here are some of our favorites. **What are your favorite words?**

A dictionary's pages contain many words, but so do its letters! Using only letters in the word DICTIONARY, spell:

1. A child's plaything

___ ___ ___

2. An insect in a colony

___ ___ ___

3. A vegetable on a cob

___ ___ ___ ___

4. Dry mud

___ ___ ___ ___

5. Falling drops of water

___ ___ ___ ___

6. Railroad cars and an engine

___ ___ ___ ___

7. A milk container

___ ___ ___ ___ ___ ___

gewgaw: a trinket

splendiferous: magnificent

collywobbles: a stomachache or feeling of nervousness

bumfuzzle: to confuse

widdershins: counterclockwise

flibbertigibbet: someone who is silly and talks a lot

xertz: to greedily eat or drink

The *Oxford English Dictionary* is one of the most widely used dictionaries in the English language. The first edition took 50 years to complete and was finished in 1928. It included more than 400,000 words and phrases from the 12th century to the present!

October 22
NATIONAL COLOR DAY

Each group of 3 words describes a color. Use your color IQ to figure out each one.

1.	Crimson	Ruby	Scarlet
2.	Azure	Cobalt	Teal
3.	Auburn	Mahogany	Sepia
4.	Amber	Citron	Canary
5.	Sage	Chartreuse	Jade
6.	Plum	Mauve	Lavender
7.	Tangerine	Marigold	Persimmon
8.	Jet	Charcoal	Onyx

October 22 is also **National Smart Is Cool Day.** Get together with your friends and share your favorite trivia!

Where do crayons go on vacation?

Colorado

October 4
NATIONAL TACO DAY

Take-Along Taco Cup

Spoon the following ingredients into a plastic cup, in this order:

- ¼ cup canned black beans
- ¼ cup guacamole
- ¼ cup sour cream
- 2 tablespoons crushed tortilla chips
- ¼ cup salsa
- 2 tablespoons shredded cheddar cheese

Americans love tacos. They love them so much that they eat about **4.5 BILLION TACOS** every year!

shredded cheddar cheese

salsa

crushed tortilla chips

sour cream

guacamole

black beans

Knock, knock.
Who's there?
Taco.
Taco who?
I don't want to taco 'bout it.

TIC TAC TACO

TO SOLVE THIS SPEC-TACO-LAR PUZZLE...

...TACO-BOUT WHAT EACH ROW IN EVERY DIRECTION HAS IN COMMON.

LOOK CLOSELY IN QUESO YOU MISS SOMETHING!

NATIONAL PIEROGI DAY

Pierogi are delicious stuffed dumplings from Poland. Many cultures make foods that feature a filling stuffed or wrapped in dough. This puzzle contains **29** such foods, from places like China, India, Mexico, and, of course, Poland. The yummy words can fit in the grid in just one way. **Use the number of letters in each word as a clue to where it might fit, and you'll have this puzzle wrapped up in no time.**

5 Letters
BAOZI
KNISH
PASTY
RUNZA

6 Letters
BLINTZ
PASTEL
TAMALE
SAMOSA
WONTON

7 Letters
BURRITO
CALZONE
CORN DOG
KALDUNY
PELMENI
PIEROGI
RAVIOLI
STRUDEL

8 Letters
DUMPLING
EMPANADA
KREPLACH
PASTIZZI
TURNOVER

9 Letters
AGNOLOTTI
STROMBOLI

10 Letters
PANZEROTTI
POT STICKER
SHISHBARAK
TORTELLINI

13 Letters
JAMAICAN PATTY

HIGH HOLY DAYS

In Judaism, the High Holy Days are the holidays of Rosh Hashanah and Yom Kippur.

Rosh Hashanah marks the start of a new year in the Hebrew calendar. Jewish people often celebrate by eating apples and honey to symbolize a sweet new year. This year, Rosh Hashanah begins at sunset on **October 2** and ends at nightfall on **October 4**. It begins the ten days when Jews think about their actions from the previous year. **Yom Kippur** means "Day of Atonement," and many Jews fast on this day and spend the day praying in a synagogue. This year, Yom Kippur begins at sunset on **October 11** and ends at nightfall on **October 12**.

SHOFAR

1. From **cardstock**, cut out two horns.

2. Glue the sides together to make a pocket. Use a **marker** to add decorations.

3. Punch two holes at the top. Tie on a **ribbon** hanger.

4. Write notes on **paper**. Place them inside the horn.

A *shofar* is a ram's horn that is blown like a trumpet on the Jewish High Holy Days. Most scholars and rabbis agree that it is meant as a wake-up call. The blast of the shofar reminds people to take time to think about what they can do to make the world a better place.

I'm sorry that I didn't listen.
I'm sorry that I was rude to my brother.
I promise to be a better friend.
I promise to be patient.

APPLES-AND-HONEY PLATE

1. From **tissue paper**, cut out apples, leaves, and a beehive.

2. Use a **sealer** (such as Mod Podge) to glue the shapes to the back of a **clear plastic plate**. Use as many layers of tissue paper as needed to get the color you want.

3. Cover the shapes with two or three coats of sealer, letting it dry between coats.

Be sure to keep the sealer on the back of the plate, away from any food!

Apples and honey symbolize a sweet new year!

Pomegranate seeds symbolize *mitzvahs*, or good deeds, and are often eaten on Rosh Hashanah.

GOOD DEED POMEGRANATE

1. From **cardstock**, cut out a pomegranate-shaped card, two circles, and pomegranate seeds.

2. Glue the circles inside the card. Glue the seeds on the circles.

3. On each seed, write a good deed you plan to do in the coming year.

To build a sukkah properly, Jewish people must follow rules found in an ancient Jewish law book called the Talmud. Here are some of the sukkah rules:

- It can be built on a boat.
- It can be built on an ox-cart.
- It can be built in a treetop.
- It can be built on top of a camel.
- It can have an elephant or a whale for a wall.
- The roof cannot be made of utensils.
- It may be built in a tree but not under a tree.
- It must have at least two and a half walls.

The roofs of sukkahs must be harvested from the ground. Materials can include evergreen branches, palm fronds, bamboo, and cornstalks.

October 16–23, 2024
SUKKOT

Sukkot (sue-COAT) is a Hebrew word that means "booths" or "huts."

Every fall, many Jewish people around the world celebrate the holiday of Sukkot. One way they celebrate is by building huts called sukkahs in their backyards. If it is warm and dry enough, they stay in those shelters for seven days and nights. This is meant to remind the Jewish people that for 40 years the children of Israel, their ancestors, lived in huts in the Sinai Desert after the prophet Moses led them out of captivity in Egypt. In modern times, it has also become a reminder that many people do not have a place to call home.

CHALLAH BREAD

The last day of sukkot, the family eats a special meal that includes challah dipped in honey and kreplach (dumplings stuffed with meat).

Follow these instructions with an adult helper to make challah (HAH-luh), a braided bread. Challah is eaten every week for Shabbat, but it is also enjoyed at special holidays like Rosh Hashanah and Sukkot.

1. In a large **bowl**, pour one cup of **warm water** and 1 packet of **dry yeast**. Stir until the yeast dissolves.
2. Stir in ¼ cup **vegetable oil**, ¼ cup **honey**, and 1 ½ teaspoons **salt**.
3. In a small bowl, beat 3 **eggs**. Pour them into the mixture in the large bowl and stir.
4. Stir 4 cups **flour** into the mixture, a half cup at a time.
5. Knead the dough on a clean, flour-covered surface for five minutes. Add small amounts of flour until the dough is no longer sticky.
6. Place the dough back into the bowl and cover it with a **clean, damp cloth**. Let it sit for two hours in a warm place to rise.

7. With an adult, preheat the oven to 350° F.
8. Push down the dough in the bowl.
9. Divide the dough into three pieces. Roll each piece on a flour-covered surface to form a long rope. Braid the three ropes together.
10. Grease a **cookie sheet** with **butter** or **cooking spray**. Place the braided dough on the sheet. Tuck the ends underneath.
11. In the small bowl, beat one **egg yolk** and one tablespoon of water. Brush the mixture over the braided dough.
12. Put the braided dough into the oven. Bake it for 25 to 35 minutes. Remove when the top is golden brown.

October 31
HALLOWEEN

Check out these frightening and fascinating facts!

THE SCOOP ON PUMPKINS

The heaviest pumpkin on record weighed **2,625 pounds.**

That's about as much as an adult giraffe!

A pumpkin that big could make about **602 pumpkin pies.**

SWEET STATS

Americans' favorite Halloween treats:

Chocolate **68%**

Candy Corn **10%**

Chewy Candy **7%**

WHAT A SCREAM!

The loudest scream ever recorded reached **129 DECIBELS (dB).** That's louder than a chainsaw.

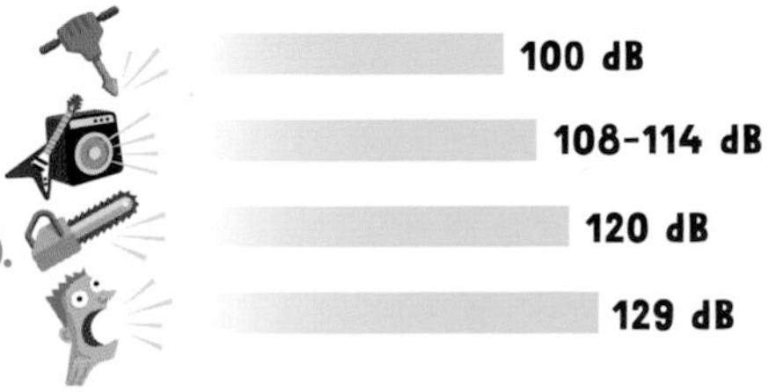

100 dB

108-114 dB

120 dB

129 dB

BY THE NUMBERS

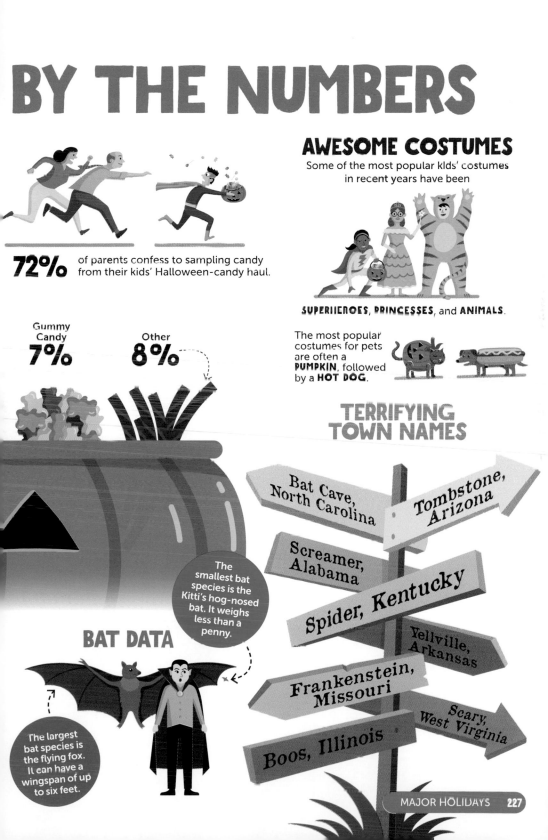

72% of parents confess to sampling candy from their kids' Halloween-candy haul.

AWESOME COSTUMES

Some of the most popular kids' costumes in recent years have been

SUPERHEROES, **PRINCESSES**, and **ANIMALS**.

The most popular costumes for pets are often a **PUMPKIN**, followed by a **HOT DOG**.

Gummy Candy **7%**

Other **8%**

TERRIFYING TOWN NAMES

Bat Cave, North Carolina

Tombstone, Arizona

Screamer, Alabama

Spider, Kentucky

Yellville, Arkansas

Frankenstein, Missouri

Scary, West Virginia

Boos, Illinois

The smallest bat species is the Kitti's hog-nosed bat. It weighs less than a penny.

BAT DATA

The largest bat species is the flying fox. It can have a wingspan of up to six feet.

October 1
INTERNATIONAL RACCOON APPRECIATION DAY

A raccoon's paws really come in handy. In fact, raccoons use the sense of touch in their paws more than their other senses. If you've ever seen a raccoon "washing" its food, it's actually doing something called dousing. Getting their paws wet heightens raccoons' sense of touch, so they're able to feel what they are holding better.

This raccoon and his woodland friends are having a blast trick-or-treating. How are these pictures the same? How are they different?

October 2
WORLD FARM ANIMALS DAY

The names of 11 farm animals are scrambled to the right. **Can you unscramble each set of letters and find the words?**

Take the letters from the boxes and write them in order in the blanks below.

What is a cow's favorite fruit?

— — — — — — — — — —

HICNECK   __ __ __ [ ] __ __ __

BABTIR   __ __ [ ] __ __ __

OAGT   __ __ [ ] __

ACT   __ [ ] __

AMLAL   [ ] __ __ __ __

ROHSE   __ __ __ __ [ ]

PACLAA   __ [ ] __ __ __ __

OWC   __ [ ] __

CUDK   __ [ ] __ __

GIP   [ ] __ __

EHPES   __ __ __ [ ] __

October 8
WORLD OCTOPUS DAY

Octopuses are talented, eight-limbed creatures. Among their many skills is their ability to change colors. This talent helps them camouflage to stay safe from predators or to hide while hunting for food. Changing colors is also how they communicate with other octopuses! If humans spoke in colors, what color do you think "hello" would be?

Having eight arms in the kitchen would definitely be helpful! **Hunt for the 6 objects in this scene while Chef Cephalopod prepares dinner.**

OCTOPUSES HAVE THREE HEARTS.

octagon   oar   orange

oak leaf   owl   ornament

October 20
INTERNATIONAL SLOTH DAY

The sloths are all celebrating International Sloth Day at Sloth-Land Adventure Park! Snoozanne wants to see a concert, Snorbert can't wait to go on a tube tour, and Dozalita is eager to try the ropes course. But all three activities have just started!
What time is it?

Sloths live for a long time—on average about 20 years. The oldest sloth grew up in Australia's Adelaide Zoo and lived to be **43 years old!**

Three-toed sloths' fur is home to moths and algae. The moths help the algae grow, and the algae is a form of food and camouflage for the sloths.

ROCK-A-BYE CONCERTS
Every 3 hours from 12:00 P.M. to 9:00 P.M.

LAZY RIVER TUBE TOURS
Every 1½ hours from 12:00 P.M. to 9:00 P.M.

TREETOP ROPES COURSE
Every 2 hours from 2:00 P.M. to 8:00 P.M.

October 31
NATIONAL MAGIC DAY

Benny Bunny is putting on a magic show for National Magic Day. Bet he's not going to pull a rabbit out of his hat!

Can you find all of the hidden objects in this picture?

golf club snake jar button pizza lollipop bell necktie

MAGICAL CONNECT THE DOTS

Connect the dots from 1 to 15 to see something a magician uses.

Take a spin around the globe to see how

October 4
CINNAMON BUN DAY

In Finland and Sweden, today is a day to celebrate Scandinavia's favorite cinnamon-flavored bread. These Scandinavian countries have their own names for cinnamon rolls!

1. Norway: *skillingsboller* ("schilling buns")
2. Finland: *korvapuusti* ("slapped ear")
3. Sweden: *kanelbullar* ("cinnamon buns")
4. Denmark: *kanelsnegl* ("cinnamon snails")

October 18
INDEPENDENCE DAY

32 years ago, in 1991, Azerbaijan adopted a constitutional act that restored its independence from the Soviet Union. The vote to support the act was unanimous among the citizens of Azerbaijan.

There are over **400 VOLCANOES** in Azerbaijan, but they don't shoot lava—they shoot mud and sometimes oil. When they aren't making a muddy mess, they let out sulfur gases, making the area smell a lot like eggs.

The blue stripe and the crescent represent Azerbaijan's Turkic origins.

Like most flags, this one is full of symbolism.

The red portion symbolizes developing democracy.

The green is a nod to Islam, the most practiced religion in Azerbaijan.

The eight-point star is a reference to how Azerbaijan was written in the old alphabet, with eight letters.

THE WORLD

eople around the world celebrate in October.

The Austrian Parliament building in Vienna was built between 1874 and 1883. The main statue in the fountain in front of the building is Athena, the Greek goddess of wisdom.

October 26
NATIONAL DAY

This day is a celebration of the Austrian Parliament passing a law in 1955 that Austria would remain a neutral country.

At the time, it was occupied by four countries (the Soviet Union, the United States, Great Britain, and France), post–World War II. By declaring neutrality, the law ended the occupation and allowed Austria to be its own country again. On this day, in addition to several rituals performed by the government, federal museums open their doors for free to Austrian citizens.

October 29
REPUBLIC DAY

This is a day to celebrate in Turkey, as people remember Turkey's victory in the War of Independence in 1923. There are fireworks, art events, concerts, and celebrations throughout the country. Can you find where the three jigsaw pieces fit into this photo of a Republic Day celebration?

SUNDAY	MONDAY	TUESDAY	WEDNESDA

ZODIAC SIGNS
SCORPIO:
OCTOBER 23–NOVEMBER 21

SAGITTARIUS:
NOVEMBER 22–
DECEMBER 21

BIRTHSTONES
TOPAZ

CITRINE

Bye-bye, Daylight Saving Time! Did you turn back your clock one hour?*

*You're off the hook Arizona and Hawaii.

3

Westward, ho! The first wagon train arrived in California 183 years ago. The group had left Independence, Missouri, on May 1, 1841.

4

National Love Your Red Hair Day

Don't have red hair? Appreciate someone else's ginger locks!

5

National Nachos Day

Grab your chips an pile on the topping Today is a great da for nachos.

6

What a wall! In 1970, China opened up the Great Wall of China to tourists from around the world for the first time.

10

VETERANS DAY

11

National French Dip Day

The French dip sandwich was invented in an L.A. restaurant in the early 1900s.

12

WORLD KINDNESS DA
You're welcome!

1

Click this! In 1970, Douglas Engelbart was granted a patent for the "X-Y Position Indicator for a Display System," what we now call a computer mouse.

17

National Apple Cider Day

A delicious fall drink!

18

In 1997, Bobbi McCaughey became the first woman to successfully give birth to septuplets (seven babies). Today, they are 27 years old!

19

National Name Your PC D

Will it be Fred, Rob or Millie?

20

CELEBRATE YOUR UNIQUE TALENT DAY

24

NATIONAL EAT WITH A FRIEND DAY

25

National Cake Day

This day takes the cake!

26

So many floats! In 192 Macy's department store sponsored its first Thanksgiving Day Parade. Although held on Thanksgiving, it wa actually a Christmas parade.

2

THURSDAY	FRIDAY	SATURDAY
FLOWER CHRYSANTHEMUM 	**DIWALI** **1**	**NATIONAL DEVILED EGG DAY** **2**
ELECTION DAY VOTED **7**	**Cook Something Bold and Pungent Day** Fill your home with smells of spicy peppers, garlic, onions, or whatever flavors say BAM! **8**	**Independence Day (Cambodia)** This holiday celebrates independence from France in 1953 with speeches and a torch-lighting ceremony. **9**
In 1989, George H. W. Bush made pardoning a live Thanksgiving turkey a national tradition. **14**	**America Recycles Day** Take the pledge to "Keep America Beautiful"! **15**	**HAVE A PARTY WITH YOUR BEAR DAY** **16**
World Hello Day *Guten Tag! Hola! Konnichiwa!* Aim to greet 10 new people today. **21**	**Go for a Ride Day** Hop on your bike or board, and get out of the house! **22**	**EAT A CRANBERRY DAY** Dried Cranberries **23**
THANKSGIVING DAY **28**	*One giant footstep . . .* In 2004, movie monster Godzilla was given a star on the Hollywood Walk of Fame. **29**	**Saint Andrew's Day (Scotland)** Scots honor the patron saint of Scotland with festivals and celebrations full of music, dance, and food. **30**

NOVEMBER

NATIONAL NATIVE AMERICAN HERITAGE MONTH

November celebrates the diverse and rich culture, history, and traditions of Native peoples. It's also a time to raise awareness about the barriers Native people have faced in the past as well as in the present.

There are 574 federally recognized Native American Nations in the United States. Two hundred and twenty-eight of these are Alaskan Natives.

More than 9.6 million Americans, or 2.9 percent of the U.S. population, are of Native heritage.

The sport of lacrosse comes from stickball games the Haudenosaunee played as early as the 12th century. They linked the game to their creation stories and call it "The Creator's Game."

A Navajo girl in a traditional handwoven blanket looks out over Monument Valley.

The names of 10 Native American nations are listed here in alphabetical order. Use the number of letters in each word as a clue to where it might fit in the grid.

APACHE
BLACKFEET
CHEROKEE
CHICKASAW
CHOCTAW
HAUDENOSAUNEE
MUSCOGEE
NAVAJO
OJIBWE
PUEBLO

Ask a teacher or librarian to help you learn about the Native history of your area.

NATIONAL MODEL RAILROAD MONTH

Passenger railroads started in the 1820s,
and toy trains made of wood and metal arrived in the 1860s.
Today, kids and adults enjoy model railroading.

Fill in the letters in the picture code to answer the riddle.

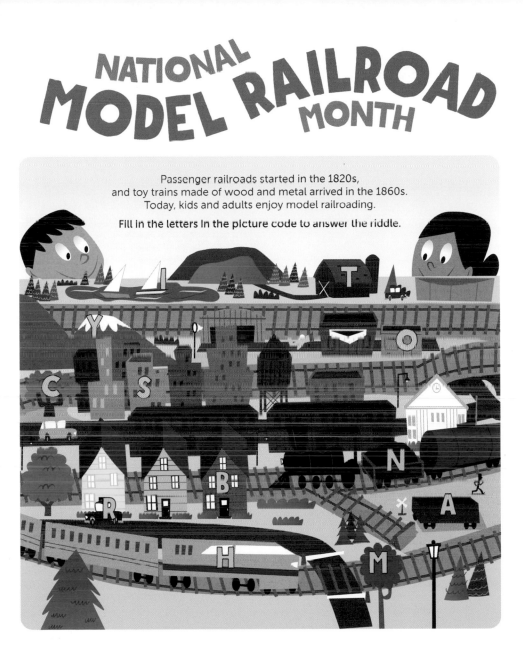

What do you call a locomotive that sneezes?

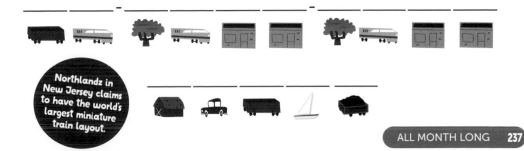

Northlandz in New Jersey claims to have the world's largest miniature train layout.

FAMILY STORIES MONTH

Everyone has a story. Ask your parents, grandparents, or other family members for theirs! Share yours, too.

What's silly in this family photo? Take turns telling a silly (but true!) story about your family.

STORY STARTS

Genealogy is the study of family history and ancestry. Be your family's genealogist! Write down or record your relatives' stories. You might ask these questions:

- What is your earliest memory?
- What was your favorite game growing up?
- Who was your best friend when you were my age?
- What was your first job?
- What was your favorite song, TV show, or movie?
- Where was your favorite place to visit?

Look around your house. An old photo album, school diploma, or favorite knickknack may spark a family member's story.

KIDS' SCIENCE QUESTIONS

Why can't you remember anything from when you were a baby?

Short-term memories last for seconds to hours. Long-term memories last for years.

Babies do form memories as building blocks for their development. Babies remember faces, copy what they see, and learn how to talk. Later on, using words to store memories helps them to recall specific events. We may not remember events from when we were babies because we didn't have the words to attach to the memories. Thank goodness for baby photos and videos!

NATIONAL NOVEL WRITING MONTH

November is also Picture Book Month.

NOVEMBER 15 is I Love to Write Day.

Every November, aspiring authors attempt to write a novel in just 30 days. Challenge yourself to write this month, even if you're not writing a novel. Here are some writing activities you can use to hone your skills.

CHARACTER PLAY

With a partner, decide on two characters from books, movies, your imagination, or the real world that could have a conversation—maybe Harry Potter and Peter Pan, Goldilocks and Baby Bear, or a lion and a hippo who both want to drink from the same watering hole.

One of you starts the conversation on paper, writing a sentence as one of the characters. The other person writes a response as the second character. Keep going back and forth until you have written for about 10 minutes. Then read your script out loud, with each person reading their character's part.

OOPS!

We all make mistakes. Luckily, most mistakes aren't serious, and sometimes they're funny when they're in the past. Write about one of your funny mistakes.

PERFECT PROFESSIONS

When writers come up with names for their characters, there are often specific reasons for them. Maybe the name sets a mood, says something about the character, or is just funny.

Here are some character names that fit their professions. Can you come up with more?

CONTRACTOR: I. M. BUILDER

DINER CHEF: PATTY COOK

SWIMMER: WILL FLOAT

AUTHOR: PAGE TURNER

CHAUFFEUR: MERCEDES D. DRIVER

VALET: PARKER CARR

TRACK AND FIELD COACH: MILES LONG

BANKER: RICH N. CASH

BODYGUARD: JUSTIN CASE

Sue Justice

Lawyer

Hunter N. Skye

Astronomer

Barry D. Treasure

Pirate

35 YEARS AGO, THE BERLIN WALL FELL.

This was the first step toward freedom for East Berliners, the end of communism in East Germany, and the reunification of Germany.

The entire wall didn't actually fall all at once. The borders were just opened, allowing people to freely cross. (Although people did start to chip off souvenirs of the wall on this night.) It took two years for the wall to be completely demolished.

In 1987, President Ronald Reagan gave a famous speech in front of the Berlin Wall. In it, he spoke to the leader of communist Soviet Union and said, "Mr. Gorbechev, tear down this wall!"

Following World War II, Germany was divided into two countries: Democratic West Germany and Communist East Germany. The former capital, Berlin, was also divided into West Berlin and East Berlin. The East Germans built the Berlin Wall to keep the people separate. Armed guards prevented anyone from crossing through it freely. The Berlin Wall has now been down longer than it was up.

TOURING BERLIN

A trip to Berlin wouldn't be complete without a visit to these sites. When you're done finding them in the word search, start in the left corner and use the leftover words to learn a fun fact about one of these locations.

WORD LIST

Alexanderplatz
Berlin Cathedral
Brandenburg Gate
East Side Gallery
Mauerpark
Museum Island
Neus Museum
Potsdamer Platz
Reichstag
Spree River
Tiergarten
Zeughaus

```
T  H  S  E  E  A  S  R  M  T  B  Z  B  P  T
S  I  U  D  E  G  A  E  U  L  E  T  R  O  I
L  E  A  R  Y  I  S  V  S  T  R  A  A  T  E
H  E  H  L  O  N  G  I  E  M  L  L  N  S  R
E  S  G  T  S  U  R  R  U  V  I  P  D  D  G
I  V  U  I  N  G  S  E  M  E  N  R  E  A  A
C  T  E  I  O  N  S  E  I  O  C  E  N  M  R
F  T  Z  H  E  U  B  R  S  E  A  D  B  E  T
R  L  I  N  M  W  A  P  L  L  T  N  U  R  E
L  A  E  S  E  F  U  S  A  E  H  A  R  P  N
H  C  U  Z  O  Z  X  G  N  G  E  X  G  L  M
K  E  P  J  O  K  E  H  D  O  D  E  G  A  S
N  M  G  A  T  S  H  C  I  E  R  L  A  T  W
M  A  U  E  R  P  A  R  K  X  A  A  T  Z  O
E  A  S  T  S  I  D  E  G  A  L  L  E  R  Y
```

___ ___ ____

_____ ___ ___

_____ _____

_____ __ ___

_____ ____.

November 10, 1969

55 YEARS AGO, SESAME STREET AIRED FOR THE FIRST TIME ON NATIONAL TELEVISION.

Big Bird, Oscar the Grouch, Cookie Monster, Count von Count, Bert and Ernie, and Grover would become household staples for American children for decades. It has since aired in more than 120 countries.

The idea for Sesame Street came from a simple question asked by a reporter "Do you think television can teach anything?"

Big Bird's costume has more than 4,000 feathers!

Sesame Street was based in a New York City neighborhood. People in New York find the subway to be a most convenient way to get around the city. Before you climb aboard this train, scan the scene at this subway platform. **Circle all the silly things you find!**

BIRD ADDITION

Sesame Street friends help kids everywhere learn how to complete all kinds of tricky tasks, like counting, reading, and even eating cookies. (Thanks, Cookie Monster!) Now help Big Bird by using your math skills to figure out what number his bird friends represent. Each bird on this page has a value from 1 to 9. No two birds have the same value. Can you use the equations to figure out which number goes with which bird?

Syri: Which is farther—New York City or the Moon?

Alex: New York City.

Syri: Why do you say that?

Alex: I can see the Moon, but I can't see New York City.

November 17
NATIONAL TAKE A HIKE DAY

These adventurous folks are taking a hike in red-rock country. However, there's definitely a few silly things in this scene. **Can you find them all?**

ABOUT 35 MILLION Americans go day hiking.

COMPASS CODE

To answer the riddle below, **start at the North (N) circle.** Then move in the directions listed and write the letters you find in the correct spaces.

Where's the best place to eat while hiking?

Where there's ____ ____ ____ ____ ____ ____ ____

____ ____ ____ ____ ____ ____

1. S 1 ____
2. SE 2 ____
3. W 3 ____
4. NW 1 ____
5. S 3 ____

6. NE 3 ____
7. W 1 ____
8. S 2 ____
9. N 1 ____
10. SE 2 ____

11. W 3 ____
12. N 1 ____
13. E 2 ____
14. NW 2 ____

NATIONAL SQUARE DANCE DAY

Swing your partner— do-si-do! In this folk dance, four couples face each other to form a square and follow the steps sung or called out by a "caller."

There are at least 10 differences in these pictures. How many can you find?

BOW TO YOUR PARTNER!

Here's how to do some of the most common square-dance moves.

Allemande Left: Turn to the dancer next to you who is not your partner (also called your *corner*). Then join left hands or link elbows, and circle around until you are back next to your partner.

Do-Si-Do: Face your partner. Step past each other, passing right shoulders. Without turning, step around, back to back, passing left shoulders, until you are in front of your partner again.

Right and Left Grand: Face your partner, join right hands, and walk past each other. Then join left hands with the next person stepping toward you. Circle around, switching hands, until you come back to your partner.

Promenade: Stand side by side with your partner and join hands, right with right, left with left. Walk together counterclockwise in a circle until you reach your starting position.

Swing Your Partner: Link right elbows and step in a clockwise circle, staying in the same spot in the square.

The largest square dance, with **1,632 PARTICIPANTS,** took place at the 66th National Square Dance Convention in 2017.

FROM ALABAMA TO WASHINGTON, as many as 31 states have listed the square dance as their "state dance" or "state folk dance."

November 11

NATIONAL SUNDAE DAY

"NICE CREAM" is a nickname for blended frozen bananas.

1. Have an adult help you blend **frozen bananas** in a blender. Add **water** if needed to make the mixture smooth.

2. Scoop the blended banana into a bowl.

3. Add your favorite sundae toppings like **fresh raspberries, jam, cereal, whipped cream,** and a **cherry.**

Enlist the help of a grown-up and make this banana nice-cream sundae today.

November 18

NATIONAL
CIDER
DAY

Ask for an adult's help with anything sharp or hot.

HOT SPICED CIDER

1. Pour 1 gallon **cider** into a large slow cooker. Stir in 3 tablespoons **honey** and ¼ teaspoon ground **ginger**.
2. Add 12 whole **cloves**, 1 **cinnamon stick**, and ½ of an **orange**, sliced.
3. Place the lid on the slow cooker. Heat on HIGH for 2 hours.
4. Ask an adult to use a spoon to remove the cloves, cinnamon stick, and orange slices.
5. Ladle the cider into mugs. Top with **whipped cream**.

November 28

NATIONAL FRENCH TOAST DAY

OVERNIGHT
FRENCH TOAST

1. Cut a 16-ounce loaf of French bread into 1-inch slices.
2. Place 5 eggs, 1½ cups milk, ½ cup half-and-half, ⅓ cup maple syrup, and ½ teaspoon salt into a large bowl. Whisk the mixture until blended.
3. Place the sliced bread into a baking dish. Pour the mixture over the bread and press the slices into it. Cover the dish with foil and refrigerate overnight.
4. Remove the dish from the refrigerator at least one hour before baking.
5. Ask an adult to preheat the oven to 375°F. Bake the French toast for 35 minutes or until golden brown.
6. For the topping, combine 2 tablespoons melted butter and 2 tablespoons maple syrup. Pour it over the French toast before serving.

FOOD 245

SAXOPHONE DAY

There's music in the air! Use the list of instruments to solve these music jokes. Each coded space has two numbers. The first number tells you which instrument to look at. The second number tells you which letter in that instrument to use.

Tongue Twister:
Six sassy saxophones sit.

Instrument List

1. DRUM
2. FLUTE
3. VIOLIN
4. TRUMPET
5. CLARINET
6. COWBELL
7. KEYBOARD
8. TROMBONE
9. SAXOPHONE

What kind of music do they play at Stonehenge?

H _ _ _ _ _   _ _ _ _
9–6 5–3 1–2 7–8   4–2 3–3 5–1 7–1

How can your hair make music?

_ _ _ _ _ _   _ _ _ _ _ _ _ _ _ _ _
6–3 5–5 2–4 9–6   7–6 9–6 2–5 5–3 1–1 6–4 9–2 3–6 7–8

Who leads the bird band?

_ _ _ _   _ _ _ _ _ _ _   _ _ _ _
4–1 9–6 7–2   5–1 6–2 8–7   1–1 4–3 6–1 7–1   2–4 9–4 8–2

How do you make a bandstand?

_ _ _ _ _ _   _ _ _ _ _ _ _ _ _ _
8–1 5–3 7–1 8–8   7–6 6–3 9–2 7–3   4–1 9–6 2–5 3–2 8–2

_ _ _ _ _ _ _
6–1 9–6 5–3 3–5 8–2 9–1

STEP TO THE MUSIC

Who took the same number of steps to their music stands? Who took the fewest?

Tim
Andy
Rachel
Caitlin

Although the saxophone is usually made of brass, it is considered a wind instrument.

November 11
NATIONAL ORIGAMI DAY

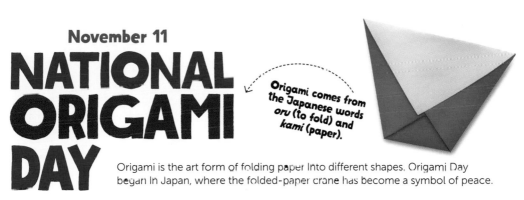

Origami comes from the Japanese words *oru* (to fold) and *kami* (paper).

Origami is the art form of folding paper Into different shapes. Origami Day began In Japan, where the folded-paper crane has become a symbol of peace.

MAKE AN ORIGAMI DRINKING CUP

1. Fold the paper in half diagonally (corner to corner).

2. Fold the left corner over the right side.

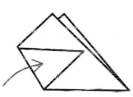

3. Fold the right corner over to the left side.

4. Fold the top front flap down.

5. Flip the cup over. Fold the other top flap down.

6. Open your cup, fill it up, and take a sip!

AN ORIGAMI ROBOT?

It's always fun to see how art can be implemented into science. Here's a robot that can fold itself and go to work!

A permanent magnet is attached.

Laser-cut lines guide the folds when heat shrinks the middle layer.

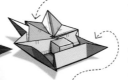

Electromagnets under the floor push and pull the magnet up and down at different angles, directing the robot's movements.

Three layers of different kinds of plastic make up the folding sheet.

Origami robots were first developed at the Massachusetts Institute of Technology (MIT). They can walk up a slope, carry an object heavier than themselves, and even swim.

The inventors believe there will be many uses for their robot. For instance, the robots might inspect equipment and workplaces since they can travel through small, narrow spaces. The robots might also be used to treat illnesses, possibly by carrying medicine directly to small places in the body or even by performing surgery. Once the robots become fast and inexpensive to make, who knows what new uses they might have.

THANKSGIVING

THANKFUL TURKEY

Cut a head, body, wings, and feet from poster board. Decorate them with cardstock, yarn, and markers.

Buddy, my hamster
hugs!
Ice CReam
wednesdays with Grandma
my Teacher
flute Lessons
Birthday parties
MY CAT

I AM THANKFUL FOR . . .

Cut feathers from cardstock. Write something you're thankful for on each feather. Glue or tape them onto the turkey.

Adult turkeys have **5,000–6,000** feathers, including 18 large quill feathers on their tails.

stories About Dinosaurs
Pickles

Save some feathers and have your Thanksgiving guests write what they're thankful for!

WHICH THANKSGIVING FOOD ARE YOU?

1. To cheer up a friend, you . . .
a. Play their favorite game
b. Talk about what's wrong
c. Make them a card full of jokes

2. Your ideal birthday is . . .
a. Playing laser tag
b. Going to the movies
c. Visiting an animal shelter

3. Which do you do for fun?
a. Try out a new activity
b. Read
c. Invite friends over to play

4. What is your favorite part of the school day?
a. Recess
b. Art class
c. Talking with friends at lunch

5. Which do you love most about Thanksgiving?
a. Goofing around with family
b. Remembering what you're thankful for
c. Helping to prepare the Thanksgiving feast

MOSTLY A's: You are turkey. You are an outgoing person who likes to be in the middle of the action.
MOSTLY B's: You are mashed potatoes. Friends and family are drawn to your quiet, warm personality.
MOSTLY C's: You are pumpkin pie. You go out of your way to do or say sweet things to brighten someone's day.

TURKEY TROT

Help Tara get to the oven to take the turkey out.

START

FINISH

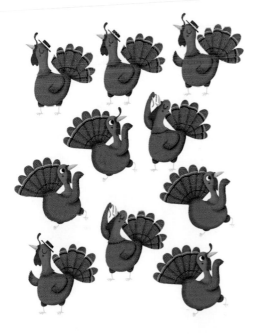

MAKE A MATCH

Find five pairs of matching turkeys.

FAVORITE FOODS

Unscramble these top 10 favorite Thanksgiving foods. Which dish is your favorite?

1. IPE
2. GUFFNITS
3. VAGYR
4. EWEST APESTOTO
5. MAH
6. ASHDEM ETTAOOPS
7. CAM NAD ESHEEC
8. ENGER ANEB ACRESOLES
9. NCOR DEBRA
10. KURTYE

The Wampanoag, or Wôpanâak, have lived in what is now New England for about twelve thousand years. Their ancestors met the Pilgrims in 1620. One year later, they and the settlers participated in several days of feasting and games that we now call the first Thanksgiving.

November 1
NATIONAL VINEGAR DAY

Vinegar is versatile. It can be used for cooking, baking, cleaning—even science experiments! Watch what happens when you mix vinegar with baking soda in the following experiment.

1. Set a **muffin tin** on a **baking sheet**. Add ¼ cup **baking soda** to each muffin cup.
2. Put 10–15 drops of **food coloring** into each cup, one color per cup.
3. Quickly pour **vinegar** into each muffin cup. Watch what happens!

WHAT CAUSES THIS REACTION?
When baking soda and vinegar mix, they create a gas that makes the mixture foam up with lots of little bubbles.

November 8
NATIONAL STEM/STEAM DAY

MOP UP AN OIL SPILL

1. Put a spoonful of cooking oil into a glass of water. Stir.
2. Watch the glass for a few minutes. What happens?
3. Dab the oil with a cotton ball. What happens?
4. See how much oil you can remove using cotton balls.

What do the letters stand for in STEM/STEAM? **SCIENCE, TECHNOLOGY, ENGINEERING, ART,** and **MATHEMATICS.** Which is your favorite subject to learn about?

TALK ABOUT IT!
Describe what happened when you dabbed the oil with a cotton ball. What other materials could you use to soak up the oil?

An oil tanker is a ship that carries a load of oil. If a tanker spills oil, people must work hard to clean up the mess.

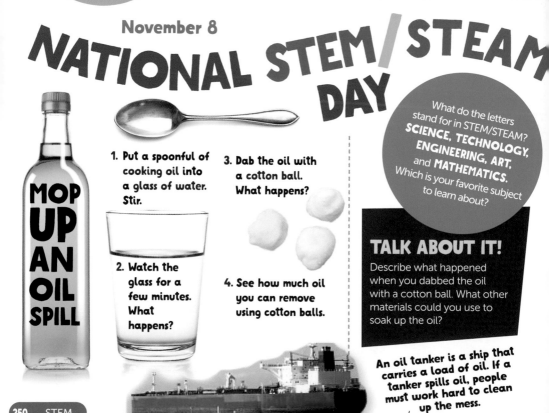

NATIONAL BISON DAY

Buffalo and *bison* are often used interchangeably, but only bison live in North America. Buffalo mostly live in Africa and Asia. Bison have a large shoulder hump, a huge head, and lots of hair, including a beard! Buffalo have rounded horns, but no hump or thick hair.

> What did the father buffalo say to his kid when he dropped him off at school?
>
> "Bison."

Use these fun facts to solve the code below. Each coded space has two numbers. The first number tells you what fun fact to look at; the second number tells you which letter to use.

Bison . . .

1. are the largest mammals in North America.
2. grow up to six feet tall and weigh more than two thousand pounds!
3. have lived in Yellowstone National Park since prehistoric times.
4. raise their tails straight up when they're about to charge.
5. run at speeds up to 35 miles per hour.
6. live to be 10 to 20 years old.
7. have excellent hearing and sense of smell but are nearsighted.

Bison trails were later used for

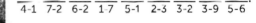

$\overline{4\text{-}1}$ $\overline{7\text{-}2}$ $\overline{6\text{-}2}$ $\overline{1\text{-}7}$ $\overline{5\text{-}1}$ $\overline{2\text{-}3}$ $\overline{3\text{-}2}$ $\overline{3\text{-}9}$ $\overline{5\text{-}6}$.

In the 1800s, sadly people hunted the bison almost to extinction. Now, conservation efforts help bison survive in smaller numbers.

MAKE A MATCH

Can you find 6 pairs of bison?

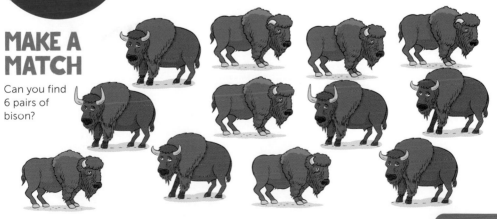

INTERNATIONAL
TONGUE TWISTER DAY

Say "It's the second Sunday of the eleventh month" five times fast. That's International Tongue Twister Day. These word workouts have been used to help learn a new language, overcome speech problems, and cure hiccups.

TOUGHEST TWISTERS

Pad kid poured curd pulled cod. This twister was created in a study by speech researchers at the Massachusetts Institute of Technology in 2013. The MIT team said those who tried to say the phrase either could not repeat it or stopped talking altogether.

The sixth sick sheikh's sixth sheep's sick. This was the most difficult tongue twister in the English language as of 1974, the last time the category was listed in *Guinness World Records*.

Iqaqa laziqikaqika kwaze kwaqhawaka uqhoqhoqha. In 1974, *Guinness World Records* also included this as the most difficult tongue twister in the world. It's in the Xhosa language of South Africa and has three clicking sounds in the last word. It means "The skunk rolled down and ruptured its larynx."

TWISTED HISTORY
Peter Piper picked a peck of pickled peppers. This first appeared in 1813 in John Harris's *Peter Piper's Practical Principles of Plain and Perfect Pronunciation*. Some say this phrase refers to a French spice grower named Pierre Poivre, who wrote about his travels in 1769. His name translates to *Peter Pepper*, but *piper* is also a Latin and an Old English word for *pepper*.

November 16
NATIONAL BUTTON DAY

People have been collecting antique and decorative buttons since at least 1938. The National Button Society was founded on this date! This fasten-ating jar holds more than just buttons. Find: 1 letter *B*, 2 dog bones, 3 rubber balls, 4 pennies, and 5 wrapped candies.

The word button is from the French word **BOUTON**, meaning "bud" or "knob."

The oldest button, carved from a shell, was found in what is now Pakistan. It is about **5,000 YEARS OLD.** But these early buttons were used as decorations on clothing, not as fasteners.

In the 14th century, wearing many buttons—especially those made of gold, silver, or ivory—showed how wealthy you were.

November 13
WORLD KINDNESS DAY

Spread kindness to someone who could use a pick-me-up. Give them a jar of sunshine!

1. Fill a clean **jar** with happy messages or quotes written on **yellow paper**. Add other small **yellow objects**.

2. For labels, decorate two pieces of yellow paper. **Tape** one piece to the jar and another to the lid.

November 19
NATIONAL CAMP DAY

Head out into the wilderness and pitch your tent. Today is National Camp Day! **Can you find all eight objects hidden at this campsite?**

baseball bat

heart

paper clip

piece of popcorn

glove

envelope

tennis ball

fishhook

Calacas (skeletons) and calaveras (colorful skulls) appear in parades, as costumes or masks, and even as chocolate or cookie shapes.

Take a spin around the globe to see how peopl

November 1–2
DÍA DE LOS MUERTOS

Mexicans in Mexico and in other countries celebrate the Day of the Dead (*Día de los Muertos*) as a time to remember family members who have passed away and to encourage their spirits to return for a visit. Many people make the celebration into a party. They have special foods, music, games, stories, and dances.

Look for these hidden objects in the picture: butterfly, candy, clock, ghost, fan, fish, footprint, loaf of bread, pumpkin, and watermelon.

November 4
FLAG DAY

Panama declared independence from Columbia on November 3, 1925. The flag designed by the family of the country's first president, Manuel Amador, was officially adopted the next day.

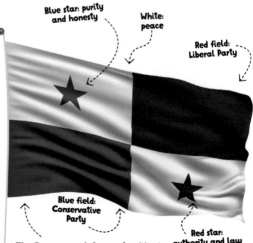

Blue star: purity and honesty

White: peace

Red field: Liberal Party

Blue field: Conservative Party

Red star: authority and law

The flag represents Panama's political parties and values of the time.

THE WORLD

around the world celebrate in November.

November 5
GUY FAWKES DAY

On November 5 in 1605, Guy Fawkes was discovered attempting to blow up British Parliament with barrels of gunpowder. Luckily, he was stopped, and today the English celebrate Guy Fawkes Day with fireworks and bonfires.

November 11
SAINT MARTIN'S DAY

In Germany, this holiday honors St. Martin of Tours, a Roman soldier who was made a bishop and later a saint by the Catholic Church. A kind man, he was said to have cut his cloak in half with his sword to share with a beggar during a snowstorm. Processions are often led by a man on horseback dressed as St. Martin in his long red cloak. School kids hold paper lanterns as he passes. **Can you find the three puzzle pieces in this photo?**

SUNDAY	MONDAY	TUESDAY	WEDNESDAY

SUNDAY — 1

"I was . . . tired of giving in." In 1955, Rosa Parks refused to give up her seat for a white patron on a bus in Montgomery, Alabama, which helped start the civil rights movement.

MONDAY — 2

National Anytime Hawaiian Day

Celebrate Hawaii's diverse culture today!

TUESDAY — 3

NATIONAL APPLE PIE DAY

WEDNESDAY — 4

INTERNATIONAL CHEETAH DAY

8

Pretend to be a Time Traveler Day

To what time will you travel?

11:00

9

A Charlie Brown Christmas debuted on CBS in 1965.

10

Honoring greatness. In 1901, the first Nobel Peace Prize was awarded. One of the recipients was Henry Dunant, who founded the Red Cross.

11

NATIONAL APP DAY

It seems like there is an app for anything you might need. What is your favorite app?

15

NATIONAL UGLY CHRISTMAS SWEATER DAY

MERRY CHRISTMAS

16

Tea Time. On this day in 1773, American colonists threw tea overboard in Boston Harbor in what became known as the Boston Tea Party.

17

Wright Brothers Day

Their first flight was on this day in 1903.

18

Answer the Telephone Like Buddy the Elf Day

22

A bright idea. In 1882, Edward H. Johnson created the first string of electric Christmas lights.

23

Farmer's Day (India)

This holiday that celebrates farmers takes place on the birthday of Chaudhary Charan Singh, the fifth prime minister of India.

24

NATIONAL EGG NOG DAY

25

CHRISTMAS

HANUKKAH begins at sunset.

29

TICK TOCK DAY

Time's a ticking. If you want to do something before the end of the year, now's the time!

30

We're not alone . . . On this day in 1924, the Hubble telescope helped prove there are other galaxies outside of the Milky Way.

31

NEW YEAR'S EVE

ZODIAC SIGNS

SAGITTARIUS: NOVEMBER 22–DECEMBER 21

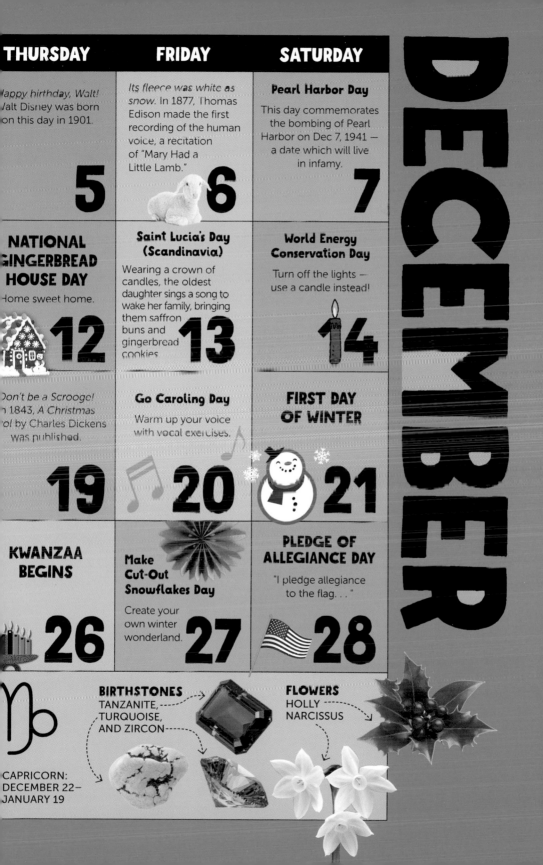

THURSDAY	FRIDAY	SATURDAY

THURSDAY

Happy birthday, Walt! Walt Disney was born on this day in 1901.

5

FRIDAY

Its fleece was white as snow. In 1877, Thomas Edison made the first recording of the human voice, a recitation of "Mary Had a Little Lamb."

6

SATURDAY

Pearl Harbor Day

This day commemorates the bombing of Pearl Harbor on Dec 7, 1941 — a date which will live in infamy.

7

NATIONAL GINGERBREAD HOUSE DAY

Home sweet home.

12

Saint Lucia's Day (Scandinavia)

Wearing a crown of candles, the oldest daughter sings a song to wake her family, bringing them saffron buns and gingerbread cookies.

13

World Energy Conservation Day

Turn off the lights — use a candle instead!

14

Don't be a Scrooge! In 1843, *A Christmas Carol* by Charles Dickens was published.

19

Go Caroling Day

Warm up your voice with vocal exercises.

20

FIRST DAY OF WINTER

21

KWANZAA BEGINS

26

Make Cut-Out Snowflakes Day

Create your own winter wonderland.

27

PLEDGE OF ALLEGIANCE DAY

"I pledge allegiance to the flag. . ."

28

BIRTHSTONES
TANZANITE, TURQUOISE, AND ZIRCON

FLOWERS
HOLLY
NARCISSUS

CAPRICORN: DECEMBER 22– JANUARY 19

DECEMBER

"HI, NEIGHBOR" MONTH

Get to know your neighbors better this holiday season—it all starts with a smile and a hello! Here are a few other ideas of how you can spread holiday joy.

1. Make a card and write a nice note inside.
2. Bake cookies to share.
3. With permission, shovel snow from a neighbor's sidewalk or driveway.
4. Make a homemade gift to give.
5. Collect food for your local food bank.
6. Tell your neighbors what you admire most about them.

TREE TREATS

Give a heartwarming gift.

1. Wash a **plastic ornament** inside and out. Decorate it with **puffy paint**. Let it dry.

2. Make a funnel by rolling and taping a half circle cut from **paper**.

3. Remove the top of the plastic ornament. Use the funnel to fill the ornament with **hot-cocoa powder, tea leaves**, or **coffee beans**.

4. Add a **ribbon** hanger and a **cardstock** tag with drink-making instructions.

December 3 is National Make a Gift Day!

LEARN
A FOREIGN
LANGUAGE
MONTH

There are **7,139** known languages spoken throughout the world.

To celebrate this month, try your hand at a new language! There are a variety of apps, books, and websites that can help you learn another language. Ask a parent or librarian to help you find the best resource for you to use.

There are many ways to say "hello." Can you match each greeting with the correct language?

1. Hola
(OH-lah)
JAPANESE

2. Konnichiwa
(co-nee-chee-wah)
CHINESE

3. Hallo
(HA-lo)
SPANISH

4. Privet
(PREE-viet)
GERMAN

5. Bonjour
(bohn-ZHOOR)
RUSSIAN

6. Ciao
(chOW)
SWAHILI

7. Jambo
(JAM-bo)
FRENCH

8. Ni hao
(Nee HaOW)
ITALIAN

Zimbabwe holds the record for the most official languages spoken in one country with a whopping 16 different languages!

UNIVERSAL HUMAN
RIGHTS MONTH

Eleanor Roosevelt was the chair of the Human Rights Commission.

On December 10, 1948, the United Nations published a document called the *Universal Declaration of Human Rights*, which states that fundamental human rights must be universally protected. People from all over the world from a variety of backgrounds helped draft the declaration, which was the first of its kind in the history of human rights.

30 YEARS AGO, SONY RELEASED THE FIRST PLAYSTATION IN JAPAN.

It cost ¥39,800 (about $366) and sold 100,000 consoles on the first day!
Test your skills at these video game puzzles. **Can you solve them all?**

DOUBLE CROSS

AA	TT	II	TH	SS	QQ	EY
HH	OO	BB	RR	AL	EE	VV
LH	NN	ZZ	YY	CC	AV	AA
II	QQ	EE	EN	DD	PP	WW
IN	GG	LL	TT	VV	EL	ZZ
XX	HH	IV	II	BB	OO	SS
TT	UU	NN	EE	SS	ES	MM

Why are cats good at video games?

☐☐☐☐ ☐☐☐ ☐☐☐ ☐☐

☐☐☐☐ ☐☐☐☐☐.

To find the *"purr-fect"* answer to the riddle below, first cross out all the pairs of matching letters. **Then write the remaining letters in order in the spaces beneath the riddle.**

PlayStation had a CD-ROM drive which allowed the system to play more detailed games. In contrast, Nintendo stored its games on cartridges, which had less memory storage capabilities.

GAME ON!

Andrew and three of his friends entered a video game competition. From the clues below, can you figure out which game each friend played and which place he or she took? **Use the chart to keep track of your answers. Put an X in each box that can't be true and an O in boxes that match.**

1. One of the girls took 1st place in Zany Zoo.
2. Andrew's game had exactly 8 letters in its name.
3. Diego's place was ahead of Briana, but behind Andrew.
4. Briana played her favorite game, Race Car Fun.

	Space Travel	Golf Guru	Race Car Fun	Zany Zoo	1st	2nd	3rd	4th
Andrew								
Briana								
Cassie								
Diego								

December 22, 1964

60 YEARS AGO, LOCKHEED'S SR71 BLACKBIRD FLEW FOR THE FIRST TIME OVER THE DESERT SKIES OF CALIFORNIA.

The SR71 was designed and built by Lockheed's Skunkworks Program. Top engineers in this program began developing advanced aeronautics in 1943.

This supersonic aircraft could fly at 3,000 feet per second, or Mach 3, which is three times the speed of sound. The SR71 flew at an altitude of nearly 80,000 feet. Commercial airlines only fly between 31,000 and 38,000 feet.

FASTEST SPACECRAFT

The Parker Solar Probe, a spacecraft studying the Sun, will reach 430,000 mph at its closest approach to the Sun.

This probe could get from Philadelphia, PA, to Washington, D.C., in one second!

GET UP TO SPEED

Start your engines. These are some of the fastest vehicles ever invented!

WHAT'S THE FASTEST THING IN THE UNIVERSE?

Light! Light travels at a speed of 186,000 miles per second. If a flash of light went around Earth instead of going straight, it would circle the globe 7.5 times in one second.

FASTEST JET PLANE

The (retired) Lockheed SR-71 Blackbird can fly 2,100 miles mph.

FASTEST LAND VEHICLE

The Thrust SSC is a jet-powered car that reached 763 mph in 1997.

Wait up!

December 19
BUILD A SNOWMAN DAY

Get outside and get active by building your very own snowman. No snow? No problem. Just get busy completing these snowman-themed puzzles instead.

There are 6 words (not pictures!) hidden in this scene. **Can you find BOOTS, CHILL, FROST, ICE, MITTENS, and SNOW?**

These pictures are all mixed up. **Write 1, 2, 3, or 4 under each picture to show how the kids work together to build a snowman.**

SAY EACH TONGUE TWISTER THREE TIMES FAST!

Silly snowmen make children smile.

Shovel snow slowly.

No nose knows snow like a snowman's nose knows.

December 21
NATIONAL KNITTERS DAY

Things have gotten tangled at the knitting club. **Can you tell which ball of yarn belongs to each knitter?**

December 13
NATIONAL VIOLIN DAY

As Thad and Aya practice their violins, find the hidden objects in this scene.

button   spool of thread   apple

flowerpot   ring

kite   envelope   spoon

Where did the whale play his violin? In the orca-stra

TONGUE TWISTER:
Vivian plays her very small violin with vigor.

December 21

NATIONAL SHORT STORY DAY

Use one of these story starters to write a story. Or write your own story inspired by the pictures.

IN A LURCH

Chris and Andy were riding the Ferris wheel at the fair. They were having a great time until, suddenly, the ride stopped with a lurch. . . .

CATCHING THE BUS

"I can't be late today, no matter what," Caitlin told herself. But no one told the bus driver. As he drove away without Caitlin, she started to panic. What was she going to do now? . . .

WACKY INVENTIONS

Theo was famous for creating wacky inventions—ones that didn't always work. But he knew his newest invention would change everything. What could possibly go wrong? . . .

December 8
NATIONAL BROWNIE DAY

Not sure what to give that special someone this holiday season?
A brownie mix might just be the answer.

ROCKY ROAD BROWNIE MIX

1. Find a **1 to 1½ quart jar** that can be closed with a lid.

2. In the jar, layer the following: 1 cup of **sugar**, ⅓ cup **unsweetened cocoa**, ½ cup **flour**, ¼ teaspoon **baking powder**, and ¼ teaspoon **salt**.

3. In a **zippered plastic bag**, place ¼ cup **mini chocolate chips**, ⅓ cup **mini marshmallows**, and ¼ cup finely chopped **pecans**. Zip the bag closed and place it on top of the mixture in the jar.

4. Write the recipe on a card. Decorate it with crayons, markers, or stickers.

5. Punch a hole in the corner of the card. String a ribbon through the hole and tie the ribbon onto the mouth of the jar.

How to Make Rocky Road Brownies

1. Preheat oven to 350°F. Spray a 9-inch baking pan with nonstick cooking spray.

2. Pour the brownie mix into a large bowl. Add ½ cup melted **butter**, 2 **eggs**, and 1 teaspoon of **vanilla extract**. Stir until well blended. Spread the mixture in the prepared pan.

3. Bake 20–25 minutes or until a toothpick comes out clean. Sprinkle the **chocolate-chip mixture** over the top. Bake another 3–5 minutes or until the marshmallows are puffy and slightly browned.

4. Cool in the pan on a wire rack, then cut into squares.

The next time you make this, use other types of toppings to create your own version of rocky road brownies!

Don't forget!

December 11
NATIONAL HAVE A BAGEL DAY

Plain, sesame, or whole wheat? Make your choice, then find the hidden objects in the scene below.

The bagel's hole isn't just for decoration. Having a hole helps the bagel to bake faster and gives more surface area with that delicious bagel crust.

eyeglasses

ruler

piece of popcorn

envelope

spoon

banana

slice of pizza

fishhook

golf club

crescent moon

football

musical note

olive

December 13
NATIONAL COCOA DAY

Try these four twists on hot chocolate. What other mix-ins can you think of?

Kickin' Hot Cocoa
Sprinkle **cayenne pepper** and **cinnamon** into a mug of hot cocoa and stir well.

Choco-Peanut-Butter Blend
Mix a tablespoon of **creamy peanut butter** into hot chocolate until the peanut butter dissolves.

Caramel Chocolate Swirl
Stir a tablespoon of **caramel syrup** into a cup of hot chocolate.

Hot Chocolate Float
Add a scoop of **mint ice cream** into a mug of hot chocolate.

The earliest known chocolate drink is believed to have been created around **1700 BCE** by the Olmecs, who lived in what is now southern Mexico. However, since sugar wasn't introduced to the Americas yet, the drink was bitter, not sweet.

HANUKKAH

Every year, in late November or December, Jewish people enjoy an eight-day celebration that began about two thousand years ago. After a victory over the Syrian-Greek army around 165 BCE, the Jews rededicated the Second Temple of Jerusalem. They found only enough oil to keep the Temple lamp lit for one day. Yet the oil burned until a new supply arrived—eight days later! Today, Jewish people remember this miracle by lighting the Hanukkah menorah—one candle for each day. The traditional potato pancakes called *latkes*, usually fried in oil, are a reminder of that miracle, too.

MAKE A MAGNETIC MENORAH

1. Place a sheet of **blue craft foam** on a protected surface. Cover your palms and fingers with **poster paint**. Overlap your thumbs and spread out your fingers, then press both hands onto the craft foam.

2. Wash and dry your hands. Cover your thumb with gold paint. Make nine thumbprints on **yellow craft foam**.

3. Cut out the "menorah" and the "flames." Glue **magnets** to the back.

4. Put the menorah and flames on a refrigerator. "Light" the candles during Hanukkah.

WHOLE LOTTA LATKES

You're making latkes for two dozen (24) people. You already have oil, salt, pepper, and matzo meal. How much will you spend on the three main ingredients if one potato is 89 cents, one dozen eggs is $2.67, and an onion is 99 cents?

> **POTATO LATKE RECIPE**
> (serves 6)
> 5 large potatoes
> 3 eggs
> 1 onion

December 26–January 1

KWANZAA

Kwanzaa is a holiday that was created by Dr. Maulana Karenga in 1966. It celebrates family, community, and culture. The holiday stems from the African tradition of giving thanks for the first fruits of the harvest (*Kwanzaa* means "first fruits" in Swahili).

There are seven principles celebrated during this holiday: **unity**, **self-determination**, **collective work and responsibility**, **cooperative economics**, **purpose**, **creativity**, and **faith**. A candle is lit each day on a kinara. Each candle represents one of these principles.

"Heri za Kwanzaa!" means "Happy Kwanzaa!"

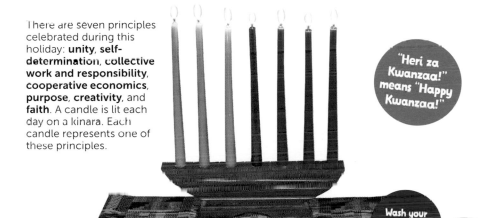

Wash your hands before you begin

Makes 12 cornucopias.

Celebrate Kwanzaa by displaying—then eating!—this tasty treat to represent *mazao* ("crops" in Swahili).

1. Peel two small **bananas**, a **mango**, two **pears**, and two **kiwis**. Wash one cup of **berries**.

2. With an adult's help, cut the fruit into small pieces. (Throw away the pear cores and the mango seed.)

3. Gently combine the fruit in a bowl. Then spoon the mixture into **waffle cones**.

4. Arrange the cones on a large plate or serving tray.

5. When it's time to eat them, you can top each cornucopia with a sprinkle of **coconut flakes** or a drizzle of **honey** or **chocolate sauce**. Enjoy!

MAZAO, one of the symbols of Kwanzaa, represents the harvest and the hard work that went into producing it.

Celebrities who have celebrated Kwanzaa include Oprah, Maya Angelou, and Angelina Jolie.

CHRISTMAS

The Christmas holiday celebrates the birth of Jesus Christ. People decorate Christmas trees with lights and ornaments, do good deeds for others, and give gifts to friends and family.

JINGLE-BELL ORNAMENTS

Make these ornaments to hang on your own tree or to give as a gift.

1. Twist one end of a **fuzzy stick** into a loop. Twist a **jingle bell** onto the other end.

2. Use **colored paper** and **stickers** to create a Nativity scene, a Christmas tree, or a bell. **Tape** the chenille stick to the back. Add a **yarn** bow.

A TREE FULL OF TREATS

Help the mouse find a clear path to the cheese at the top of the tree!

TRICKY TREES

Each of these trees has the numbers 1 through 6 running along the sides. And, in each triangle, each side adds up to the number in the middle. Can you place the numbers in each triangle so that everything adds up correctly? Each of the numbers 1 through 6 is only used once in a triangle.

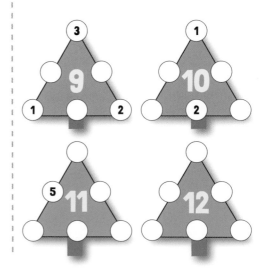

Santa and the gang are celebrating a successful Christmas.
While they party, can you find all the hidden objects in the scene?

banana	button	glove	toothbrush
bell	carrot	ladder	umbrella
bow	fork	spoon	watermelon

Why did the Christmas tree go to the barber?

It needed to be trimmed.

What is a Christmas tree's favorite candy?

Orna-mints

What do you call a Christmas tree with an apple?

A pineapple

What do you call a cat sitting on the beach on Christmas Eve?

Sandy Claws

WORLD WILDLIFE CONSERVATION DAY

December 4

This holiday exists to bring awareness to the many wonderful species of wildlife that need our help. Here are a few ideas of how you can help animals in need, not just on this day, but every day.

RECYCLE

Humans make a lot of garbage. Being careless with our garbage is hard on the environment—and some of our favorite animals. Recycling can help control the amount of waste we pile up. Recycling can also protect animal habitats. In fact, the Minnesota Zoo asks that its visitors recycle their phones. The mineral coltan that is used to make phones is mined from lowland gorilla habitats. Recycling phones helps save the gorillas!

STEP-BY-STEP DRAWING

Follow the steps to draw a panda.

1.
2.
3.
4.
5.

There are only **1,800 GIANT PANDAS** living in the wild.

BE SUSTAINABLE

Switching to using metal or other reusable straws can be a huge help. Plastic straws end up in the ocean and hurt animals like sea turtles. If more of us can use reusable straws, then fewer straws will end up as garbage.

Reusable straws are made from metal or glass, and biodegradable straws are made from paper or bamboo.

TAKE CARE WITH GARBAGE

Remember to always throw garbage away in the proper place to keep it out of animal habitats. And make sure things like plastic soda rings are cut so animals, like this seagull, don't trap their heads inside.

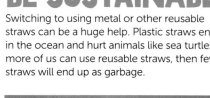

December 11

INTERNATIONAL MOUNTAIN DAY

This day encourages us to take care of our mountains. Earth's peaks are home to 15% of the world's population. What's more, they provide about half of the world with its drinking water. Join this hiker as she appreciates the beauty of the mountains.

Can you find the 13 objects hiding in the scene?

HOW DO PEAKS PROVIDE DRINKING WATER?
Rain and melted snow run down mountains. This water eventually flows to the streams and rivers that supply people's drinking water.

baseball bat

cowboy boot

fish

fork

comb

frog

hat

wedge of orange

needle

paintbrush

slice of pizza

sailboat

watering can

December 14

INTERNATIONAL MONKEY DAY

What do you get when you mix a monkey and rainbow paint?

A messy house

We're not monkeying around—today is the day we celebrate these cute primates. In the puzzle below, fill in the squares so the six letters appear only once in each row, column, and 2 x 3 box. Then read the highlighted squares to find the answer to the riddle.

RIDDLE: What key opens a banana?

Answer:
A _ _ _ _ _ _ _

Letters: E K M N O Y

					O
E			Y		M
K			O	Y	
	E	O			N
O		M			K
			M		

Tongue Twister

FIVE FUNKY MONKEYS MUNCHING FIVE FRIED MUNCHIES

December 9
NATIONAL LLAMA DAY

We've got lots of love for llamas! Find one trio of identical llamas, four pairs of identical llamas, and one llama with no match in this scene.

BONUS! Say this tongue twister five times fast: Mama Llama's pajama drama.

December 3

NATIONAL MAKE A GIFT DAY

A HANDMADE GIFT MEANS A LOT— AND SO DO COMPLIMENTS!

Add something to your gifts that your friends and family are sure to love; kind words. Wrap your handmade gift in solid-colored paper, and use a marker to write compliments or thank-yous on the paper. You might thank your mom for helping you with your homework. Or let your brother know he's great at telling jokes. A thoughtful note is a valuable gift!

December 20

GO CAROLING DAY

What is your favorite carol to sing? Sing along while you find all 12 hidden objects.

flower

chair

sailboat

coat hanger

hamburger

heart

mitten

candle

watermelon

baseball

ice-cream cone

fork

Take a spin around the globe to see how

December 6

⦿ ST. NICHOLAS DAY

In Belgium, on December 5, children put out their shoes by the fireplace, along with food and water for St. Nicholas's horse. The next morning, the shoes will be filled with treats like chocolates, cookies, oranges, and toys.

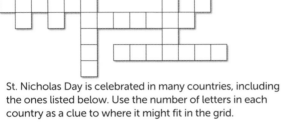

St. Nicholas Day is celebrated in many countries, including the ones listed below. Use the number of letters in each country as a clue to where it might fit in the grid.

AUSTRIA	ENGLAND	ITALY
BELGIUM	FRANCE	MEXICO
CANADA	GERMANY	RUSSIA
CROATIA	ICELAND	TURKEY

December 12

⦿ JAMHURI DAY

In Swahili, one of two official languages of Kenya, the word *jamhuri* means "republic." This holiday celebrates Kenya's independence from the United Kingdom on December 12, 1963, as well as Kenya's becoming a republic a year later on December 12, 1964. Kenyans celebrate the holiday with speeches, parades, and feasts to honor the country's culture and heritage.

Kenyan dancers perform a traditional dance during Jamhuri Day celebrations.

THE WORLD

December 24
NOCHE BUENA

Filipinos celebrate Christmas Eve with a midnight church mass and a traditional feast called Noche Buena, which means "good night" in Spanish. During the Christmas season in the Philippines, beautiful star-shaped lanterns, known as *parols*, light up the night sky and cast a soft glow on streets and homes. The stars remind Christians of the star of Bethlehem, which they believe guided three wise men to the baby Jesus.

Make a Philippine Parol

1. As shown in the diagram, fold a piece of **cardstock** in half. Mark the center of the side opposite the fold. Draw lines from the center to each lower corner. Cut out the triangle, and unfold it to form a diamond. Repeat with four more pieces of cardstock. **Tape** the diamonds together to form a star

2. For a tassel, cut twenty 10-inch pieces of **yarn**. Fold ten of them in half and tie them together at the fold. Tie another piece of yarn below that. Trim the ends of the tassel. Repeat with the other ten pieces of yarn

3. Punch a hole in the top point of the star and the two lower points. Tie the tassels to the lower holes. Tie a piece of yarn in the top hole for a hanger.

4. Decorate the star with **glitter glue**.

December 26
BOXING DAY

Most of the 53 countries in the Commonwealth—nearly all of which are former territories of the British Empire—celebrate Boxing Day. This holiday is spent with family and friends. People often shop or watch sports, and eat leftover Christmas food.

Deondre, Jada, Ashlyn, and Luke are wrapping presents. Follow the ribbons to figure out who's wrapping each gift.

JANUARY

I celebrated the **start of 2024** by _____
_____
_____

For **National Puzzle Day** on **January 29**, I tried
_____
_____
_____

My **favorite January holiday** was
_____
_____

FEBRUARY

On **February 2, 2024,**
the groundhog
☐ **DID**   ☐ **DID NOT**
see his shadow.

I made **valentines** for
_____
_____
_____
_____

My **favorite February holiday** was
_____
_____

MARCH

On **International Day of Happiness** on **March 20, these** are the things that made me happy: _____

_____

_____

_____

_____

My **favorite March holiday** was

_____

_____

March 26 was Make Up Your Own Holiday Day. The **holiday I created** was _____

_____

_____

This is how you celebrate it: _____

_____

_____

_____

_____

_____

_____

_____

APRIL

On **April Fools' Day**, I was surprised by _____

_____

_____

_____

I celebrated **Earth Day** by _____

_____

_____

_____

My **favorite April holiday** was

_____

_____

MAY

I spent time with
my **family** in May by

_____

_____

_____

_____

Here is **something new I tried** in May:

_____

_____

_____

_____

My **favorite May holiday** was

_____

_____

JUNE

I celebrated the first day of summer **by**

_____

_____

_____

_____

_____

My favorite June holiday was

_____

_____

_____

I took photos this month to celebrate events like **Nature Photography Day** on **June 15.** Here is my favorite photo from June:

PASTE YOUR FAVORITE PHOTO HERE!

JULY

I celebrated **Independence Day** by

_____
_____
_____

I played these **sports** or **games** in July:

_____
_____
_____

My **favorite July holiday** was

_____
_____

AUGUST

I read _____ **books in 2024!**

For **National Book Lovers Day** on **August 9,** I read _____
_____
_____
_____

Here are some **foods I ate outside** in August:

_____
_____
_____
_____

My **favorite August holiday** was

_____

SEPTEMBER

I spent time with my friends
this month by

_____

_____

_____

_____

_____

My favorite
September holiday was

_____

_____

September 12 is the National Day of Encouragement.
Here are some things that make me feel encouraged:

_____

_____

_____

_____

_____

_____

_____

_____

OCTOBER

For **National Do Something Nice Day** on **October 5**, I _____

_____

_____

_____

For **Halloween, my costume** was

_____

_____

My **favorite October holiday** was

_____

NOVEMBER

On **International Tongue Twister Day** on **November 10,** my favorite tongue twister was

_____

_____

_____

I celebrated **Thanksgiving by**

_____

_____

_____

My **favorite November holiday** was

DECEMBER

For **Pretend to Be a Time Traveler Day** on **December 8**, I would travel to

_____

_____

_____

My favorite December holiday was

_____

_____

I sang or **played these songs** in December:

_____

_____

_____

_____

_____

_____

_____

_____

2024 MEMORIES

I learned these three things about myself in 2024:

1. _____
_____
_____
_____

2. _____
_____
_____
_____

3. _____
_____
_____
_____

My favorite part of 2024 was

_____
_____
_____
_____
_____
_____
_____

I tried these three new things in 2024:

1. _____
_____
_____

2. _____
_____
_____

3. _____
_____
_____
_____

My hope for next year is _____
_____
_____
_____

JANUARY

PAGE 7: TANGLED LEASHES

PAGE 7: WHAT'S YOUR DOG IQ?
1. A; 2. A; 3 B; 4. B; 5. A

PAGE 8: TOTEM TWOSOME

PAGE 8: DOGGON IT!

PAGE 9: EGYPTIAN EXHIBIT

PAGE 10: FUNNY FOOTBALL

PAGE 11: WINTER X GAMES

PAGE 13: NATIONAL THESAURUS DAY

PAGE 14: NATIONAL POPCORN DAY

PAGE 15: NATIONAL BLONDE BROWNIE DAY

PAGE 21: PENGUIN PATTERN
The pattern is +4, −1.
1, 5, 4, 8, 7, 11, 10, 14, 13, 17, 16, 20, 19, 23, 22, 26, 25, 29, 28, 32

PAGE 21: PENGUIN PUZZLER
Ben's locker combination is 12, 18, 24.
BONUS: AN ICEBERG-ER

PAGE 22: MY PET DRAGON

PAGE 23: NATIONAL PUZZLE DAY

PAGE 24: SAINT KNUT'S DAY (SWEDEN)
julstjärna = Christmas star
julklappsstrumpa = Christmas stocking
julgranskula = Christmas ornament
julgransbelysning = Christmas tree lights

PAGE 25: SAINT DEVOTA'S DAY
1. C; 2. H; 3. F; 4. A; 5. G; 6. D; 7. B; 8. E

FEBRUARY

PAGE 30: CHERRY MATCHUP

PAGE 31: CHILDREN'S DENTAL HEALTH MONTH

PAGE 31: RIDDLE SUDOKU

C	O	S	N	W	R
W	R	N	S	O	C
S	W	O	C	R	N
N	C	R	W	S	O
O	S	C	R	N	W
R	N	W	O	C	S

Why do kings and queens go to the dentist?
TO GET CROWNS

PAGE 32: THE BEATLES HITS
1. Here Comes the SUN
2. Sergeant PEPPER's Lonely Hearts Club Band
3. Let it BE
4. I Want to Hold Your HAND
5. PENNY Lane
6. BLACKBIRD
7. While My GUITAR Gently Weeps
8. Yellow SUBMARINE
9. STRAWBERRY Fields Forever
10. Lucy in the Sky with DIAMONDS
11. I am the WALRUS
12. Drive My CAR

PAGE 33: AT THE OBSERVATORY

PAGE 34: NATIONAL GIRLS & WOMEN IN SPORTS DAY
1. B; 2. C; 3. A; 4. A; 5. C; 6. B; 7. B; 8. A; 9. C; 10. A
ALEX FINISHES FIRST!

287

PAGE 35: SUPER BOWL LVIII

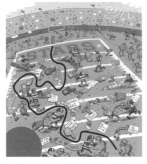

What do football champions put their cereal in?
SUPER BOWLS

PAGE 35: SUPER BOWL SUPER STATS
1. C; 2. A; 3. B; 4. A

PAGE 36: OPERA DAY

PAGE 37: GET OUT YOUR GUITAR DAY

PAGE 37: NAME THAT GUITAR

WILLIE NELSON: TRIGGER
B.B. KING: LUCILLE
ERIC CLAPTON: BLACKIE
EDDIE VAN HALEN: FRANKENSTRAT
BRIAN MAY: RED SPECIAL

PAGE 38: NATIONAL FROZEN YOGURT DAY
HERE ARE ANSWERS WE SPOTTED. YOU MAY HAVE FOUND OTHERS.

PAGE 40: LUNAR NEW YEAR

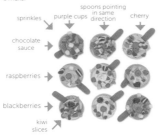

PAGE 41: VALENTINE'S DAY

PAGE 42: WASHINGTON'S BIRTHDAY

HOOVER: HOOVER DAM
KENNEDY: KENNEDY SPACE CENTER
(THEODORE) ROOSEVELT: TEDDY BEAR
LINCOLN: LINCOLN MEMORIAL
JEFFERSON: JEFFERSON MEMORIAL
WASHINGTON: WASHINGTON MONUMENT

They served in this order: Washington (1st president), Jefferson (3rd), Lincoln (16th), T. Roosevelt (26th), Hoover (31st), and Kennedy (35th).

PAGE 43: LEAPING LEMURS

PAGE 43: A LEAP OF LOGIC

TAYLOR: Spot, 3rd place
MADISON: Hoppy, 1st place
CAMERON: Freddie, 2nd place

PAGE 44: WEATHER STUMPER

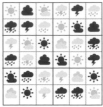

PAGE 45: THE HOOVER DAM

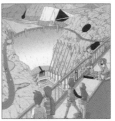

PAGE 47: NATIONAL LOVE YOUR PET DAY
The mischievous pet is the dog.

PAGE 49: NAVAM FULL MOON
POYA DAY (SRI LANKA)

MARCH

PAGE 52: WOMEN'S HISTORY MONTH
1. Marie Curie
2. Amelia Earhart
3. Maria Tallchief
4. Valentina Tereshkova
5. Junko Tabei
6. Sandra Day O'Connor
7. Aretha Franklin
8. Mo'ne Davis
9. Kamala Harris

PAGE 53: UMBRELLA FUN

When can 6 people share one umbrella without getting wet? *WHEN THE SUN IS OUT*

PAGE 53: NATIONAL MUSIC IN OUR SCHOOLS MONTH

ANSWERS

PAGE 54: NATIONAL NOODLE MONTH
T; F; T; T; F; T; F

PAGE 56: SKY HIGH

PAGE 57: EIFFEL TOWER

PAGE 58: SPACE BASKETBALL

PAGE 58: TO THE HOOP!
Why are basketball players messy eaters?
THEY'RE ALWAYS DRIBBLING.

PAGE 59: HOME RUN

PAGE 60: READ ACROSS AMERICA DAY

PAGE 60: PIANO PATH

PAGE 61: TOP ACT
1. *BEAUTY AND THE BEAST*
2. *THE ADDAMS FAMILY*
3. *THE LITTLE MERMAID*
4. *INTO THE WOODS*
8. *LITTLE SHOP OF HORRORS*
9. *THE WIZARD OF OZ*

PAGE 62: NATIONAL PI DAY

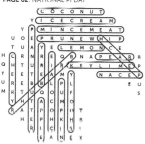

PAGE 66: LEPRECHAUN SHENANIGANS

The red-circled leprechaun is the mischief-maker. He took a guitar and hid it above Under the Rainbow Restaurant.

PAGE 66-67: EASTER SUNDAY

PAGE 66: A VERY YUMMY EASTER
Carly: *STRAWBERRY MUFFINS*
Anthony: *APPLE TART*
Kiera: *COCONUT CUPCAKE*
Dan: *LEMON PIE*

PAGE 67: RABBIT SEARCH

PAGE 67: GLOBAL EASTER TRADITIONS
Manchester, England, is the made-up tradition.

PAGE 68: WORLD WILDLIFE DAY

PAGE 69: EARTH HOUR
CHINA, 1:30 a.m.; UKRAINE, 7:30 p.m.;
NEPAL, 11:15 p.m.; MALI, 5:30 p.m.

PAGE 70: INTERNATIONAL MERMAID DAY

PAGE 71: NATIONAL CRAYON DAY

PAGE 72:
INDEPENDENCE DAY (GHANA)

PAGE 73: HOLI (INDIA)

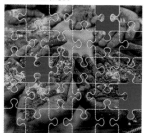

289

APRIL

PAGE 76: FLYING NUMBERS

Why was 6 mad at 7? *BECAUSE 789*

Why is a circle always so hot? *BECAUSE IT'S 360 DEGREES*

How do numbers celebrate? *WITH HIGH 5S*

What does a dollar have in common with the moon? *THEY BOTH HAVE 4 QUARTERS.*

How does 10 feel without its number 1 friend? *LIKE A 0*

What happened when 19 and 20 got into an argument? *21*

PAGE 76: TIC TAC KITE

PAGE 77: NATIONAL HUMOR MONTH

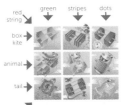

PAGE 77: LOOK BOTH WAYS!
1. H; 2. G; 3. C; 4. J; 5. A; 6. I; 7. B; 8. F; 9. D; 10. E

PAGE 78: NATIONAL GARDEN MONTH
1. A; 2. B; 3. C; 4. B; 5. A; 6. B; 7. C; 8. C

PAGE 78: NATIONAL GUITAR MONTH
B AND C

PAGE 79: POSTAGE PAW-BLEMS
THIS PACKAGE WILL COST THE MOST TO SHIP.

BONUS: YES, PURRNELOPE HAS ENOUGH MONEY TO SEND ALL FOUR PACKAGES.

PAGE 79: 24 TO THE DOOR

9 + 12	2 x 11	15 + 9	17 + 7
7 + 15	35 − 11	8 x 3	25 − 2
3 x 4	6 x 4	20 + 3	18 + 7
18 + 6	40 − 16	5 x 7	33 − 10

PAGE 79: SUM FUN!
1. 7
2. 8
3. 29
4. 64
5. 7
6. 3,600
7. 10

WORLD LARGEST BOX OF CHOCOLATE WEIGHS 3,725

PAGE 80: NORTH POLE
1. SLEDDING
8. GLOVES
13. SNOWFLAKE
21. ELVES
25. SCARF
29. FREEZES
35. SLUSH
39. HOT COCOA
46. ANTARCTICA
55. ARCTIC
60. COAT
63. TEETH
67. HEATS
71. SNOWMAN
77. NUMB
80. BLOW
83. WINTER
88. RINK
91. KNITS
95. SPRING

PAGE 81: SOLAR SYSTEM

PAGE 82: PLAY BALL!
1. CODY
2. HECTOR
3. CLAUDIA
4. SETH
5. JACOB
6. ARIEL
7. TROY
8. LINDSEY
9. LAURA

PAGE 82: HOME RUN!

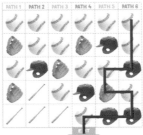

PAGE 83: INTERNATIONAL DANCE DAY

PAGE 83: DINOSAUR DANCE-OFF

What do you call a dinosaur that's been dancing all night? *MY-FEET-ARE-SORE-US*

What kind of dinosaur liked to dance? *THE DISCO-SAURUS*

PAGE 83: THE BOSTON MARATHON

PAGE 84: PUZZLING PAIRS
1. COLD, CHILLY; 2. FEAR, FRIGHT; 3. SPOT, SPECK; 4. DART, DASH; 5. PLATE, PLATTER; 6. BRING, BEAR; 7. SWAY, SWING; 8. TRIP, TOUR; 9. GRIP, GRASP; 10. SHAVE, SHEAR

PAGE 84: WALLY AND WENDY HAVE NOT YET READ *EARLY BIRD GOT THE WORM!*

PAGE 84: JUST WING IT

PAGE 86: BOBBIE'S BURRITOS
The order should be F, C, E, A, B, D.

PAGE 86: NATIONAL DEEP DISH PIZZA DAY

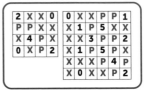

PAGE 87: NATIONAL JELLY BEAN DAY

PAGE 88: EID AL-FITR
A *fanous* is a *LANTERN*

PAGE 91: TEST YOUR ECLIPSE KNOWLEDGE
ANSWERS: NO, YES, YES, NO, NO, NO.

PAGE 92: ZOOKEEPER'S BYE-BYE
1. CROCODILE
2. BABOON
3. BUFFALO
4. SHEEP
5. GECKO
6. BUTTERFLY
7. KANGAROO
8. POLAR BEAR
9. CHIMPANZEE
10. RATTLESNAKE

PAGE 93: TREEMONTON TOWERS

PAGE 94: NATIONAL UNICORN DAY

PAGE 95: TAKE OUR DAUGHTERS AND SONS TO WORK DAY

THE ARTIST HASN'T ARRIVED YET.

PAGE 96: DO YOU KNOW THAT DRAGON? (ENGLAND)

1. F; 2. C; 3. E; 4. A; 5. D; 6. H; 7. B; 8. G

PAGE 97: FLY IT HIGH (SIERRA LEONE)

MAY

PAGE 100: ASIAN/PACIFIC AMERICAN HERITAGE MONTH

1. Chloe Kim
2. Maya Lin
3. George Takei
4. Nathan Chen
5. Jose Antonio Vargas
6. Duke Kahanamoku
7. Patsy Mink
8. Kalpana Chawla

PAGE 101: STRAWBERRY WORDS

1. RAY	6. STAR	11. WATER
2. WET	7. WEST	12. STRAY
3. RAT	8. WEBS	13. SWEAT
4. BEAR	9. RARE	14. YEAST
5. EAST	10. STAY	15. SAWYER

PAGE 102: DRUM MATCH
1. E; 2. C; 3. B; 4. G; 5. A; 6. F; 7. D

PAGE 103: NATIONAL PET MONTH

PAGE 104: WELDING THE DETAILS

PAGE 105: TRAIN HUMOR
HOW ARE A TRAIN AND AN ORCHESTRA ALIKE? *EACH HAS A CONDUCTOR.*

HOW DO TRAIN ENGINES LEARN TO PLAY SPORTS? *THEY HAVE COACHES.*

PAGE 106: KENTUCKY DERBY

WHY DID THE PONY HAVE TO GARGLE? *HE WAS JUST A LITTLE HORSE.*

PAGE 110: EAT WHAT YOU WANT DAY

1. APPLE	6. COOKIE
2. POTATO	7. EGGS
3. PEAS	8. BEANS
4. CUCUMBER	9. FISH
5. MILK	10. CHEESE

PAGE 111: NATIONAL HAMBURGER DAY

PAGE 112: CINCO DE MAYO
1. D; 2. A; 3. F; 4. B; 5. E; 6. C

PAGE 113: MOM MATCH

PAGE 114: JUMBLED FLOWERS
LILY
TULIP
LILAC
DAFFODIL

PAGE 114: FLOWER OR NOT

BLUEBELL	*CLEMATIS*
SNAPDRAGON	*HYDRANGEA*
CHRYSANTHEMUM	*FOXGLOVE*
RHODODENDRON	
GLADIOLUS	

PAGE 114: COUNT THE CODE
What did the dog do after he swallowed a firefly? *HE BARKED WITH DELIGHT!*

PAGE 114: HIDDEN FLOWERS

As **Ter**ry says, vanilla is better than chocolate

A superhe**ro sel**dom fails.

Ms. Go**rda is** your new teacher.

This **fir is** taller than it was last year.

On the **porch, I d**on't get sunburned.

PAGE 115: MEMORIAL DAY

PAGE 116: PLANETARIUM FIELD TRIP

PAGE 118: NO SOCKS DAY

PAGE 118: NATIONAL FROG JUMPING DAY

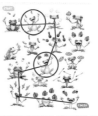

BONUS: PEANUTS, PEAPODS, PILLOWS, PUMPKIN, PICKLES, PINEAPPLES, PEACOCKS, PIZZA, PEAR, PENCILS, AND PRESENTS.
BONUS: 32

PAGE 119: INTERNATIONAL MUSEUM DAY

PAGE 119: MUSEUM LOGIC

SEAN: ART, FRIDAY
SOFIA: FASHION, SUNDAY
LAWRENCE: SPACE, SATURDAY
KELSEY: RAILROAD, MONDAY

PAGE 121: VICTORY DAY (RUSSIA)

JUNE

PAGE 124: CAMPFIRE JOE

PAGE 125: AFRICAN AMERICAN MUSIC APPRECIATION MONTH

1. BANJO
2. TROMBONE
3. TUBA
4. SAXOPHONE
5. TRUMPET
6. CLARINET
7. PIANO
8. DRUMS
9. BASS
10. GUITAR

Why do farmers play soft jazz for their corn? IT'S EASY *ON THE EARS.*

PAGE 126: CANDY COUNTER

PAGE 126: NATIONAL FRESH FRUIT AND VEGETABLE MONTH

1. In the showroom, a **car rot**ated on a platform.
2. Maya looked **up each** book Liam recommended.
3. The dog's **bark al**erted the cat.
4. "I'm getting a new bicycle Mon**day**," said Darnell.
5. Adrianna gets **up ear**ly every morning.
6. I bought a tea**pot at O**scar's sale.
7. Pete and his mom baked his tea**cher rye** bread.
8. That clown can **spin a ch**air on his hand.

PAGE 127: SENSING THE OUTDOORS
MISSING SENSE: TASTE

PAGE 128: SECRET CIPHER DISK
CRACK THIS CODE: *YOU ROCK!*

PAGE 129: SAME AND DIFFERENT

PAGE 129: CAKE MATCHES

PAGE 130: INTERNATIONAL DAY OF YOGA

PAGE 131: HOCKEY STICK CHALLENGE

THERE ARE **18** HOCKEY STICKS

PAGE 131: HOCKEY MATH
20 - 15 = 5
60 - 20 = 40

PAGE 132: NATURE PHOTOGRAPHY DAY

PAGE 133: WORLD MUSIC DAY

PAGE 133: MUSIC MADNESS

WHAT KIND OF MUSIC DO MUMMIES LIKE? *WRAP*

WHAT IS A BUBBLE'S LEAST FAVORITE TYPE OF MUSIC? *POP!*

WHAT DO YOU GET WHEN A MUSICIAN LOSES THEIR BEAT? *A TEMPO-TANTRUM*

PAGE 134: NATIONAL DOUGHNUT DAY

PAGE 135: NATIONAL HERBS AND SPICES DAY

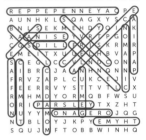

PAGE 139: FIRST DAY OF SUMMER

Best deal: buy the green sunglasses and get a pair of sandals free for a total cost of $20.00.

PAGE 140: COME OUT OF YOUR SHELL

PAGE 140: TURTLE MATCH UP

PAGE 143: NATIONAL SUNGLASSES DAY

PAGE 144: DIA DOS NAMORADOS (BRAZIL)

JULY

PAGE 148: ICE-CREAM MONTH
CRISS-CROSS ICE CREAM

PAGE 148: ICE-CREAM MONTH
SCOOPIN' IT UP

How many cones did the shop sell on Friday?

$4 + 4 + 4 + 4 + 4 = 20$ → **20**

How many cones did the shop sell on Saturday?

$4 + 4 + 4 + 4 = 16$ → **16**

PAGE 149: NATIONAL BERRY MONTH

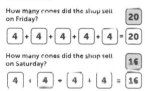

PAGE 150: JUMBLED ANIMALS
ZEBRA
CAMEL
PANDA
CHEETAH
POLAR BEAR

PAGE 150: GUESS WHO?
JAGUAR, ELEPHANT, PEACOCK

PAGE 150: LAND OR SEA?
LAND: *KOMODO DRAGON, ALPACA, CHINCHILLA, BONGO*
SEA: *BRITTLESTAR, MANATEE, STINGRAY, BARRACUDA*

PAGE 150: PENGUIN POSES

PAGE 151: PLASTIC-FREE JULY
1. paperback
2. paperweight
3. dishcloth
4. tablecloth
5. eyeglass
6. hourglass

PAGE 152: ZOOKEEPER'S PATH

PAGE 153: MOON LANDING

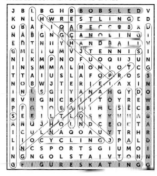

PAGE 154: SUMMER OLYMPIC GAMES

PAGE 155: SUMMER OLYMPIC GAMES

PAGE 160: INDEPENDENCE DAY
Vermont was not one of the 13 original colonies.

PAGE 163: WORLD SNAKE DAY

PAGE 165: NATIONAL WATERPARK DAY

We found *PEAR, KARATE,* and *PARKA* in *WATERPARK*

PAGE 166: LA FÊTE NATIONALE (FRANCE)

PAGE 167: INDEPENDENCE DAY (LIBERIA)

Liberia's capital city is *MONROVIA.*

AUGUST

PAGE 170: FAMILY FUN MONTH
CANOEING CREW

PAGE 172: IN THE WHEELHOUSE

PAGE 174: NATIONAL GOLF MONTH

1. C; **2.** B; **3.** A

PAGE 176: NATIONAL CLOWN WEEK!

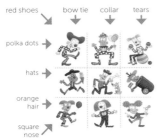

red shoes   bow tie   collar   tears

polka dots →

hats

orange hair →

square nose →

PAGE 176: CIRCUS LINGO
1. F; **2.** H; **3.** A; **4.** E; **5.** G; **6.** D; **7.** B; **8.** C

PAGE 177: NATIONAL TELL A JOKE DAY

Why was the dog excited to go to school?
The class was having a SMELLING BEE.

Why did the dog study before class?
In case the teacher gave a PUP QUIZ

BONUS: There are 71 bones.

PAGE 178: CAMPFIRE DAY AND NIGHT

I'm squishy and sweet and airy and light.
I'm brown when I'm roasted. Inside, I'm still white.
Need s'more hints? This might do the trick:
I'll be at the campfire stuck on your stick.
MARSHMALLOWS

PAGE 179: EAT OUTSIDE DAY

We found these things that rhyme with *grill* and *eat*: windowsill, spill, daffodil, quill, windmill, anthill, duck bill, pepper mill, gill, sheet, tweet, feet, cleat, meat, parakeet, dog treat, beet, sweet, wheat, seat, street. You may have found others.

PAGE 180: MANY NATIONS SEARCH

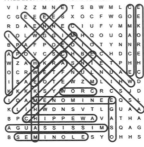

PAGE 182: SHOOTING STAR DAY

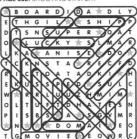

What is a shooting star?
It isn't a star at all. It's a meteor.

PAGE 183: NATIONAL DOG DAY

PAGE 184: NATIONAL ROLLER COASTER DAY

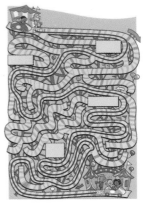

PAGE 185: NATIONAL BEACH DAY
The scenes occurred in the following order:
B, A, F, H, D, C, G, E

PAGE 186: ROYAL EDINBURGH MILITARY TATTOO

SEPTEMBER

PAGE 190: NATIONAL HISPANIC HERITAGE MONTH

1. Octaviano Ambrosio Larrazolo
2. Roberto Clemente
3. Rita Moreno
4. Franklin Chang-Diaz
5. Dr. Antonia Novello
6. Dolores Huerta
7. Carlos Santana
8. Sonia Sotomayor

PAGE 191: NATIONAL CHICKEN MONTH

PAGE 192: BETTER BREAKFAST MONTH

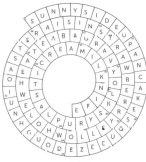

PAGE 193: NATIONAL HONEY MONTH

What kind of haircut does a bee get?
IT GETS A BUZZ CUT.

PAGE 193: NATIONAL SHAKE MONTH

PAGE 195: JOHNNY APPLESEED

PAGE 196: NATIONAL GYMNASTICS DAY

1. fish
2. flag
3. fork
4. pear
5. crown
6. banana
7. candle
8. carrot
9. hammer
10. pencil
11. fried egg
12. umbrella
13. hockey stick

How do you get a cat to do tricks?
PUT A DOG IN A CAT COSTUME.

PAGE 197: INTERNATIONAL MINIATURE GOLF DAY

PAGE 199: INTERNATIONAL COUNTRY MUSIC DAY

PAGE 201: NATIONAL FORTUNE COOKIE DAY
SMILE! YOU ARE ONE SMART COOKIE!

PAGE 201: COOKIE SUDOKU

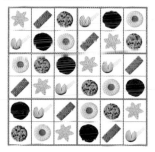

PAGE 202: LABOR DAY

A "SHEAR" PLEASURE. (HAIRDRESSER)

I'M DRAWN TO IT. (ARTIST)

IT'S A PIECE OF CAKE! (BAKER)

OUT OF THIS WORLD! (ASTRONAUT)

I GET A KICK OUT OF IT! (SOCCER PLAYER)

MOVING RIGHT ALONG. (TRAFFIC OFFICER)

AN APPLE A DAY COULDN'T KEEP ME AWAY!
(DOCTOR)

PAGE 203: NATIONAL GRANDPARENTS DAY

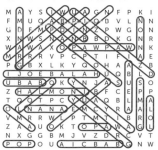

PAGE 204: CONSTITUTION DAY

ACROSS
4. ALEXANDER HAMILTON
5. RHODE ISLAND
7. GEORGE WASHINGTON

DOWN
1. JOHN ADAMS
2. BENJAMIN FRANKLIN
3. THOMAS JEFFERSON
6. JAMES MADISON

PAGE 205: FIRST DAY OF FALL

PAGE 207: NATIONAL ELEPHANT APPRECIATION DAY

Why do elephants have trunks?
BECAUSE THEY LOVE TRAVELING

PAGE 208: NATIONAL SKYSCRAPER DAY
1. A; 2. C; 3. B; 4. B; 5. C; 6. A

PAGE 208: INTERNATIONAL SUDOKU DAY

What did the nut say
when it sneezed?
"CASHEW!"

PAGE 209: INTERNATIONAL TALK LIKE A PIRATE DAY

PAGE 210: ENKUTATASH (ETHIOPIA)

PAGE 211: FIESTAS PATRIAS (CHILE)
GUITAR
HARP
PIANO
ACCORDION
TAMBOURINE

OCTOBER

PAGE 214: GLOBAL DIVERSITY AWARENESS MONTH
1. CHINA
2. ICELAND
3. JAPAN
4. NORWAY
5. GREECE

PAGE 217: PADDLING PARADE

PAGE 218: NATIONAL ROLLER SKATING MONTH

PAGE 219: WORLD SERIES CHAMPIONSHIP

FLY CATCHER

What baseball team does a joker like best?
THE NEW YORK PRANKEES

PAGE 221: DICTIONARY DAY
1. TOY
2. ANT
3. CORN
4. DIRT
5. RAIN
6. TRAIN
7. CARTON

PAGE 221: NATIONAL COLOR DAY
1. RED
2. BLUE
3. BROWN
4. YELLOW
5. GREEN
6. PURPLE
7. ORANGE
8. BLACK

PAGE 222: TIC TAC TACO

Here are answers we spotted. You may have found others.

LETTUCE ON TOP / SOUR CREAM / CHILI PEPPER	LETTUCE ON TOP / TOMATOES ON BOTTOM	LETTUCE ON TOP / TOMATOES IN MIDDLE / OLIVE
MEAT ON TOP / SOUR CREAM	MEAT ON TOP / TOMATOES ON BOTTOM / CHILI PEPPER / OLIVE	MEAT ON TOP / TOMATOES IN MIDDLE
CHEESE ON TOP / SOUR CREAM / OLIVE	CHEESE ON TOP / TOMATOES ON BOTTOM	CHEESE ON TOP / TOMATOES IN MIDDLE / CHILI PEPPER

PAGE 223: NATIONAL PIEROGI DAY

PAGE 228: INTERNATIONAL RACCOON APPRECIATION DAY

Here are the differences we found:

PAGE 228: WORLD FARM ANIMALS DAY

CHICKEN	LLAMA	DUCK
RABBIT	HORSE	PIG
GOAT	ALPACA	SHEEP
CAT	COW	

What is a cow's favorite fruit?
CATTLELOUPE

PAGE 229: WORLD OCTOPUS DAY

PAGE 229: INTERNATIONAL SLOTH DAY
It is 6:00 P.M.

PAGE 230: NATIONAL HAIR DAY

PAGE 231: NATIONAL MAGIC DAY

PAGE 231: NATIONAL MAGIC DAY

IT'S A MAGICIAN'S HAT!

PAGE 233: REPUBLIC DAY (TURKEY)

NOVEMBER

PAGE 236: NATIONAL NATIVE AMERICAN HERITAGE MONTH

PAGE 237: NATIONAL MODEL RAILROAD MONTH

What do you call a locomotive that sneezes?
AH-CHOO-CHOO TRAIN

PAGE 240: TOURING BERLIN

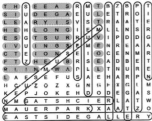

THE EAST SIDE GALLERY IS THE LONGEST SURVIVING SECTION OF THE BERLIN WALL.

PAGE 241: BIRD ADDITION

$$1 + 4 = 5; 2 + 2 = 4$$
$$3 + 1 + 1 = 5$$
$$4 + 4 = 8; 3 + 4 = 7$$

$$\begin{array}{r}11\\+87\\\hline 98\end{array}\qquad\begin{array}{r}24\\+42\\\hline 66\end{array}\qquad\begin{array}{r}65\\+13\\\hline 78\end{array}$$

PAGE 242: COMPASS CODE

Where's the best place to eat while hiking?
WHERE THERE'S A FORK IN THE ROAD.

PAGE 243: NATIONAL SQUARE DANCE DAY

PAGE 246: SAXOPHONE DAY

What kind of music do they play at Stonehenge?
HARD ROCK
How can your hair make music? *WITH A HEADBAND*
Who leads the bird band? *THE CON-DUCK-TOR*
How do you make a bandstand? *TAKE AWAY THEIR CHAIRS.*

PAGE 246: STEP TO THE MUSIC

Tim and Rachel took the same number of steps.
Caitlin took the fewest steps.

PAGE 249: TURKEY TROT

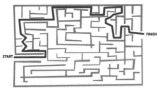

PAGE 249: MAKE A MATCH

PAGE 249: FAVORITE FOODS

1. PIE
2. STUFFING
3. GRAVY
4. SWEET POTATOES
5. HAM
6. MASHED POTATOES
7. MAC AND CHEESE
8. GREEN BEAN CASSEROLE
9. CORN BREAD
10. TURKEY

PAGE 251: NATIONAL BISON DAY

Bison make a later sound for MILLIONS.

PAGE 251: BISON MAKE A MATCH

PAGE 252: NATIONAL BUTTON DAY

PAGE 253: NATIONAL CAMP DAY

PAGE 254: DÍA DE LOS MUERTOS (MEXICO)

PAGE 255: SAINT MARTIN'S DAY (GERMANY)

DECEMBER

PAGE 259: LEARN A FOREIGN LANGUAGE MONTH

1. SPANISH
2. JAPANESE
3. GERMAN
4. RUSSIAN
5. FRENCH
6. ITALIAN
7. SWAHILI
8. CHINESE

PAGE 260: DOUBLE CROSS

AA	TT	II	(TH)	SS	QQ	(EY)
HH	ÖÖ	BB	RR	(AL)	EE	VV
(LH)	NN	ZZ	YY	CC	(AV)	AA
II	QQ	EE	(EN)	DD	PP	WW
(IN)	GG	LL	TT	VV	(FI)	77
XX	HH	II	BB	OO	SS
TT	UU	NN	EE	SS	(ES)	MM

Why are cats good at video games?
THEY ALL HAVE NINE LIVES.

PAGE 260: GAME ON
ANDREW: GOLF GURU, 2ND
BRIANA: RACE CAR FUN, 4TH
CASSIE: ZANY ZOO, 1ST
DIEGO: SPACE TRAVELER, 3RD

PAGE 263: BUILD A SNOWMAN DAY

PAGE 263: BUILDING TOGETHER

PAGE 264: NATIONAL KNITTERS DAY

PAGE 264: NATIONAL VIOLIN DAY

PAGE 267: NATIONAL HAVE A BAGEL DAY

PAGE 268: WHOLE LOTTA LATKES
YOU'LL SPEND $24.43.

PAGE 270: A TREE FULL OF TREATS

PAGE 270: TRICKY TREES

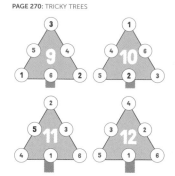

PAGE 271: CELEBRATING CHRISTMAS

PAGE 273: INTERNATIONAL MOUNTAIN DAY

PAGE 273: INTERNATIONAL MONKEY DAY

What key opens a banana?
A MONKEY

PAGE 274: NATIONAL LLAMA DAY

PAGE 275: GO CAROLING DAY

PAGE 276: ST. NICHOLAS DAY (BELGIUM)

PAGE 277: BOXING DAY
(COMMONWEALTH COUNTRIES)

United States Congress/WC (100), United States State Department/WC (100), Unknown/WC (100), UroshPetrovic (212), User5387422_776/GI (97), Vac1/GI (84), VeenaMari/GI (61), VIDOK/Getty Iamges (213), VIDOK/GI (189, 235), vikif/GI (135), VikiVector/GI (69), Visit Roemvanitch/GI (103), Vstock LLC/GI (125), VvoeVale/GI (50, 168), Watcha/GI (123), wildpixel/GI (74), WSM radio/WC (199), wynnter/GI (13), xxmmxx/GI (201), XXMMXX/iStock (14), YinYang (168), yogesh_more/GI (187), Zakharova_Natalia/GI (149), zkruger/GI (17), zoom-zoom/GI (51), Zoonar RF/GI (147), 7oya2222/GI (168).

Illustration Credits: Emily Balsley (51), Barroux (99, 212), Constanza Basaluzzo (10, 43, 169, 188, 235), Paula Becker (84), Galia Bernstein (119), Chris Biggin (265), Iryna Bodnaruk (32, 70), Helena Bogosian (78, 230, 252), Paula Bossio (111, 271), Robin Boyer (21), Tim Bradford (261), Jim Bradshaw (222), Scott Buroughs (131), C.B. Canga (8), Mattia Cerato (81), Jon Chad (45), Anna Chernyshova (268), Hayelin Choi (239), Dave Clegg (43, 92, 119, 146, 253, 267), Josh Cleland (71, 79, 110, 177), Dave Clugg (148), Garry Colby (34, 76), Daryll Collins (58, 83), Gareth Conway (188), David Coulson (15, 19, 26, 45, 51, 75, 81, 99, 152, 168, 188, 204, 231, 251, 256, 262), Jeff Crowther (12, 26), Jef Czekaj (108, 196), Mike Dammer (50, 147, 168, 212, 234, 235), Tim Davis (36, 40, 57, 163, 209), Mike DeSantis (0, 192, 215), Jack Desrocher (116, 120, 188, 221), Chuck Dillon (136, 242), public domain (26), Jim Downer (188), Lorin Driggs (217), Liz Goulet Dubois (209, 235), Avram Dumitrescu (159), Joey Ellis (44), Valerio Fabbretti (42), Carolina Farias (43, 191), Ruth J. Flanigan (86), Luke Flowers (31), Guy Francis (265), Keith Frawley (181, 188, 234, 253, 256), Mark Fullerton (101), Anna Garcia (229), Viviana Garofoli (83), Claudine Gevry (32), Patrick Girouard (155), Ethel Gold (261), Barry Gott (238), Melanie Grandgirard (249), Dean Gray (?), Peter Grosshauser (27, 223, 248), Mary Hall (133), Samara Hardy (32), Jennifer Harney (32), Christopher Hart (108), David Helton (129), Jannie Ho (32, 123, 127), Denise Holmes (212), Paul Hoppe (104), Marie Horvath (98), Jessika Innerebner (229), Deborah Johnson (32), Dave Joly (37, 76, 129, 213), Chris Jones (197), Colleen Kelley (128), Kelly Kennedy (2, 6, 13, 32, 33, 50, 53, 59, 60, 78, 98, 116, 124, 146, 164, 165, 168, 169, 184, 188, 189, 208, 263, 273), Steve Kirk (92), Dave Klug (7, 99, 169, 170, 175, 199), Genevieve Kote (143), Hilli Kushnir (113), Gary LaCoste (20, 90, 146, 169, 228, 266), Christina Larkins (65), Rita Lascaro (75), Bonnie Leick (118), Pat Lewis (22, 78, 118, 126, 133, 139, 149, 171), Ron Lieser (124), James Loram (83), Loufane Loufane (51), Mike Lowry (55), Tammie Lyon (188), Steve Mack (7, 26), Anni Matsick (117), Erin Mauterer (123), Katie McDee (105, 146), Rachael McLean (140), Deb Melmon (264), Valentina Mendicino (274), Susan Miller (243), Judith Moffatt (53), Gary Mohrman (32), Paul Montgomery (117), Julissa Mora (27), Mike Moran (8, 25, 41, 56, 60, 77, 82, 95, 104, 126, 142, 146, 174, 181, 189, 193, 202, 213, 219, 231, 235, 237, 241, 249), Mitch Mortimer (54, 151, 228, 244), Dan Moynihan (108), Shaw Nielsen (256), Bob Ostrom (222), Jim Paillot (27, 168, 176, 189, 221), R. Michael Palan (32, 58), Debbie Palen (178), Diane Palmisciano (122), Sean Parkes (152), Gina Perry (109), Mike Petrik (265), Tamara Petrosino (197), Dave Phillips (12), Colleen Pidel (26, 51, 74, 122, 137), Rich Powell (15, 30, 84, 119, 126, 136, 162, 163, 179), Robert Prince (99), Alessandra Psacharopulo (67), Merrill Rainey (174), Kevin Rechin (10, 36, 80, 108, 135, 171, 243), Pauline Reeves (185), Dana Regan (213), Scot Ritchie (172), Andrew Roberts (160, 161, 226, 227), Claudine Rose (188), Natascha Rosenberg (26), Andy Rowland (241), Amy Safford (234), Jane Sanders (2, 26, 27, 74, 98, 234, 235, 256, 257), Rico Schacherl (50, 147), Hank Schneider (89), Joe Seidita (18), David Sheldon (140), Steve Skelton (103), Jan Smith (32), Sally Springer (195), Jackie Stafford (165), Jim Steck (114), Rick Stromoski (136), Anna Süßbauer (193), Gary Swift (75), Jason Tharp (21), Beegee Tolpa (239), Ekaterina Trukhan (74, 213), Jackie Urbanovic (218), Sharon Vargo (118), Jessika

VonInnerebner (123), Tracy Walker (89), Brian Michael Weaver (14, 21, 26, 31, 32, 35, 50, 64, 108, 146), Monica Wellington (105), Chuck Whelon (93), Brian White (32, 94, 207, 260), Pete Whitehead (12, 14, 152, 262), Liz Williams (30), Mark Winter (130), Daniel Wiseman (27), James Yamasaki (107), Ron Zalme (272), Kevin Zimmer (2, 4, 47, 62, 63, 69, 79, 95, 101, 112, 115, 138, 142, 144, 185, 195, 203, 205, 218, 220, 225, 246, 248, 258, 264, 267, 270, 275, 277), Jennifer Zivoin (254), Diana Zourelias (22, 75, 183).

Contributing Writers: Amie Jane Leavitt, Carmen Morais, Annie Rodriguez, Curtis Slepian, Cheryl Solimini

Graphic Design & Layout: Colleen Kelley

Expert Reviewers: Kelsey Dayle John, Ph.D., NARS Consultants (Native Americans for Restorative Stewardship)

Published by Highlights Press
815 Church Street
Honesdale, Pennsylvania 18431
ISBN: 978-1-64472-919-9

Manufactured in Dongguan, Guangdong, China
Mfg. 03/2023

First edition
Visit our website at highlights.com.
10 9 8 7 6 5 4 3 2 1